DEMONS!

The Devil, Possession & Exorcism

DEMONS!

The Devil, Possession & Exorcism

〽

Anthony Finlay

BLANDFORD

ACKNOWLEDGEMENTS

A thank you to all the people I have spoken to or interviewed with regard to their views on the subject; to all the people who have helped me in a myriad ways, especially my editor, Pat Pierce, for her punctilious attention to detail; to the authorities who have allowed me to quote; to the librarians and assistants in the libraries I have used: The British Library; The London Library; libraries in the South East (mainly Bromley and Croydon Libraries); and the Public Record Office, Kew; to Internet providers at the libraries and elsewhere.

Many thanks to the Anglican and Roman Catholic Churches who made the task easier by provision of pertinent literature; and to personnel of these Churches for allowing me to talk to them on this 'difficult' subject and for giving me permission to use their ideas, and to attend relevant conferences.

I would particularly like to express my appreciation to the parish priests Canon John Watts of Orpington, Reverend Peter Thomas and Mrs Thomas of Bromley and Reverend Paul Wakelin of Northfleet, Kent.

And finally, if any acknowledgements have not been made to relevant authors and/or publishers I apologize – I have made every effort to trace them.

A BLANDFORD BOOK

First published in the UK 1999
by Blandford
Cassell plc
Wellington House
125 Strand
London WC2R 0BB

A Cassell imprint

Text copyright © 1999 Anthony B. Finlay

Distributed in the United States by Sterling Publishing Co., Inc.
387 Park Avenue South, New York, NY 10016–8810

British Library Cataloguing-in-Publication Data
A Cataloguing-in-Publication Data entry for this book is available from the British Library

ISBN 0–7137–2720–9

Printed and bound in Great Britain by MPG Books Ltd, Bodmin, Cornwall

CONTENTS

Acknowledgements *4*

Preface *6*

Introduction *8*

ONE: Ancient Origins of the Devil *11*

TWO: Demonic Belief and Power *34*

THREE: The Prince of Darkness Evolves *53*

FOUR: A Mania for Witchcraft *78*

FIVE: The Power of Possession *99*

SIX: Exorcism – Expelling Demons *120*

SEVEN: The Exorcist and the Possessed *135*

EIGHT: Changing Attitudes to the Devil *153*

NINE: The Devil – Critics and Supporters *171*

TEN: Today – Still a Need to Believe *188*

ELEVEN: Demystifying the Devil *204*

TWELVE: The Wiles of Satan versus the Bible *219*

Appendices *234*

Bibliography *247*

Index *252*

PREFACE

This book is not just about demons (devils), but is concerned also with their master, the Devil (notice the capital 'D'). It tells the story mainly of the Judeo-Christian Devil, although there is some tracing of the demonic back into antiquity. Accordingly, it reflects the development of the Devil and his demons largely over the last two thousand years. The study is from the European point of view, principally English or British.

Demons! is not intended to be a history of demonology through the ages alone, but I trust the work throws up some important questions about the subject: questions that remain unanswered to *everyone's* satisfaction. I can try to answer some of them from a clerical point of view, but I would not presume to dictate to others what they should believe.

Demonology is the study of demonic power and influence; as such it encompasses possession, exorcism and, to an extent, witchcraft – in so far as witches were thought to be in league with the Devil. In the course of the study, certain fundamental tenets and dogma of Christian faith are examined. Some seminal books of ages past are mentioned, for they reveal attitudes to then current religious problems, as well as having considerable influence on future thinking and action.

I have attempted to outline the changing attitudes to all things demonic, citing various 'movements' and notable people who were in the vanguard of 'progress': thinkers and writers, both literary and political. Scepticism was usually their common characteristic.

A study of the diabolic would be incomplete without some mention of spiritualism (or spiritism), and the associated growing interest in the occult, Satanic cults and breakaway sects. This book therefore aims to cover the development of demons and the thinking about them from Biblical times to the present.

'Case studies' concerning possession and exorcism form a not inconsiderable part of the book; some are personal recollections. Accounts of 'demonized' individuals are given, in the hope we may the better be able to judge what is 'genuine' and what is spurious.

The depiction of the Devil in literature, poems, plays and fiction reflects current feeling – even beliefs about the diabolic and the demonic. I have also tried to distinguish between the views of the Roman Catholic and Protestant Churches on this topic of demonology.

This study, therefore, arises from the words, and actions therein, of Scripture, mainly those of the New Testament. The method chosen is generally chronological. This story of the demonic has no particular axe to grind – it is up to you what you think. I just present the facts, raise some questions, give some personal experience from, I own, a Christian viewpoint.

The revised standard version of the Bible (Collins, 1952) has been referred to throughout; this version retains much of the flavour and indeed phraseology of the King James Version of 1611. However, some of the quotations appearing in the book are clearly modern in expression (where I thought a more up-to-date translation was called for) and these have been taken from the New Revised Standard Version of 1995 (Oxford University Press).

A major topic in *Demons!* is that of the problem of evil – as it is for any study involving the Devil and demonology. Demons of course are evil by their very nature, but we are also concerned with the evil principle in life. The two are not the same.

The literature on the Devil (or Satan) is vast; much more sparse is that on demons (or devils) with a small 'd'. A survey of the extant writing on the subject is given, to an extent, through the references in the text and a bibliography. Trying to be comprehensive would require half a lifetime.

It is hoped that this book will fill a gap: its scope is some two millennia – or more! My aim is to entertain and inform. The intention is to produce a readable and interesting study of a very important subject to be of both academic and general interest.

INTRODUCTION

'Angels are part of the universe; they do not constitute a world on their own, but form one world with the physical universe…' (Aquinas, *Summa Theologiae*). These words, taken from St Augustine, seem particularly apt as an introductory sentence. Devils are fallen angels; therefore devils are also part of the world we know, spiritual and material. 'Angels were created happy… and have a natural love for God…' until they, or some of them, transgressed. Then the opposite was true. But this happiness (for loyal angels, as for mankind) 'can be earned only by any action motivated by love'. The angels sinned, says Thomas Aquinas, by choice, 'by turning to their own desires, without attending to God's will'.

The above was written about 1270 when belief in demons was great – and continued to be so for the next five hundred years or more. The Roman Catholic Church was then at the zenith of its power. Although the Renaissance period showed a slackening of belief, the Devil (and his demons) have made a successful come-back as witness the pronouncements in the *Catechism of the Catholic Church* (Vatican, 1994).

AN UNWELCOME REVIVAL

The 'white witch' is one of the symptoms of a revival of ancient belief. Business, they say, is booming for white witches, who claim always to do good. It seems some people turn to these practitioners of 'Wicca', as they call it, to halt a downturn in their lives or to sort out their love life. As an aid to this the 'witches' may cast spells.

There is a Church of Witchcraft claiming thousands of members, and a Pagan Federation. Some white witches are officially organized into businesses, so popular has the movement become. The modern witch, however, is far removed from the traditional conception of the old hag in weird black clothes. She (or he) is more likely to be an ordinary person in the street. Although there is no evidence of supernatural powers on the part of the witches, it may be that their positive attitude to problems induces a 'feel-good' factor. It is, however, less than credible when some white witches make statements like: 'Witches cast spells by harnessing the power of the mind through various rituals'; or if someone needs healing: 'I'll ask them if they want me to cast a healing spell'.

The growing acceptance of paganism and witchcraft is not without its perils. Antagonistic elements still show in a type of witch-hunting manifested in physical and/or verbal attacks, especially on local leaders of the cult, such as self-styled high priests and priestesses.

Belief in the depredations of demons is as strong as ever – in certain areas of life. Much non-traditional belief is focused on the agency of departed human spirits. The traditional belief is that most activity in this sphere is due to spirits, nearly always bad, who have never been carnate. But belief in demons is now very much alive.

The following happened in 1997. I can still see the newspaper heading:

CULT FAMILY KILLS TEENAGER TO RID HER OF DEMONS
Faith Luxor aged seventeen was suffocated to death with a plastic bag by her mother and sister in a cult ritual to free her from 'demons'. The mother believed her daughter was possessed by demons and this was the only way to rid her of the evil spirits. Mrs Luxor was a believer in a strange hybrid creed mixing elements of West African theology and Cuban voodoo. Faith's sister and mother were involved in weird household rituals and animal sacrifice, in which Faith herself never took part.

Mrs Luxor did not believe in medicine and when Faith became ill she blamed it on demon possession which she tried to eradicate by several attempts at exorcism. Her failures led her to conclude that 'the only recourse was to kill the girl'.

Credence in demons has been a mark of Man since the earliest times. They and a ruling spirit of evil have a long history going back millennia before Christ. With the establishment of the Christian faith, belief in the Devil and his cohorts also became more firmly established. At that time the old personage and appearance of Satan (a synonym for the Devil) underwent several changes, but he was mainly malignant and the enemy of God.

DEMONOLOGY AS A STUDY

Demonology as a subject worthy of study came slowly, but by the fifteenth and sixteenth centuries a plethora of books had already been written on the subject – all of course revealing great belief in its actuality. So much so, that some breakaway sects became quite obsessed with Satan and took to worshipping him.

Demonology is the study of the history of demons (of which the Devil is one): their origin, development, influence and power. At least, that has been my tenet in writing this book. One has to weigh the traditional view with those of science, medicine, psychology and psychiatry, all comparatively recent developments which attempt to explain strange activities manifest in cases of possession, particularly. I have presented evidence (for supernatural existence), but have tried to avoid dogmatic conclusions. Readers can come to their own.

Certainly down the years there have been many unexplained phenomena generally attributed to evil spirits. Some seem to offer very convincing evidence for a reigning supernatural power – but who can definitely say? In the times of the New Testament people were certain, but they had precious few sciences to help them. Now, only traditional Christians of the main faiths are still sure – and especially the Roman Catholic hierarchy. For them demons are not peripheral. We are as strongly engaged in spiritual warfare as ever we were.

Satan is (or was) malevolence personified – and for many of those in religious orders throughout the ages this is exactly what he was: the manifestation, in corporeal form, of the Prince of Darkness. He is *the* cause of sin, aided by his cohorts, the demons, who are ready to do his bidding.

Satan, it must be said, features little in the Old Testament, but comes alive in the New Testament. Accordingly, since Jesus' ministry and His death, the Church has seen as one of its main aims the eradication of all things Satanic, including heretical sects and cults – as it still does. A development one way has always been countered by an argument the other, by bulls, encyclicals and statements.

In some ways, a history of demons is a history of religion, or at least of Christianity, as demonology ran *pari passu* with ecclesiastical development. The Christian Church has always regarded itself as the implacable enemy of all things diabolic. In the early days, idolatry was one such thing because it denoted a straying away from the only true ways of the Church and had, as Aquinas (*Summa Theologiae*) pointed out, a double cause:

> … *men… exaggerating into worship their great affections for some men or their delight in skilfully fashioned images, or their wonder at the beauty and strength of God's creatures, and [because of] demons who present themselves for worship in the idols men have made…*

Satanism, therefore, and spiritualism, have more than a passing mention in these pages as aspects of diabolic activity. The first has always been with us; the latter is a comparatively recent, and growing, phenomenon.

A study of any kind has limits. I have, however, tried to cover what I believe to be the ancient and modern machinations of demons and their leader. The classifications of demons (the demonologists were very fond of categorizations, which meant knowing the appearance and dwelling places of the evil spirits) were regarded as important aids to understanding and combating them.

An element of confusion has been introduced into the study of the Devil and demons because of a simple matter of mistranslation or misinterpretation by scholars from the earliest times, particularly when the original Hebrew version of what came to be called the Bible was translated into Greek. Basically, confusion centres on the meaning of vital words like 'Devil', 'demon' and 'Satan' (*see* page 12). Adding to the problems is the fact that 'daimon' [*sic*] was usually thought of as a good spirit, helpful to mankind, whereas of course 'demon' had almost from the beginning a bad connotation.

We end as we began with a quotation. It is from the Letter of Paul to the Romans (8:38–9)

> *For I am persuaded that neither death nor life, nor angels, nor principalities, nor powers, nor things present, nor things to come, nor any height nor depth nor any other creature shall be able to separate us from the love of God…*

The 'Principalities' and 'Powers' of which the prophet speaks are some of the spiritual beings with which we shall be concerned in the chapters to follow.

CHAPTER ONE

ANCIENT ORIGINS OF THE DEVIL

F rom the dawn of the earliest civilizations mankind has been haunted by thoughts of demons as malevolent beings whose purpose was to lead men into evil ways. In an age where virtually nothing could be explained, this would account for the misery and unhappiness in the world all around them. Scientific knowledge of disease and natural phenomena was negligible, and accordingly superstition reigned supreme.

Something deep in the human psyche has always, even today, produced a belief in restless spirits of the dead who return to plague the living or their habitations. These souls of the departed have, from time immemorial, been thought of as being malevolent towards the living, because it was believed that they returned only to avenge a wrong done to them while alive. Therefore, they were to be feared, and if possible to be appeased or exorcized.

THE DEVIL IN HOLY WRIT

Belief in demons was already ancient when the Old Testament was being written in the millennium before the birth of Christ. There is, however, no reference to demons in these writings and very little to the Devil, or Satan, as he is generally called.

The New Testament is very different altogether, and numerous mentions are made of Satan as the embodiment of evil, as distinct from 'a' satan or adversary allusively referred to in the Old Testament. Usually, it is from the concept of Satan as revealed in the Bible that our idea of demons is derived: Satan is the King of the Demons who are descended from him. For example, many cases of bodily possession by demons are described in the New Testament, as is their expulsion by the power of exorcism, generally by Jesus. Demons, and their father, the Devil or Satan, we believe came into existence as a result of 'the fall', whenever that was. Surprisingly, there is no detailed reference to the fall of the angels in the Bible, certainly not in Genesis, where Adam and Eve were tempted, it is supposed, by Satan, an already fallen angel.

The gradually evolving concept of the Devil is of a being who is the implacable enemy of God and Christians; devils are equated with demons, who are malignant fiends. The word 'devil', deriving from the Greek *diabolos*, originally meant 'accuser'. When the Old Testament was translated from Hebrew into Greek, confusingly, the word *diabolos* was used for the Hebrew 'satan', a being whose purpose was to try to test Man and who, at that stage, was not actually evil. Some of his handiwork can be seen in his tormenting, by God's permission, of the righteous Job. A further error was perpetrated when this Greek version of the Old Testament was translated into Latin and *diabolos* became either 'Devil' or 'Satan'.

New Testament allusions to the Devil or Satan, deriving from the Greek *satanas*, are plentiful; a picture begins to emerge of Satan as the adversary not merely of mankind, but of God also. English translations of the Bible made the Hebrew 'satan' and the Greek *satanas* interchangeable with 'Satan', causing more confusion. Later on, 'devil' and 'demon' became equated, although demons were not originally all evil; some were thought of as good, a type of guardian spirit. 'Demon' meant slanderer. The Greek version of the Hebrew Bible (called the Septuagint) used the word 'demon' as something essentially evil. The result was that eventually originally different spirits became confused and subsumed under such labels as 'demon', 'devil' or 'fiend'. Satan became the recipient of all these labels, and all references in the Bible to an enemy of God devolved on him. More difficulty is presented by the varying names bestowed on him in his role as arch-fiend: Lucifer, Asmodeus, Beelzebub and so on.

The Judeo-Christian concept of the devil, which is mainly what we are concerned with here, has traditions going back to a past which was already old when the Gospels were being written. The Hebrew race had been much subjugated even before the time of Christ, so writers of the Gospels, particularly those of the New Testament, inevitably were influenced by the beliefs of their conquerors, especially in the area of religious belief, in which a demonology loomed large.

The predominant theme of these AD writers was the conflict between good and evil: good represented by Jesus' life on earth; and evil represented by Satan or the Devil. So there appeared to be two entities, mutually exclusive, both with supernatural powers. In a world created by an omnipotent, wholly good God, how could the readily observed phenomenon of evil in the world be allowed to exist? Indeed, how could it have been created in the first place by an all-loving God by whom all things were created?

For some civilizations a belief in polytheism (more than one god), some of the gods being beneficent, some maleficent, was the answer to this particular riddle. For Judaism, and the later Christianity, there was no such solution, for they were monotheistic (believing in only one god).

Traditionally, the Jewish race was founded by Abraham, to whom the promise was made by God that the land of Israel should eventually belong to him and his descendants. In accordance with this promise, in about 2000 BC Abraham led his people from Mesopotamia, where they were then gathered, into Egypt. Some 550 years later Moses led the Exodus from Egypt, 'the land of bondage', and his people later conquered Palestine (as Israel was originally known) under Joshua. The new kingdom was divided into Israel and Judah, both parts of which were overrun by the Babylonians, who deported many of the inhabitants. During this period, from about 600 to 550 BC (the Babylonian exile), many characteristic Judaic beliefs arose, among which was the idea of one omnipotent God.

Moses' teaching, as seen in the first five books of the Bible, known as the Torah, laid down religious principles and morality. Religious leaders, called rabbis, encouraged adherence to the Torah. In subsequent centuries, various interpretations of Scriptures were written down in the Talmud (basically, the Old Testament), so that the Torah and the Talmud became the focal point of the Jewish faith. Strictly speaking the Talmud is a compilation of oral tradition and law, accompanied by commentary on them. There are two versions of the work: the Palestinian Talmud, dating from about AD 450, and the Babylonian Talmud, dating from about AD 500. The latter tends to be more acceptable to traditional Jews.

An understanding of the events, indeed faith, presented in the Gospels is impossible without a basic knowledge of the influences throughout the ages on the writers – whoever they were! Historically the Gospels have been attributed to people known as Matthew, Mark, Luke and John, but it is possible that more than one hand was involved under each person's name. Moreover, it has never been decisively proved that any of these writers were eye-witnesses (with the probable exception of John) to events in the life of Jesus. The crucial point is that the writers of the Gospels were evangelizing for the new religion of Christianity, seeing as their primary task an interpretation of events enacted thirty and more years earlier that would testify to Jesus as the promised Messiah. In this task many echoes of earlier civilizations are apparent.

We have seen that Abraham led his people out of Mesopotamia to begin the Hebrew travels. Mesopotamian demonology, therefore, had great influence on Hebrew and Christian thought. Their demons were generally hostile: some were thought of as jailers of the dead in hell; others were ghosts of those who had died unhappy deaths; and some haunted desert places or tombs. There were demons of every human ill. Lilith, the terrible night fiend, a female, attacked men and sucked their blood. Usually these demons were conceived of as misshapen and ugly, part animal, part human. Protection depended largely on worship of a good deity and the carrying of certain amulets and charms.

INFLUENCES ON HEBREW DEMONOLOGY

Palestine was conquered by the Assyrians in 720 BC, but was subsequently overrun by the Babylonians. What is now called the Middle East, which of course included Palestine, was mainly under Persian domination for some 200 years. A period of independence for the Hebrews was short lived; differences arose and civil war broke out leading to Roman intervention in 65 BC. In AD 70 the temple at Jerusalem was destroyed by the Romans. Palestine was then conquered in the seventh century by Muslim Arabs, who went on to rule for about 900 years. Early in the fifteenth century, the Ottoman Turks conquered the country, remaining for some three centuries.

For many years, therefore, the Hebrews were under the yoke of the Egyptians, a long period of captivity that had its influence on future writings. Egyptian religion had many gods, but they were all aspects of one God. For them the universe was the creation of this one all-powerful God, represented by the sun god; but he had an adversary, Seth, who although not the embodiment of evil was nevertheless associated with death and destruction. He tended to haunt desert and desolate places like the demons of the later Christianity.

Babylonian religious belief had a much less ordered cosmos than the Egyptian. As a result, this gave rise to a world of hostile demons, often the spirits of the dead, which were responsible for almost every ill that might befall – a precursor of the Christian belief in corporeal possession by demons.

Eventually, as we have seen, the Hebrews settled in the land of Canaan (Israel), where the central religious tenet was a belief in conflict between Baal (at that time benevolent) and another god, Mot, lord of death and misfortune. Other influences were Greek and Roman beliefs. These beliefs held in veneration many gods representative of various elements in the natural world, although in so far as there was one supreme god, for example Zeus or Jove, these religions can be thought of as monotheistic, adducing a single divine being or principle.

The gods of earlier, pagan communities were later demonized – a common development in the history of nations – so that a ready-made corpus of detestable beings, so to speak, was at hand. Some religions strongly believed in a pure (!) spirit of evil, as in the Persian, where one being, Ahriman, is wickedness and evil personified. It was said that, like Satan, he was consumed by covetousness and envy, and rebelled against his loving god; for his sin he was cast down into darkness and void. As in the Christian story, Ahriman is the tempter of the first human couple, who, like Adam and Eve, fall into sin. As in the later Biblical accounts, at the centre is a powerful spiritual struggle between the forces of good and evil.

In distinction, it must be said, the Greeks and Romans believed in a number of hostile spirits without having one predominant personality of evil. The Greek word '*daimon*' did not automatically mean an evil spirit – it could be a kind of guardian – but mistranslations resulted in a plentiful demonology for subsequent Christian writers.

The Greeks themselves were influenced by earlier civilizations such as those of the Minoans and the Myceneans. Their gods were manifestations of the one God. Thus, individual gods possessed both good and evil qualities.

In the classical period, each god was perceived as a synthesis of diverse elements deriving from earlier sects. In the Greek demonology this was Pan, one of history's enduring figures. Pan is usually depicted as goat-like and hairy in appearance, with horns and cloven feet. A phallic deity like his father, Hermes, he symbolized sexual licence. There were, however, many other minor malicious spirits, but none embodied a Principle of Evil. As we have seen, the Greek *daimon* did not always denote an evil being, but the term shifted its connotation over time until in Plato's writing, or soon afterwards, it became an evil and destructive entity: like a satan who became *the* Satan.

Through their philosophical enquiries the Greeks attained a moralized standard of behaviour to which both men and gods conformed. The Principle of Evil (the Devil) became not just something opposed to the gods, but morally evil in itself. Development of the idea of the Devil went hand in hand with beliefs about demons. In Greek thought these demons were, like the gods, morally ambivalent. An important concept was that of Hades, the underworld, a place of punishment for the wicked. The god Hades became leader of an army of evil spirits whose job was to torment the living. One can readily see in this the basis of the Christian hell.

THE CONCEPTION OF AN EVIL BEING

A reading of the Old Testament reveals a God who is harsh and unyielding – not a wanted characteristic in an all-loving, merciful being! Attitudes had to change. This led to the conception of a spiritual being, one that was evil, opposed to God. Satan, the Devil, of the kind seen in the New Testament, hostile to God and Man, had been created.

But how had the being originated? The common belief was that Satan, Lucifer, call him what you will, had wished to be like God Himself and, basically out of jealousy and overweening pride in himself, had rebelled against God. Conflict had ensued in which Satan was defeated, as a result of which he was cast out of Heaven along with other angels he had influenced. These lesser angels became devils, and later demons. This all happened soon after the creation.

In another version accounting for the fall of Lucifer/Satan, he became envious of Adam and Eve's apparently blissful state, and determined to end their reign in the Garden of Eden, especially when God wished him to bow down to the newcomers. Consequently, he took the shape of a serpent; speaking through its mouth, he beguiled the first man and first woman into committing sin by eating of the forbidden fruit. When Satan's treachery was discovered by God, he was expelled from paradise and forever damned.

The rapidly growing host of demons was also accounted for by the story that some of the angels, 'seeing the daughters of men, that they were fair', had lusted after human women, came down from heaven and mated with these earthlings. As a result, strange giant-like beings were created, who subsequently became demons and who themselves created demonic beings through their own couplings.

Yet another version has Adam having another wife, the night demon, Lilith, the mother of Adam's offspring who became demons. Some of these stories are related in the books of the Bible, some narrated in the books known as the Apocrypha: that is to say, books not accepted by the rabbis as forming part of the true scriptural canon. Nevertheless, these books shed valuable light on matters which exercise the minds of Biblical scholars. They are most easily understood as books composed by Hebrew writers, bridging books which span the overlapping periods at the end of the activity of the Old Testament writers and the beginning of the composition of the New Testament.

In another interpretation of the existence of demons, they derived from the minor evil spirits of the Near East, and this was itself derived in part from the practice of regarding the deities of pagan peoples as demonic. The Devil is their prince – as well as being the prince of evil humans. In the New Testament, the Devil is still a creation of God, albeit a fallen angel, but he acts as the chief of fallen angels and of all evil powers. Demons aided and abetted the Devil in his wicked designs; above all, they were tempters who did all they could to lead mankind astray. It seemed that they assailed the virtuous and righteous more than most, especially the religious, and most particularly the saints. Visions and manifestations promising worldly pleasures were, it seems, common.

PRINCE OF THIS WORLD

Of course in the first century or so AD, Christianity was a minority religion, struggling for recognition and expansion. It had no corpus of defined doctrine. For the early Christian Church, God was timeless and eternal and ruled a cosmos informed by love, reason and free will. Some of the angels sinned (because they were allowed to by God) in so far as they had free will. Man was then created, also with free will. Consequently, Adam and Eve were not forced to sin, and in yielding to the Devil's temptation were exercising their free will. This first sin alienated mankind from God and left us subject to the Devil's temptations. In this sense he rules the earth; he is 'prince of this world'. Christ's incarnation restored our freedom and set us free from the bondage of sin.

God, it was felt, permits demons to torment humanity as a trial of steadfastness, of goodness, of loyalty to Him; such affliction, indeed all pain and misfortune in the world, may warn us of the dangers of evil; they may be just punishment for sin or weakness or transgression of some kind. Because of Man's fall from grace, all subsequent men and women are born tainted by original sin, and concupiscence is the result: a predilection for material things, wealth and lust are some effects. Before this original sin of mankind, the Devil had no power over us. After we sinned, exercising our free will, the Devil was allowed certain powers over us. When God made Himself Man He Himself was subject to the temptations of Satan, as witness the accounts of the temptations in the desert and on the mountain top.

The Devil appeared to his victims in many disguises. Naturally, it suited later clerics to invest the Devil with a hideous connotation, frightening in appearance, changeable in shape and form, and capable of being virtually ubiquitous. Clearly, the belief was that painting a terrifying picture of the Devil was more likely to keep the people in line than mere promises of unworldly delights to come if they behaved themselves!

The Devil could appear as an animal, perhaps a deformed one, or something in between a man and a beast. He is usually black, possessing horns and a tail, and cloven feet. He might be giant sized or small but threatening. After all, he took the shape of a snake in order to tempt Eve. He might, on the other hand, take the shape of an attractive person to beguile us. The Devil is almost always male. He and his henchmen live at the centre of the universe, as conceived at that time. For, where God, the angels, the Devil and the demons dwelt was of great moment.

A SPIRITUAL COSMOLOGY

The early Fathers, 'the Apostolic Fathers', were Christian writers on faith, theology and morals in the first few centuries AD who constructed an elaborate cosmology. Simply stated, Satan and the devils lived in hell at the centre of the earth, while God and the angels lived in heaven or in the (upper) air (the ether). The centre of the cosmos was the heavy region of hell – furthest away from God.

From the earth, looking up towards heaven, our gaze would pass through

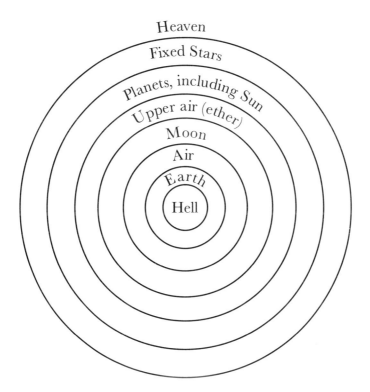

Early Christian cosmology

several spheres. Above the earth was the air, in which dwelt the more corporeal of the angels, perhaps the fallen ones. The sphere of the moon was just above the air. Beyond the moon was the upper air in which dwelt the good angels, less material than the others. Outside them were to be described the spheres of the planets: the Sun, Mars, Jupiter and so on. Past the planets was the sphere of the fixed stars. The final sphere moved the whole universe and outside this was the realm of God, all beauty and light. This cosmology was deliberately constructed to reflect a spiritual, religious bias: it is hierarchical, both spiritually and materially. Morally, also, it is intelligible.

Our propensity to wickedness draws us down to the lower earth where dwell the Devil and his demons; striving for virtue and goodness raises us up, as we aspire to the fount of all goodness and purity, God, and His faithful angels who live in the outer, ethereal regions of the universe. This universe was created by God in order to increase the sum total of happiness and goodness for Man, who must have free will so he may choose goodness. This cosmos had no beginning and will have no end: for the early Christians, the cosmos existed eternally. The purpose behind the creation of the cosmos was a statement, a manifestation of God's power, His all-abiding omnipotence and dynamism. (*See* diagram, page 17.)

It was believed that the angels who dwelt in the upper air also had their hierarchies. Three levels encompassing three ranks obtained: the highest were the Seraphim, Cherubim and Thrones; middle ranking were the Dominations, Virtues and Powers; the lowest ranking were the Principalities, Archangels and Angels.

Satan had been a Seraph, one of the highest order of angels, until he fell like a bolt of lightning, crashing through the spheres on his headlong dive to earth. Striking the earth, he caused a great impact, opening up a crevice which led straight to the centre of the earth. This centre where Satan dwelt was known as Hell.

THE ESSENTIAL EVIL OPPOSER

Satan by no means spent much time in hell. He seems to have spent most of his time leading mankind into sin, and to do this he had to haunt the earth's surface. Although not getting as much mention as such an influential being should in the writings of the Gospels, Satan is essential for belief in Jesus as the living God: the betrayal and death of Jesus would not make sense without him.

Originally he was not evil, simply an opposer. In the Hebrew Bible, 'Satan' is not the name of a particular character. He is a messenger, albeit supernatural, a member of God's court. Dissidents among the Jews, certain sects opposed to mainstream Judaism, began to characterize their enemies as 'satans' – adversaries – and in due course this figure became transmuted into the malevolent 'Satan' of (later) Christianity.

The Gospels basically tell the story of Jesus as a struggle between Him and Satan, beginning with the temptations at the start of Jesus' public life and ending with the crucifixion. This is most clearly seen in the Gospel According to John.

Luke further relates how, after the failure of the temptations in the desert, Satan returned in person to try again; he entered Judas, so beginning the process leading to the crucifixion. One interpretation of the Gospels shows how both demonic and divine energies can dwell within human beings and can either bring about their destruction – or lead them to God. In the Bible a cosmic drama is being played out. The message is: by his death Christ has conquered Satan, and the exercise of judicious choice by humanity promises a glorious life to come.

FALL OF THE EVIL ONE

For Christianity this Satan is revealed in the Bible, but belief in an Evil One is by no means found exclusively in Holy Writ. He has appeared in all the world's mythologies, in Hindu (Vitra), in Persian (Ahriman), in Greek (Zeus) and also in most of Scandinavia (Loki). It may be true, however, that more references to a Satan (of Christianity) are also to be found in the Bible, though many are obscure. What may be claimed is that similar stories to those found in the Bible, especially concerning the entities of good and evil, are also found in all the ancient pagan literature which records those nations' annals. All possess some reference to a fall from favour or from grace whereby an initially good being is transformed by his own fault into something evil and menacing.

For Christians the abiding reason for the creation of the Devil and his cohorts was the fall from heaven occasioned by pride. As Christ said to His disciples (Luke 10:18): 'I saw Satan like lightning falling from heaven'. Satan's sin would therefore appear to be an attempt to equate himself with God, to share His sovereignty. When he offered Christ the kingdoms of this world (as one of the three temptations), he was in fact offering what he could not deliver; only the sins and follies of this world are his to offer.

The fall of the angels has differing accounts in the accepted canon, the Apocrypha and the apocalyptic literature (unaccepted as the true word of God). In the Book of Enoch, one of the uncanonical books, it is related how the angels saw and lusted after the daughters of men. They went down to earth, and as a result of their liaisons giants were born who wreaked lawlessness and bloodshed on the earth. These giants in turn gave rise to a race of evil spirits.

In another part of the Book of Enoch the angels who fell are alluded to as stars who cast themselves down from the heavens. They were judged and found guilty by the Lord. In the Book of Jubilees, another non-canonical apocalyptic book, the main motive of the angels who came down to earth was to improve men and instruct them in righteousness. Later, however, they yielded to the charms of women.

We also read here of 'satans' who existed in heaven before the fall of the angels. At this time the satans and the fallen angels are distinguished. In the Book of Enoch the sin of the fallen angels comprises their becoming subject to Satan, their leader. Other apocryphal books (Books of Adam and Eve) relate the manner in which Satan tempted Adam and Eve and brought about their downfall. Satan, apparently questioned by Eve as to his motives, said that basically his motive was his jealousy of Adam. Rabbinic literature adduces that evil spirits were created, but created on the eve of the first Sabbath, so that there was no time to give them bodies. Adam, it seems, mated during his separation from Eve with numerous female spirits, while Eve did the same with many male spirits. In both cases their progeny was malevolent.

PROVING JESUS' DIVINITY

What must never be lost sight of when reading the Gospels is that the writers were seeking to prove the divinity of God made Man, that is, Jesus, as being the true incarnation of Godhead and the true Messiah. Proof of this would inescapably establish the religion derived from Jesus' teaching as the one incontrovertible true Church for which Man had been waiting and in whose trust lay eternal salvation. Indeed, the Gospel writers were zealots for whom spreading the word as they understood it was the paramount duty in life.

Unfortunately for them, heresy early raised its ugly head, so that even in the first century AD the as yet infant Church was riven. Several sects rose up over the subsequent centuries advocating variants on the traditional teaching, some of which openly worshipped Satan, such as the Bogomils in the tenth century. In the following century several strange organizations came into being, members of which practised obscure rites and rituals; central to their beliefs was worship of the Principle of Evil, namely the Devil and his demons.

In the Gospel writings it is very clear that belief in hostile spirits was common; it was taken for granted that people could be plagued by evil beings, as witness the many allusions to the activities of devils, as they were always referred to (never demons), especially in connection with the phenomenon of possession. The Biblical alternative phrase to devils was 'evil' or 'unclean' spirits. Christ on earth cast out many evil spirits and gave the Apostles power to do the same in His name (Mark 16:17): 'These signs shall follow them that believe; in my name they shall cast out devils...'

THE CREATION

Much debate surrounds the actual moment of creation of the angels and one might be forgiven for remarking: so what? It is purely a point for Biblical scholars or theologians to argue over. This is not the case. Explanations of the fall (of the angels and of Man) hang on it. Some thinkers believe that the angels existed long before the Son of God was begotten. The Greek Fathers usually, and the Latin ones on occasion, believed that the making of the angels preceded the creation of most of the world, so they were present at, and were used at, the creation of the world itself.

However, the most commonly adopted viewpoint is that the angels were created along with the rest of creation. St Augustine, one of the great early medieval religious thinkers, held the view that the angels and the earth were created simultaneously.

People of other traditions believed that earth and heaven were made before the angels and, not only this, but that the making of light came before the creation of the angels. Lucifer, the apostate angel, was as his name indicates the Bearer of Light in his palmy days when he dwelt with God. Light was created by God, and Lucifer was his instrument in extending that light into the darkness of ignorance and of the physical void. It may also refer to Lucifer's shining beauty – a beauty that was drastically lost by the fall. According to traditional belief, Lucifer's beauty was totally and immediately destroyed.

Lucifer was still essentially a spiritual being, but became more corporeal through his descent; after all, he would have to have a body to suffer the torments of hell's fires. The ability to take bodily form by all the angels is, however, understood. There are many instances in the Bible of angels appearing in bodily form. They are clearly freer than Man in respect to space and time, yet they have been created and are therefore finite compared to God. They are equally obviously preternatural in their mental and physical powers.

The same can be said of the Hebrew demons, whose conception derived from other cultures, such as that of Canaan and Mesopotamia. They could be responsible for plague, pestilence and famine. Many she-devils, whose ringleader was Lilith, went about at night attacking sleeping men. Some spirits were accompanied by howling dogs; Leviathan, related to Babylonian myth, haunted the sea; and Behemoth was a monster who killed people on sight. Hebrew demons could cause all manner of misfortunes. The goat was a common manifestation of the devil, which clearly led to the virtually ubiquitous depiction of the Devil (and devils) as having animal characteristics.

GOOD ANGELS AND THE INCARNATION

An interesting, even curious, phrase is the scriptural reference to 'elect angels', that is to say, those that did not sin (1 Timothy 5:21); the interpretation of this seems to be that some angels were predestined for loyalty and goodness.

It is instructive to compare this notion with the current (and long-standing) belief in predestination for mankind – as some religious organizations have held (and still do hold). The corollary is that part of the angelic host was placed on probation as it were, but then difficulties arise from the accepted theory of the omniscient nature of God. No doubt, like infinity and eternity, there is much about Godhead and the Scriptures that mortal minds cannot comprehend – or even begin to rationalize.

In the Scriptures, angels are most frequently used as messengers (the meaning of the word 'angels') and to 'assist' in certain momentous Biblical events, but they do not actually administer God's providence and are never substitutes for God. These are the 'good' angels. The evil angels oppose God's will and owe their allegiance to an erstwhile high-ranking angel who sinned: Satan. These manifestly do come between God and Man. From the many names given him, we readily see that power, malice and hostility are his chief attributes: Satan (adversary); Belial (wickedness); Beelzebub (lord of the flies or dung heap);

and the Devil himself (slanderer) are but some of them.

Because Man was the target of the Devil's attacks – due to Satan's implacable hatred of the first humans in their paradise, the Garden of Eden – God ruled that the battle against Satan should be spearheaded by a man: Jesus was that man, the Son of God. The fall of Man had to be atoned for by the rise of a man who was the embodiment of God, with some of God's attributes, but a real man of his times nevertheless: Jesus Christ.

Ultimately the Devil had to be defeated. If he were all-conquering, as he could have been with ninety per cent of mankind, paradise, the Kingdom of God, would have been sparsely populated, at least with the souls who had made it to the everlasting life of happiness with God!

Accordingly, the birth of Jesus to Mary and Joseph is to be seen as the first salvo fired by God in his plan to defeat Satan. By the Incarnation Christ died to redeem all mankind: Man was at least given the chance to regain access to the eternal life which he had rejected by his first sin. 'He who believes in me shall never die' – nothing could be more unequivocal, provided one lived according to the principles of the Messiah. In other words, Man was free to resist or to submit to the Devil on account of his free will. Though Christ died to save the human race, nothing was guaranteed: but the opportunity to attain the good things in this life and in the life to come was in place again. The resurrection was the ultimate proof that Jesus was indeed God made Man, the true Redeemer. The miracles had been indications; the Resurrection the proof. The human soul now had the ability to be as the angels in their spiritual entity; this similarity was clearly stated by God in His words (Luke 20:35–6): 'those who are found worthy... will be as the angels in heaven are, children of God now that the resurrection has given them birth'.

For the angels not in heaven – the fallen ones, now devils – no repentance was possible. Because of their nature, their supreme intellectual power by which all things were conceived and done intuitively, they were incapable of reconsidering anything. Their sin was unforgivable because they could not retract. Their banishment from heaven was not a banishment from creation, however. The Devil had an important part to play in the world – this is the reason why he exists. We have seen the Devil's role in trying and testing Man. We need to remember that his portrayal in the Old Testament is as a creature of God, by no means a rival being. It is only when we come to the New Testament that we see the Principle of Evil, the Devil, in his own right.

CHRIST'S POWER OVER SATAN

Until the Incarnation and Jesus' ministry, where the New Testament accounts begin, Satan the Prince of this World had reigned supreme. When Jesus began exorcizing, He gave this power to His disciples, but on one occasion gently admonished them, saying (Luke 10:17–20): 'instead of rejoicing that the devils are made subject to you, you should be rejoicing that your names are enrolled in heaven'. It is clear that Christ claims power over Satan and his devils; that he leaves to His Church a power over devils; that He sees His mission on earth as combating and overthrowing Satan and his henchmen.

Satan is more than once described in the Bible as the ruler of this world. The way this is to be understood is that his kingdom is our world and our time. Hell may be Satan's kingdom, but so is the world as long as Man is to be tempted. In fact 'the world' generally in the New Testament is a term of opprobrium, for the term means that part of humanity which fails to conform to God's precepts. For the Gospel writers the Devil always had the best tunes. The worldly struggle was between life (in this world) and death of the soul (in the next).

However, Satan will not be Prince of this World for ever. At the Last Judgement, at the end of time, Satan will lose his title and become only Prince of Hell. This much is clear from the Scriptures. It is equally clear that until that time the demons are free to haunt the world, seeking victims. This may seem hard to understand, but because God is just, He is so to fallen angels as to Man. Satan is granted rights also. As some theologians have put it, God would be unjust to Satan if anyone else could achieve holiness without effort and without meriting it.

DEVELOPMENT OF CHRISTIANITY AND DEMONOLOGY

From the foregoing it is clear that Greek and Jewish concepts of the Devil were synthesized in Christianity, which states that there is only one omnipotent, wholly good God. These attributes derive partly from Judaism and partly from Hellenistic (or Greek) thought. Christianity developed as a monotheistic religion: God as the fount of all, evil (for a purpose and with His permission) as well as good. For some thinkers the dualist element in Christianity is incontrovertible. Dismissing the Devil leaves the Deity unbalanced, lop-sided. The argument is: without the Devil belief in God is likewise abolished. The one complements the other. Belief in one is necessary for belief in the other.

Christianity attributed powers to demons similar to those given them by the rabbinical literature, so that by the end of the New Testament period no differentiation was made between demons and the fallen angels. In Hebrew writing demons are spiritual beings who are permitted by the Lord to tempt us as punishment for our sins.

In the New Testament the Devil is the enemy of the Kingdom of God and the wreaker of mischief among mankind. Later on he came to rule hell, to suffer in hell himself and to administer punishment to sinners there. He was aided in his work of torturing the damned by a host of demons, generally depicted as black, horned and tailed. In the New Testament, demons are associated with a number of animals: lions, bears, scorpions and other creatures.

The Devil himself is most often likened to a serpent, though not often portrayed as one. Wings are traditionally attributed to the Devil, probably deriving from his origin as an angel and his speed of flight as he rules the air. At the time of the New Testament the Devil was the personification of evil: he occasioned harm to humans, often of a physical nature; he accused and punished sinners; he led the host of demons; he was the (temporary) ruler of this world until the end of the world, when he would be defeated; he tempted people to sin; and he had inherited all the evil qualities derived from earlier pagan beliefs.

TRADITIONS SEPARATE

After the time of the New Testament writing, Jewish and Christian traditions began to separate. Christian tradition came to identify the Devil and the demons with the fallen angels, with the Devil as the chief of the demons. Judaism followed the path of circumscribing the role of the Devil: that is, Jewish writers thought and wrote about the Devil as a being of lesser influence in human affairs.

Christianity addressed such questions as the nature and rank of the angels. It discussed the time of the fall and Satan's motives. It asked questions arising from matter in the Scriptures and in the process developed a theology of possession and exorcism. It associated the Devil with heretics, Jews and infidels. The opposition of the powers of the Devil and God/Christ is the informing theme of the later thinking.

Some of this thinking is encountered in the writings of the greatest medieval Catholic thinker, St Thomas Aquinas (1225–74), whose position can be summed up as follows. God created a world in which sin is possible; evil is possible; rebellion is possible. If there had been no free choice of evil, Man could have chosen only from good things so in a way there would have been no free choice and certainly no testing of Man. This world order was created by God, as was the Devil, therefore one may say that sin and all things evil were permitted by God. It is not surprising that Satan was inclined to the sin of pride because of the very superiority granted him by God. However, nothing is possible outside the Supreme Maker's will. Everything, therefore, good or evil, has its cause and beginning in Him. God, the infinitely compassionate, therefore must have felt sorrow as well as justified anger when Lucifer fell. He had to condemn Lucifer, but cannot hate him because the Godly nature is all-loving. The Devil's tragedy is that he cannot redeem himself and God cannot restore him to his highest position in heaven because, as we have said, the Devil, once an archangel, cannot repent, and therefore cannot respond to God's love.

MAN AS INTERMEDIARY?

Could Man have been the intermediary? Perhaps, it has been argued, Man was created in the hope of Satan's redemption. Man could have been the instrument of the Devil's hostility to God; Man could have tempted Satan in return and could have led him back to his true origin. The first humans should have been the means of Satan's return to Paradise. Instead, God's love was betrayed. In accepting the word of the tempter, Adam and Eve thwarted God's design. As Papini puts it in his book *The Devil* (page 47): 'the celestial giant has fallen into the pit; the earthly emperor is maimed and poisoned'. The important point is that Man was redeemed by the death on the cross.

On the other hand, the Devil's hatred of all things good derives from his realization that he is eternally dependent on his Creator. He knows that if he has not been dispossessed, not destroyed, it is only because God has given him a role to play in the world – has seen in fact his value: as a tempter *par excellence*. In this role he has had resort to many disguises of the flesh and has taken possession of the minds of men and women. Some people have been so evil as to be construed as incarnations of the Devil: Nero, Attila, Ivan the Terrible and Hitler are but some of them, and there are many more depending on one's viewpoint. Literature, of course, provides many instances: Mephistopheles, and the many variations on the Faust story.

It has been said that Satan peoples his hell, but at the same time he peoples heaven. In other words, it is only by overcoming wickedness that human beings attain beatitude. There is no true merit which does not entail struggle and ultimate victory over the Demon (or demons). Without the curse of original sin Man would not be subject to temptation. Even the crucifixion could not obliterate that.

According to St Augustine of Hippo (AD 354–430), God offered His Son to the Devil as bait, as it were, which he of course reached out for, but could not attain, Christ being not merely Man but God incarnate. The Devil was defeated, but not destroyed, which will happen only at the Second Coming. During the early years of the Christian Church the concept of the Devil as a malevolent being grew, especially at first in the eyes of the clerics. He was soon realized as being an ideal recruiting sergeant to the still fledgling Christian faith. His faithful followers, the demons, wrought, it was believed, untold ills.

At the time of Jesus many demons recognized Him, declaring Him to be the Son of God. They communicate with each other (Matthew 12:43 ff) and are capable of trembling at God's name. Their chief aim is to lead people away from the faith, but they perform all manner of depredations, including injury, attempted murder and possession of human bodies, and can perform miracles, albeit of a deleterious nature.

They assailed the common people and the religious mystics equally. The latter believed that the Devil attacked them more because they had more to lose, in their intense search for union with God. The Devil, it was believed, loved to interfere with the process of prayer and meditation. He may even make us feel pride – a sin – in our spirituality being greater than other people's. He will attempt to distract us from our true purposes, especially if we are mystics, contemplatives or clerics. Spiritual attack and physical assault, perhaps both, are frequently resorted to. Lust, gluttony, fear, despair are a few of his snares.

UNDERSTANDING EVIL

This study of belief in demons throughout the centuries is in many ways basically an attempt to understand the phenomenon of evil. We have discussed the perplexing question of the presence of evil in a world created by a God who can do no evil, therefore cannot create evil. Remaining is the question: does belief in the

Devil and his demons help to answer this? It is too easy to say that evil men are led astray by the Devil or by demons. To adduce this is to deny we have any responsibility, ultimately to deny our free will.

We have all read in the media of people who claim they heard voices in their subconscious urging them on to wicked deeds, hoping to offer this as a defence for their actions. Of course, it may be that these people were temporarily deranged and did imagine voices – but if they were not deranged and the voices were real? How can we ever know the truth? Current thinking that the concept of the Devil and his demons is just a metaphor for the acknowledged presence of evil is prevalent – but many believe otherwise.

It is true that the figure of the Devil has become trivialized in recent times, even suffered the ignominy of being banished altogether as a mere will-o'-the-wisp, so that reading of the Scriptures becomes selective and we read into them what we will and leave out what we don't like. But it must be acknowledged that the Devil is deeply rooted in Scripture and supported by tradition. Whether one is a Christian or not seems to me to be irrelevant in judging this question. History can be read by a person of any faith.

The Devil's historical development is the only sure knowledge we have. There are many inconsistencies: this much is admitted. For Christians, the being known as the Devil may be a metaphor, but it is a figure of speech for something real that undoubtedly brings evil into the world. If the Devil is a metaphor, so is God, the Omnipotent, whose power also must be called into question if one is to be consistent. Naturally, free will must be considered in any debate. As we have said, free will is necessary to Man and to his chances of attaining paradise. We observe there is a great deal of evil in the world, perhaps more than the exercise of freedom on the part of mankind warrants. It may be that the free choice of evil by the Devil, Lucifer as he was, accounts for much of it. As J. B. Russell says in his book *Lucifer: The Devil in the Middle Ages* (page 311):

> *The Devil is a metaphor for the evil in the cosmos… he represents the transconscious, transpersonal evil that exceeds the individual human evil will; he is the sign of the radical… evil in the cosmos.*

However we look at it, Satan, even in the time of the setting down of the Old Testament (*see* Chronicles 1:21), and certainly in the New Testament, had become an autonomous being. Not far behind were his legions of demons. Literature grew up from about the second century BC to about the first century AD which is known as apocalyptic. It is so called because it is full of allegedly supernatural revelations about the future or known as Apocrypha (*see* page 16) because they were thought to embody spurious matter, and this literature bears numerous references to evil spirits.

The Dead Sea Scrolls present a very similar picture of the demonology current at the time of the writing by the Jews of the Apocrypha. This demonology, seen in the scrolls and the Apocrypha, tells of a Satan who is directly opposed to

God. We learn of the tremendous struggle between them and that there are now two kingdoms: that of Christ, and that of the Devil. The New Testament Devil is assisted, as in the Jewish Apocrypha, by hosts of demons, lesser beings than himself who wage incessant war on humanity.

THE EVIL ONE IN ALL THINGS

Certainly, at the time of Christ, the Devil or the Evil One played a very important part in the lives of the people. Satan's name appears often in the Synoptic Gospels (the Gospels of Mark, Matthew and Luke). Jesus Himself refers much less than do his contemporaries to Satan, although it is clear that He did believe that mental illnesses were due to demon possession – as did the rest of the populace. Was Satan mainly a symbol of moral evil for Christ, as some writers allege? It is beyond doubt that Christ always represents the Devil as the Enemy, and as a man He could only ring true as man-made flesh if he thought like his contemporaries. For most of Jesus' ministry the disciples did not know that their leader was the Son of God. The pagan peoples who surrounded Christ saw in Him a type of magician who performed miracles by the aid of the Devil; believers in Him, Christians, worshipped Him as the Son of God.

For Christ's coevals, the evil principle was conceived as a independent entity. Moral authority was to the Jews represented by Yahveh, the Creator, the lord of the universe. An objective standard of right and wrong in this universe was before Jesus' time indeterminate except by reference to the gods who were malevolent or benevolent. After the Incarnation, people's Christian perceptions became, eventually, much clearer regarding these subjects, with the exception of course of the subsequent adherents to sects. For the people of Judea, Christ might be in all things – but the Devil was certainly in all things! The scriptural message was that Satan promised independence, but in reality delivered only oppression. Real liberty is only delivered by God. Good only really exists by comparison with evil; God exists as God because there is a Devil (and demons). As Carus writes in *The History of the Devil* (page 488):

> *Indeed we must grant that the Devil is the most indispensable and faithful helpmate of God. To speak mystically, even the existence of the Devil is filled with the presence of God.*

There are numerous references to Satan in the Scriptures, especially in the works of Paul, which show that Satan was viewed as the head of the kingdom of evil. It is quite clear that to St Paul, as to the disciples and as to Jesus, this evil kingdom and its ruler are realities. The demonology of the Gospels, concepts which were current at the time, was reflected in the apocalyptic literature, which was widely known. All references to Satan in the Scriptures need not be taken literally (although some groups do).

As we are aware, much of Christ's teaching is in parables, which by their very nature are open to interpretation. I believe that some of the most significant of

Biblical narratives are to be regarded as metaphorical – as a symbol of what the writers wanted to convey. It must be remembered that the Gospels were written decades after Christ's death, and it is likely that much, or at least some, became transmuted down the years. Of course, the writings of Scripture are traditionally regarded as the inspired word of God and it may be so. Proof one way or the other is not possible.

Lest it be thought that Satan and his demons were permitted to have things all their own way, it is emphasized in the apocalyptic literature that they are to be 'bound'; that is to say, imprisoned in some remote place, for thousands of years, before being released again to wreak their evil anew. Eventually, of course, Satan and his cohorts will finally be destroyed at the Day of Judgement. At the present time, it may be thought that the Devil is no longer bound!

Free to Find a Solution

It must be emphasized at this point that, simply because Jesus appeared to accept the current beliefs in the reality of demons (and the Devil) and the prevailing views of the cosmos and suchlike, which as a convincing man he had to, it does not follow that these views corresponded with the reality of things as we now know them. That many people believe Jesus was wrong in his views does not invalidate the utterances he made two millennia ago. Langton has summed it up nicely, when he said in his *Essentials of Demonology* (page 224):

> So far as the teaching of Jesus is concerned, we are left free to find a solution of the problem of evil... in any manner that best accords with the total facts of life, whether these are presented by anthropology, psychology, or spiritual experience.

Belief by Christians in the Devil is based on explicit evidence in Holy Writ. But Christians do not believe in two equal Powers: one of good, one of evil; they deny that evil is as ultimate as good. Christianity states that Man need not inevitably be destined for struggle and death, and that his disloyalty to God could only arise from without himself. It was through the agency of the Devil that Man sinned. Christianity further believes that the Redemption freed Man from bondage to mortal sin and from the fleshly prison-house of the soul, and that ultimately Satan would be destroyed. The wiles of the Devil, the snares of the flesh, it is further adduced, cannot be overcome except by grace from God.

THE REDEMPTION

The apotheosis of this Redemption was the Resurrection, which broke Satan's dominion. By His death on the cross, Christ freed men from a spiritual death of their own. The Resurrection, and the ascent into heaven after meeting with some of His apostles, was a victory of good over evil. Man now had the means to attain everlasting and glorious life – provided he did not yield to the embodiment of evil – the Devil – who dominated early Christian thinking. The demons, who were fallen angels fascinated by earthly women, attained, along with their leader, 'full stature with the development of Christian doctrine', as Fishwick puts it

(*Faust Revisited*, page 20). Perhaps Eve was one of these women who attracted Satan at the same time as he was bent on vengeance. Certainly, tempted by Satan in the guise of serpent, Eve rejected the God who had created her out of Adam's rib. The descendants (legitimate) of Eve (and Adam) hated God and crucified Him – unless we can lay the blame on the Romans.

SATAN IS ETERNAL

Belief in Satan was made official by the Council of Constantinople in AD 547. He was declared eternal. He had been given the seal of ecclesiastical approval. From now on it was heresy not to believe in him. How far the crucifixion and the Redemption had achieved freedom from the wiles of the Devil was an unexplainable poser, to judge from the continuing prevalence of wickedness in the world after Christ's death.

The idea was quickly taken up by the Church and the doctrine was accepted. The crucifixion of Christ was, in the context of a struggle between God and the Devil, seen as a ransom theory, a type of transaction between them both whereby Satan's victim, Man, would be liberated by the Son of Man. Christ's victory was won by paying a kind of ransom to the Devil through the death on the cross.

Parallel to the ransom theory was the combat theory of long standing, the conflict between a Principle of Evil and a Principle of Good. These combat stories developed along two differing lines, one leading to Catholic Christianity and the other to aberrant forms of dogma propagated by breakaway sects. The latter were viewed as heretical by the early Church, which was orthodox in its theology. Christianity was in the first few centuries AD best viewed as a Jewish apocalyptic sect whose messianic belief resulted in its rapid expansion. Competing versions of Christianity lent vitality to the function of Satan, who became the foremost heretic, the Prince of Darkness. The combat story came to be seen as parallel to the heresy struggle and therefore its latest transformation. Satan was the first apostate, and just as the creation had been perverted by him, so heretic sects were viewed as manifestations of his power in action.

THE DEVIL AND HIS DEMONS

Satan therefore acquired his almost autonomous status over time with many accretions from pagan and early Christian writing. The 'Christian' Devil became a formidable personal foe only as the Church and the scriptural writing developed. The height of his power and effect was reached in the Middle Ages when the Christian/Catholic Church was also at the height of its power. By the end of the Middle Ages, at the dawn of the Renaissance, his power begins to diminish – but only very slowly. In the meantime, Satan had grown into a figure of majesty and of awe, pictured everywhere as demonic, half beast and half human. He is always, in the Middle Ages at least, represented as exceedingly ugly. It was held that the Devil and demons had bodies, more incorporeal than ours, but could also be mere spirit or change shape when occasion demanded.

The corollary of all this is that having bodies they must have natural needs, among which are the need for alimentation and a desire for the reproductive act – hence the incubi and succubi beliefs which we will later discuss (*see* page 40). The usual representation in the art of the time is of a disfigured angel wearing bat-like wings, possessing a hairy body, with one or two horns, pointed ears and either cloven or clawed feet. Demons were usually portrayed as smaller, but equally repulsive if not more so, generally with tails and horns. With the Renaissance, depictions of the Devil began to alter (not so the demons), so that he was sometimes seen as an attractive figure, appealing to mankind, all the easier to lead men and women astray. He could, however, remain invisible to catch Man off guard.

Another aspect of Satan reveals him as royalty, seated on a throne, holding a sceptre and wearing a crown – the Prince of this World. He possessed not only temporal, physical power, but also the great gifts, it was believed, of intelligence and knowledge, as did his cohorts of demons. Although he had this immense power over mankind, it was not unlimited. Man consists of body and soul. The Devil does not hold sway over both. The body of Man was held to be able to be influenced, even taken over as we shall later see, and in this sense the body was Satan's ally. His first recourse therefore is to tempt the body with tantalizing allures, often of a sexual nature, and if these do not work, to try to make the spirit itself demoralized and despairing.

Regarding possession (*see* Chapter Five), Satan himself is not generally alleged to have taken possession of Man; but his demons as his followers have this function. In cases of demonic possession related in the Bible, demons are judged to have a forcible occupancy of people who were not regarded as especially wicked persons. When Jesus met such people, he pitied them rather than blamed them. Morally wicked, however, are the people who are spoken of as being under the influence of Satan.

The great teachers who flourished about AD 100–200, and the great theological thinkers in the period approximately AD 300–500, have certain basic ideas which link them in the principles they advocated. There was an accepted body of teaching by about AD 1000 which clearly came down from tradition and from writing. This denotes a dependency of one teacher on another, arising fundamentally from the consistency of Christian teaching down the ages. One tenet is the belief that the Devil, or his minions, can take possession in such a way that certain organs and senses are, as it were, taken over; they are also capable of creating obsessions by which certain visions or entities are presented to the victim in order to lead him or her from the path of righteousness.

Of course, it would be naive to assert that even these great original thinkers were not influenced by very ancient beliefs in evil spirits among primitive cultures. From the earliest times, Man has sought to propitiate these spirits or gods. Systems of mythology and demonology developed from these beliefs. As we have seen, Assyrian, Babylonian and Persian influences were some of the most ancient and abiding. After the elaborate demonology of the above, the books of the Jewish Christians are much less clear about their own evil spirits.

In Jewish demonology some beliefs and ideas were established before the Jews came into contact with their captors. Jewish demonology indicated that demons swarmed everywhere – much like the Christian belief later. The various systems of demonology have, however, much in common; thus the demonology of Christianity owes much to Jewish, Roman and Greek ideas which themselves drew on the beliefs of the ancient civilizations already mentioned. These influences turned demons into devils and transformed worshipped gods into evil forces.

Sybil Leek in *Driving Out the Devils* (page 73) says:

> *The word 'demons' is used as a generic term in the early versions of the Bible denoting objects of pagan worship. Subsequent translations use the word 'demon' to convey the idea of evil spirits or bogeys. Demons have survived as figures of speech long after they ceased to be figures of belief… Gradually specific demons emerge from ancient Near Eastern sources… mentioned in the Old Testament. The ambiguity occurs because most of the specific demons occur in the most poetic passages… and can only be construed as figures of speech. In fact, locating a demon as a consistently evil spirit is not easy to do.*

Possessing Spirit

Satan himself, it must be said, had an ancestor in the personality of Ahriman, the evil god of the Persians; this has been mentioned earlier (*see* page 19), but it is worth emphasizing in any attempt to understand the later Christian Gospels and the motives of the writers. Ahriman, like Satan, brought about the moral fall of Man, and also appeared in the guise of a serpent. Ahriman also has his legions of followers, demonic spirits all. Jews and Persians had a long cheek-by-jowl existence, so the great similarity is not surprising.

Satan only gradually became the adversary of God and Man, but he never waged war openly on God, preferring to attack humans in a variety of ways, of which possession by his demons appears to have been foremost. In order to believe in Jesus as the Messiah, the writers of the Gospels had to portray Christ as stronger than the possessing spirits. Jesus furthermore had to be convincing in his sincerity; thus Jesus had to share the belief of his countrymen with regard to Satanism. He would have been aware, however, of the incongruity of the existence of a benevolent God side by side with that of a created power of evil. The Reverend Albert Reville encapsulates this point in his *History of the Devil* (page 21):

> *Nowhere does Jesus make belief in the Devil one of the conditions of admission into the Kingdom of God; and were the Devil a mere idea, a bare symbol, these considerations would remain literally the same.*

The doctrine of angels and devils became a belief in which Hebrew polytheism and Christian monotheism could jointly meet – and develop. One development was the conception by Christianity of the Jewish Messiah as being the Saviour of a fallen humanity. To the early Christians, Satan was the direct antagonist of the Saviour. From this time the Devil grew enormously in power and caused terrible fear among the populace. He might, on the other hand, bring great worldly favours so that the idea of sorcery grew up, whereby a pact with the Devil could create a person of magical powers.

As a result, from about the thirteenth century, the crime of sorcery was punishable by death, at least in the eyes of the Church. It must be said that the medieval Church – that is, the Roman Catholic Church – encouraged belief in the Devil and his wiles and prolonged his reign. On the other hand, it must equally be said that medieval churchmen were undergoing development of their own thought, baffled by many of life's mysteries, trying to reconcile the preservation of tenets of the faith with facets of, to them, modern life. Demons and the Devil explained a lot!

DISSIDENCE

One of the problems troubling the establishment (the Church) down the ages was the failure to define what the current understanding was *vis-à-vis* the Devil. At times groups have seen the Devil as the equal of God, while others have seen him as seemingly equal but in reality subordinate. Both viewpoints were heretical according to orthodox teaching. The early Church was plagued by a sect called Gnostics whose central belief was that the Devil had a role to play of equal importance to God's. The influence of this movement lasted centuries, and was especially strong in the second and third centuries. While it lasted, Gnosticism was a painful thorn in the Church's side.

United by the Devil

Dissidence within their own ranks of course did not do the early Christian Church much good, and with the death of the disciples aberrant cults mushroomed. It has to be remembered that in those early formative years, the fledgling faith (Christianity) consisted of converted Jews and Romans with other admixtures of races. This did not make for homogeneity or conformity, bearing in mind that these peoples came not only from different races, but originally from differing faiths. Incongruously, belief in the actuality of the Devil served to unite Christians under one banner: as it were, all were marching against the enemy of mankind.

However, the Gospel writer John, late in the first century AD, had made clear that Satan and his followers will merit eternal damnation. It is here that the first glimpse of Satan as a majestic power is seen. John's Gospel was written as an eye-witness account of Christ's life and is an attempt to explain the meaning and significance of Jesus' deeds on earth. Other authors of the collection of narratives and prophecies we call the Bible – the 'Book' – were expounding their particular viewpoint, proselytizing in the truest sense in their advocacy of the new religion of Christianity.

To the sceptic, the miracles related in the Bible may be exaggerations of natural phenomena, or accounts of happenings that were given the gloss of the supernatural in order to heighten belief in Jesus' divine origin. It is very difficult to judge. Arrogance that one knows the interpretation is not seemly. One can only speculate; but no speculation is needed if one accepts that the Testaments contain the revealed word of God: that is, the writers were divinely inspired. However, no text in the Hebrew Scriptures was contemporaneous with the events chronicled. The telling was reshaped, remodelled and added to over time as beliefs changed.

Whatever the current dogma, or tenet of faith in the ever-changing interpretation of the Bible over the years, Mark's famous words, luminous and pregnant with symbolism, gladdened the spirits of all true believers (Mark 13:24–6):

> *But in those days, after that time of distress, the sun will be darkened, the moon will lose its brightness, the stars will come falling from heaven and the powers in the heavens will be shaken. And then they will see the Son of Man coming in the clouds with great power and glory.*

It must foretell the final demise of Satan and his devils.

Whenever the phenomenon of the stars falling from heaven is to be, it will clearly be contemporaneous with the Second Coming of the Son of Man. While Mark was writing the prophetic words above, he was also concerned, like John as we shall see in the following chapter, with emphasizing current beliefs in, and the power of, evil spirits.

CHAPTER TWO

DEMONIC BELIEF AND POWER

For millennia, people, educated and uneducated alike, believed in a demonology which had its origin in Biblical stories and even earlier. Something which gripped the imagination of mankind for most of the Christian era, and to a large extent directed their lives, must be worthy of study.

Long periods in history were times of uncertainty in almost every area, except for the belief in the Devil and demons. Jesus was the overwhelmingly superior power and had authority over the Devil and demons; it is worth noting that even His attitudes to demons reflected those of His time. Additionally, the demons themselves reflected the concerns of Man from time immemorial and the concerns of the early Church.

DEMONIC POWER

'Are we not right', the Jews asked, 'in saying that you are a Samaritan and have a demon?' 'I have not a demon,' Jesus answered.

The quote is from the Gospel of St John (8:48–9) where he relates how the descendants of Abraham openly rejected Jesus' message. This extract is significant not only because it is the first reference to demons in the Bible which is not connected with exorcism, but also because the expression 'having a demon' indicates the accepted belief that Man could be possessed by the Devil or one of his demons. It was obviously taken for granted as a distinct possibility by the populace and by Christ also. Belief in demons was clearly endemic.

This is one of two references in the New Testament to demons, apart from those referring to the idea of possession and exorcism. The other occurs in the Book of Revelation (16:12–14), the last book of the New Testament, written by a

Christian prophet, John, about AD 100, concerning his visions of a new heaven and a new earth. In describing the seven plagues which were to hit Babylon sometime in the future, he writes of the seven angels who were to visit the plagues on the country:

> *The sixth angel poured his bowl on the great river Euphrates… and I saw… three foul spirits like frogs; for they are demonic spirits, performing signs…*

From these two instances it is clear that belief in evil spirits as entities, able to enter and haunt mankind, was one certain idea in a time of little certainty about anything else – at least in the area of intellectual inquiry. These scriptural instances also show that the Devil or demons had the ability to take diverse forms, human and non-human, and even to assist their 'victim' or subject by means of their diabolic, supreme power.

Nowhere in the Bible does Jesus rebuke his fellow countrymen, or even so much as hint at it, for their whole-hearted belief in demons. On the other hand, He never stated that belief (or disbelief) in the Devil and his demons was essential to salvation. Jesus' attitude to evil spirits was, we have to conclude, consonant with the general acceptance of the time regarding the reality of demons.

Malignant Demons

There are many references to possession by evil spirits and to the deliverance of the possessed by Jesus and his disciples in the New Testament. As we have already said, demonology was an ancient belief when the Old Testament was being written in the millennium before Christ. The Biblical demons are always malignant. However, unlike some of their antecedents, which sometimes could be beneficent, they almost always occur in the role of spirits which have taken over human beings – or occasionally animals.

In Luke (8:26–39), we read of the astonishing story of the Gerasene (or Gadarene) demoniac from whom a legion of demons was expelled into a herd of swine, illustrating the continual conflict on earth between Jesus and demons. Notice the demon speaks in most instances in the Bible separately from the possessed person. Elements in the story are common to most examples of possession related in the Bible: the manner of speaking, the locale, before-and-after contrasting behaviour and unnatural abilities.

From the many references in the New Testament to possession by the Devil, or demons, it is clear that these spirits are always hostile, subverting God's purpose for Man. It is instructive to note that, although the people and even His disciples at first did not recognize Jesus as the Son of God, possessing demons, as spiritual beings, did. This is clear from the way the demons addressed Jesus (Mark 3:12):

> *And whenever the unclean spirits beheld Him, they fell down before him and cried out, 'You are the Son of God'.*

A knight and the Devil

In a sense, therefore, Jesus and his disciples were victorious over Satan's devils in respect of their God-given power of expelling these demons.

But, it may be asked: where did the demons go (except in the case of the Gerasene demons, which entered into the herd of pigs and were drowned)? Presumably these spirits were free to roam about, seeking fresh victims. Occasionally they returned to their victim – a phenomenon which I shall mention later in our consideration of exorcism. This aspect is never made clear – except as above. In this respect, the triumph was purely temporal. But it sufficed to impress the people – and in Jesus' case, to impress the disciples, although it must be emphasized that the facet of impressing was but a concomitant of Jesus' true purpose of restoring normality to the afflicted person. For Jesus (and his disciples) the invading demons were acting under Satan's direction and as such were his instruments, doing his work and fulfilling their purpose.

Of course, underlying these Biblical references is the belief that ultimately the Devil and his demons will be defeated: 'That which gave Jesus his authority over demons was his perfect obedience to the will of the Father' (Everett Ferguson, *Demonology of the Early Christian World*, page 28).

Demons, to the Gospel writers, were fallen angels who, seeing Man as a sort of rival, tormented him and tried always to lead him astray. It was natural for them therefore to make frequent allusions to the depredations of the demons, who, because they were at that time always spiritual entities, could be conceived as perverting Man by entering into him or her and trying to exercise control. In several ways, demons were depicted as having characteristics or emotions akin to those of humanity: intelligent speech, fear, even hunger and thirst, though these were later developments.

They were always supernatural beings of enormous intelligence and physical power. They could work miracles of a deceptive nature and were not restricted by space or time. They promoted falsehood, especially in fomenting the growth of idolatrous sects and false religions. They afflicted men and women both mentally and physically. They could, for example, produce blindness and dumbness (*see* Matthew) and deformity (*see* Luke). Demons attacked the righteous and believers more than anyone else, so the writers of the Gospels were particularly rigorous in stressing the doctrine that ultimately God controls Satan and his activities.

REPRESENTATION OF DEMONS

Just as the idea of Satan as an evil one came into Hebrew thought slowly but insidiously over the centuries, so the conception of the Devil's helpers also developed over time. Religious authorities recognized the value of belief in demons as a control over their flocks, as did some of the assailed clerics and hermits, who related their encounters with demons the more to impress other people. Some of these narratives were frankly fanciful and intended to mislead; some of the encounters the narrators believed they had genuinely experienced. However, it must be said that in the context of great personal privation, semi-starvation, prolonged withdrawal from stabilizing human contact, asceticism, bodily chastisement and concentration on thoughts of eternity, obsession with ideas of good and evil, and religious mania, it is perhaps not surprising that tales of personal encounter with evil spirits were common among such people.

Early monastic thought was dominated by the perceived struggle between body and soul. Hermits and others who dedicated their lives to God withdrew to deserts and other remote areas to escape worldly temptation. But they could be attacked even there by evil demons just as much as the common people could be as they went about their daily business. In their attacks, the demons could take many different forms and create fantasies in their victims' minds. Sometimes, it seems, the demons simply tried to frighten their quarry; at other times they tried to tempt their victims away from the way of righteousness by appealing to some basic emotion, often lust, in appropriate human guise or by attempts to pollute the mind by inducing evil or lustful thoughts. Many are the stories of demons taking the shape of a variety of attacking animals or converting themselves into desirable young women.

Above all, it seems, demons hated religious people in the midst of their devotions and contemplations, and would do almost anything to distract them, resorting to dancing and singing and other diversions. They are extremely cunning in their understanding of human weaknesses. They can speak any language. They can travel on their wings with the speed of thought. They can always see us but we cannot see them unless they take corporeal form. Demons, like the angels, have a hierarchy within which they can specialize in wickedness. Although they attack mind and body they cannot enter the soul. They attack when they perceive we are vulnerable, or in low spirits. This is neatly encapsulated by J. B. Russell: 'The monastic struggle against the demons lent the concept of the Devil', he writes in *The Prince of Darkness* (page 932), 'particularity, immediacy, and an intensely threatening nearness.'

Hierarchies of Demons

The hierarchies of demons were modelled on those of the angels. In the first hierarchy was Beelzebub, the prince of the Seraphim; and in descending order: Leviathan, the leader of heretics; Asmodeus, the tempter of the flesh; Balberith, the evil spirit of murder; Astaroth, who personifies sloth; Verrine, the spirit of intolerance; Gressil, the instigator of impure thoughts; and Sonneillon, the inciter of hatred. In the second hierarchy is Carreau, the spirit of implacability; Carnivean, who leads men and women into obscenity; Oeillet, who is contemptuous of Man's vows, especially of poverty; Rosier, the author of unlawful love; and Verrier, who tempts Man to break the vow of obedience. In the third hierarchy is Belias, the prince of pride and misleader of women; Olivier, who urges cruelty and inhumanity; and Invart, the specialist in possessing religious women.

These demons were also grouped into classes. The grouping of the fifteenth-century demonologist de Spina is as follows: fates; poltergeists; incubi and succubi; armies; familiar spirits; nightmares; those produced by sex with humans; those in disguise; those who assailed saints; and those who persuaded women to attend sabbats (witches' meetings). Whether there is any significance in the order is not clear. Neither are other categories clear. Much obfuscation in writing about demonology derives largely from the fact that thinking was naturally in the realm of the speculative: opinion and nothing more. What reality there is, the Bible (for the believer) provides.

The above demons were only the leaders of countless hordes. Millions, it was believed, existed and dwelt everywhere. The seven deadly sins had their prime instigators: Lucifer, pride; Satan, anger; Mammon, avarice; and the rest of the sins whose presiding spirits have just been listed.

Sixteenth-century demonologists in particular were industrious in their categorizations of evil spirits. Their work, though fanciful to modern eyes, was influential in its day and fomented the pandemic belief in demons, taken swiftly on

Belphegor, the biblical demon of evil

board by the Christian Churches. Consequently, it was quite common for nuns especially to confess to possession by one of these chief devils. It can only be supposed that by naming a prominent demon, nuns believed they were advancing their credibility as witness victims, at the same time as achieving a fame otherwise denied them. To actually know the name of the oppressing devil had great kudos!

We have to an extent examined the etymology of the words 'devil' and 'demon' and how over time these two words came to be virtually synonymous. To a large extent this confusion of terms was responsible for the growth in belief in demons and demonology.

The concept of the Christian Devil and his demons was largely established by the 'desert fathers', hermit-like men who lived in the early centuries AD and who wrote down ideas and descriptions of evil entities from memories of the gods of pagan civilizations. Their devils could be either animal or angelic in disguise; they could cause great commotion and usually did; they often emitted a foul stench. They did not always assume corporeal shape themselves but often entered into a human or animal to beguile or to betray. The spirits were subordinated one to another eventually, so that a spiritual world ranged hierarchically from the highest deities to the lowest, minor devils, imps and goblins.

CLASSIFICATION

Where the spirits dwelt (good and bad) was of considerable moment to the early Christian adherents, to judge from the elaborate cosmology they created to explain such entities as 'hell' and 'heaven'. Demons were therefore classified not only according to function but also according to habitation. Guazzo, one of the most influential writers on demonology, gives a list where demons are thus characterized. In his 1608 *Compendium Maleficarum*, we can read of a variety of devils such as the 'fiery', who dwelt in the upper air; the 'aerial', who dwelt in the air around us; the 'terrestrial', cast from heaven to live permanently on or in the earth; the 'aqueous', who lived in the waters; the 'subterranean', who dwelt in caves and caverns; and the 'heliophobic', who hated light, and never appeared in daytime.

Incubi and Succubi

There appears to be another kind of devil, not much written about at first, but figuring strongly in later witchcraft trials. These were the incubus and succubus demons who assaulted humans in their sleep. Incubi were believed to be male demons who lay on women, especially nuns, in their sleep and had intercourse with them. Sometimes the victims were aware but terrified of their assailants; sometimes they seemed not to be. Succubi (or succubae strictly) were female demons who either deceived men into acts of intercourse, or by their great powers were able to cause men to submit to their actions, against their will. Again, members of the religious orders were especially prone to be their victims. These particular evil beings assumed great moment in the age of the witchcraft mania, and I shall refer to them again in a later section (see page 47). It is now advantageous to explain this belief further because it had much significance.

Many learned writers accepted the theory of the incubus and succubus demons, including St Augustine and St Thomas Aquinas. By the thirteenth century this belief was conceded. Greatly exercising ecclesiastical thought at the time was the question of demons taking bodily form, possessing sexual organs and the transmission of semen. Father Sinistrari, a noted demonologist of the late seventeenth century, writes of the Devil who 'shapes for himself a body endowed with motion, by means of which body he copulates with the human being'.

Aquinas, some 400 years earlier, spoke in his *Summa Theologiae* of the children who may be born of this devilish intercourse 'through the semen taken from some other man for this purpose, seeing that the same demon who acts as a succubus for a man becomes an incubus for a woman'. The collecting of human semen by spirits puzzled churchmen, and various theories were advanced to account for it. According to some writers, semen was collected from men in their sleep; others adduced that devils collected human semen emitted in nocturnal emissions or masturbation.

Naturally, as it was believed that most devils were male, attention was focused on the incubi and their female victims. However, it was not always made clear that the women involved were quick to confess the visitation by the demon, sometimes, we are told, nightly. This would be consonant with the misogyny of the times, women being regarded as distinctly inferior to men in every way, morally as well as intellectually, deriving from the contempt in which the first sinner, Eve, was held. For many religious thinkers the doctrine was 'axiomatic' (Del Rio, 1589/90) and an 'indisputable truth' (Binsfeld, 1590). Many people, male and female, attested to the attacks of the incubus demon. Nuns and female saints were particularly likely to be sought out.

It was also a matter of some deliberation whether these demons experienced physical pleasure during their copulations. The consensus seemed to be that they did to a degree, but that was secondary to their purpose of degrading their victim, and showing contempt for God. Categorization appeared to be something of a mania among the clerics and religious thinkers of the age, and indeed there were types of victim: the willing, the unwilling and those bewitched. Sinistrari was particularly obsessed with considerations of incubi and succubi. It is clear how the concept of the 'demon lover' arose!

The aim of succubi was the same as that of the incubi: to divert from the straight and narrow. Male saintly figures were commonly most tempted by the succubi. Most struggled victoriously, but some succumbed. Succubi bent on seducing men did not attack physically (as they could have done) but relied on their blandishments. As with the witchcraft delusion, this belief in sexually active demons lasted for centuries.

The worthy Father Sinistrari wrote obsessively about these sexually-attacking demons in his book *Demonality* (page 127). In it he argued every possible facet of the phenomena, endeavouring to explain the act of ethereal–material intercourse. His attitude is interesting as it clearly indicates a well-held belief of the time. We have mentioned that it was believed devil congress with female humans gave rise to giant beings, half man, half demon. Sinistrari did not believe that human sperm had been used, and said that we are

> *therefore bound to infer that giants are born of another sperm than man's, and that, consequently, the Incubus Demon for the purpose of generation, uses a sperm which is not man's.*

He goes on to adduce several authorities of like mind, and adds that it is his opinion that the incubus demon 'when having intercourse with women bigets [*sic*] the human fetus from his own sperm'. Incubi, he claims, must have senses because they can have various moods when about to seduce. In this sense they are not purely evil spirits, but neither are they human. Evil spirits possess Man largely by the agency of a witch or wizard but these incubi and succubi are different, he states: 'It is of his own accord, and without the cooperation of either witch or wizard, that he inflicts his molestations.' Their bodies, he writes, are made of 'the most subtle part of one of the elements', earthly, aqueous, aerial, and so on, as we have seen earlier. In the act of intercourse the demon can appear shadowy and indistinct, but can if he wishes to inflict greater degradation on his victim take the shape of a holy man, or of a kinsman or even of an animal.

Sinistrari is also exercised by the question: which is more grievous: incubus intercourse, sodomy or bestiality? He arrives at the conclusion that when having intercourse with an incubus, 'man does not degrade but rather dignifies his nature' – the thinking being that demons once were angels. He concludes that men and women who mix with incubi and succubi 'sin through intention' and are just as guilty as if they had sinned with devils.

MANIFESTATION

One belief which united everybody was the immortality of the demons: they were originally angels after all, albeit terribly altered in nature and transmogrified now that they had fallen. Their true materiality was, however, a different thing altogether and remained something of an enigma throughout the centuries.

We have seen that categorization of demons served to individualize them, and at the same time gave them a prominence among the populace which helped to keep them to the fore with all their terrors. Accordingly, there were demons devoted to almost everything: hours of the day, winds, the corners of the earth and so on. They were beings of immense power, of course, and could wreak great evil – but ultimately were under God's control. If there was any comfort for the ordinary priest and peasant, this was it.

It must be pointed out that there were alternative beliefs alleging that demons caused evils of their own free will and by their own power. Because demons had genuine power of their own (as some thought), it was equally held that demons, if they did indeed possess a degree of autonomy (under Satan), could be influenced to bring this power to aid certain people: heretics, cult leaders, doers of wicked deeds, apostates, witches and wizards. This itself led to the practice of sorcery and magic, both vehemently condemned by the orthodox Christian Church.

The traditional view of the Church was that forces of evil had no power of their own – or at least, it hoped so! Hence the demons' strategy of trickery, whereby they endeavoured to retain and demonstrate their power by luring men into wickedness. Actually entering men's bodies and controlling their minds was one of the chief ways by which the demons demonstrated their continual power. They were held responsible for all manner of disease and misfortune, which added to their image, of course. Belief in this naturally lessened individual culpability for wrongdoing or wrong thinking.

Harnessing the power of devils was the motive force behind the power of superstition, sorcery, divination and all manner of Spiritism, soothsaying, prophecy, casting spells and related activities. An important issue was that of controlling these powerful beings. God could, but could men? Appeal to the Lord for grace, prayer and an iron will would, it was believed, combat the demons. It was therefore possible – but very difficult. One special person, how-ever, could help another in a case of possession – an exorcist, calling on God's power. In contrast, the sorcerer or magician tried to usurp heavenly power (it was alleged) and for this alone he or she had to be condemned.

Many ancestors of these Christian demons were limited in their power (as were the demons in the Christian faith), but with the difference that the limita-tions were set not by a supreme good god, but by gods of the lower world. Even so, they appeared to have almost autonomous powers. Clearly, the hair-raising portrayals of the later Christian demons derive in large part from this pagan demonology, especially that of the Babylonians and Assyrians. The latter had their 'official' religion, but the people believed in a type of underground religion characterized by sorcery and magic. The main feature was the belief in a demonic leader heading a numerous band of evil spirits.

Persian (Zoroastrian) religion is concerned more with the eternal conflict between good and evil, between the good god, Mazda, and the bad god, Ahriman, whom we have already mentioned. Clearly, the Babylonian religion was based on a duality of godheads and in this regard differs from the funda-mentals of Christian belief, which is monotheistic.

In contrast again are the sacred Jewish books, which broach the subject of demonology but briefly. There are references to devilish agencies, but in com-parison with the abundant demonology of the Persian and Babylonian litera-ture, it is sparse. Although, as some writers state, Jewish demonology borrowed in no arguably direct line from Persian and Babylonian writings, these latter writ-ers must have had a considerable influence on the development of Jewish (later Christian) demonology. It would be unnatural if this were not so. The demonology of the Bible would be incomplete and indeed in need of exegesis if reference were not made to its Jewish, Assyrian and Persian antecedents in which the sources of many of the Biblical narratives lie. These various systems of belief have much in common. Succinctly, Leek, in her *Driving Out the Devils* (page 70), writes:

> *A demon can be broadly defined as an anonymous god, a personification of one or another of certain vague and less definable powers that exerted influence along with the major deities.*

Certain demons were given names: Utukku, the spirit of the dead, who haunted desolate places; Alu, the spirit of disaster, half human, half animal, who dwelt in ruins; Ekimmu, the spirit of suicide and violent death, who roamed the land aimlessly looking for victims; Gallu, the spirit of assault and attack, who prowled the streets nightly; Ilu, the spirit of the essence of evil, who can lurk any-where; Rabisu, a frightful fiend who brought about destructive nightmares; and Labartu, a blood-sucking monster, lion-headed, who endeavoured to kill on sight. Some demons caused specific disease: Namtar, who brought plague; Ashakku, who caused wasting illnesses; and Shabriri, who brought about blindness. There were many others held responsible for the manifold ills that flesh is heir to.

It is clear that no matter what the race origin of demonology, the demons are always held to be malign. The (or their) gods on the other hand could be, and often were, almost benign, or at least more favourably disposed to humanity. For example, they could be appeased with appropriate forms of obeisance.

The ritual of sacrifice in the Old Testament is obviously a development of this belief. The gods themselves were spirits, of course, but as Langton remarks in *Essentials of Demonology* (page 32),

> *Gods are oft-times quite evidently simply spirits which, for a variety of reasons, have attained to greater prominence.*

A consideration of Greek belief concerning demons reveals a strong sense that demons acted as mediators between gods and Man. As they were also generally believed to be the souls of the dead, who in life were good or bad, it was logical to suppose that the demons themselves could be good or bad. This of course was not so in Christian belief. In this, heathen deities were always in reality demons. Nevertheless, Greek semi-demons influenced the Christian concept: Gorgons, whose look could turn men into stone; Sirens, who lured men to destruction by the sweetness of their singing; the Sphinx, a fearsome creature with ravening jaws; Harpies, who carry all things to destruction; and Erinyes, angry ghosts, the spirits of the dead who seek vengeance on humanity.

The origin of demons in the early Christian world has been discussed and various theories obtained. Another view held that demons already existed at the time of the fall of the angels, who themselves gave rise to a troupe of evil spirits whose mission was to persuade men and women to sacrifice to the demons as gods. Whatever the belief of the Christian world at any one time, much of the belief arose from the close association of human society with the animal kingdom, particularly in those days; hence the frequent notion of spirits possessing animal-like characteristics. Naturally it is possible to claim that much of the attribution to specific demons of this and that arose purely from the imagination, fostered of course by the clergy.

It has to be emphasized, though, that in a sense belief in spirits has always existed in the Christian Church and still does in so far as this belief is fundamental to Christian and Jewish faith. This belief is in the continued existence of good and bad human souls: the survival of the soul after death.

DEMONS AND THE EARLY CHURCH

The genesis of all demonology may lie in the belief, lost in the mists of time, in animism: the belief basic to all peoples dating back millennia that vital phenomena are produced by an immaterial soul distinct from matter which attributes living souls to inanimate objects and to natural phenomena. This belief leads to a spiritual, not a materialist, theory of the universe.

As a consequence, once tribes had begun to cohere there arose a special group of men to interpret spiritual phenomena: the priests. From the beginning it was understood that these men were able to influence supernatural creation and could intercede on people's behalf – for the ultimate attainment of abiding with God (or gods) in the next life. Consequently, they became very powerful. At first self-appointed and self-created, they were later officially designated. Naturally, every cultural, societal or racial clash resulted in acrimony and hostility between the priest groups representing the separate races or religions. Many, if not most, wars have had religious fervour, some might say intolerance, as their basis.

Equally, it may also be claimed that it was this attitude which made all the deities that Christianity attempted to suppress into devils. Their existence was never denied: they offered too good a ready-made demonology! Apart from their obvious coercive attributes, the demons reflect the tribulations of the Christian faith over the (early) centuries. But perhaps even more, they reflect the concerns of Man from time immemorial: concerns with cold and hunger; harmful physical phenomena and animals; and enemies, darkness, disease and death. They all had their demons, their destructive forces. The degradation of these spirits took some time. Demons 'have become of evil repute mainly through the anathema of theology' (Mercure Conway, *Demonology and Devil-Lore*, Vol. 2, page 37).

It was always believed that, apart from the gods of the pagans, the devils were originally ethereal forms, some of which took hard the fact that God had not had time before the Sabbath dawned to give them bodies, or the semblance thereof. As a result, they were envious of the carnal pleasures that human beings could enjoy and this motivated them to seek to bring about the corruption of these first humans. Their master, the Devil, found (according to some accounts) a willing ally in his plan to corrupt, in Lilith, the first female devil or demon, which accounts for many depictions of the moment of betrayal as the serpent having a female head. The story goes that Lilith married Adam and also at another time was the consort of Satan. In both liaisons, demons were born. Lilith became one of the most notable demons, roaming the world, seducing and strangling men and attacking children.

Lilith is generally portrayed and written about as an attractive woman, but whether this was her true form, or the form she chose to take at least on the occasion of her trickery in the Garden of Eden, is not known. If she suffered the same fate as the other demons she would be exceedingly ugly. But perhaps her master had plans for her in her other guise. Almost always, demons are described as horrible beings. Pictures of demons half man, half animal can be seen virtually universally. Perhaps one of the more horrific is the portrayal of the demon of the south-west wind: dog's head, lion's paws, eagle's feet, four spread wings and with a fleshless skull.

Ethereal or Corporeal?
One school of thought emphasizes that demons did have bodies of an ethereal nature which became denser after their fall, becoming akin to the density of air or fire. If they had bodies they must of necessity desire food and drink – food

certainly. The smoke arising from sacrifice, human as well as animal, was one of their favourite foods, it was said. It was believed that, although the Devil and his demons did not die, they could become ill. On the other hand, some fathers of the Church held that demons were without bodies, incorporeal. When they assumed materiality they generally took human shape, deformed usually and exceedingly ugly.

There has been no shortage down the centuries of eye-witness descriptions of demons, often by saints. These were always horrific: huge heads, beetling brows, savage eyes, horns, cloven feet, with loud harsh voices and oftentimes breathing fire. The Middle Ages saw demon agency at its height, which often testified to the protean forms that could be assumed by demons. The latter, it seems, could take the form of classical gods and of famous literary figures. One of their favourite guises was that of attractive females to corrupt males or of handsome young men to corrupt females. Sometimes they even took the form of a husband or wife to the potential victim; or took the form of a priest in a state of what would now be termed indecent exposure.

At other times they could take the shape of an animal to frighten and torment their prey. Certain animals were more associated with the Devil or demons than others, such as dragons, serpents, scorpions, toads, flies and goats. No doubt the trials of animals in the Middle Ages (when, for example, a pig might be convicted of murder) arose partly from this manifestation. On occasion the demons even transformed themselves into inanimate objects, such as a goblet of wine or a purse of money. The demons had the power to enter dead bodies and to give the bodies the appearance of life, which may account for the legend of zombies. The bodies thus entered, we are to believe, were always those of people who had led unsavoury lives on earth. The teaching of the Church was that devils could not invade the corpses of people of good repute. Just the sight of the Devil or his demons could cause affliction, sometimes death.

Ranking According to Power

The classes and orders of the demons, according to some ancient theologians, were necessary in order to make them more effective as seducers from the straight and narrow, and certain groups had specific aptitudes. This concept is not so far-fetched as it may seem, since it was of the utmost importance to the medieval churchmen to know as much about the demons as possible, to help them (the churchmen) combat evil. Ranking of demons might be according to the degree of power exhibited or might be according to the sins that they induced. We are reminded of the importance accorded to knowing the name (or names) of the invading demons in the New Testament and even in exorcisms of the present day.

Demons know the past and the future – but only up to a limit decreed by God. The phenomenon of a possessing spirit reciting the secret history of the exorcist is often attested to; their knowledge of the future is said to be based on their extraordinary powers of rapid movement, their supreme intelligence and their supernatural ability to make informed guesses about future happenings. However, they could not enter the mind, but could only conjecture what was happening. If they could have done this, there would have been little hope for Man! It is clear from the utterances of possessing devils that they had encyclopedic knowledge, knowing, among other things, sciences and languages, theology and scriptural writing. One deficiency, it seems, was philosophy, because summoned-up devils, so the story goes, could not help with philosophical questions. However, just as with humans, demons differed with regard to their knowledge and degree of ability. Some were more expert in some fields than in others.

No doubt the demons were powerful, and knowledge gives power. They can permeate all things, Man being but one of them. Particularly vulnerable to attack by evil spirits, Man can be saved only by the power of God's grace. The human body can be easily attacked as a preliminary to corrupting the soul. Not only this, but the demons can cause any manner of unpleasantness, among which is the ability to affect the weather: storms, thunder and lightning and the like. Earthquake was one speciality as the demon made his violent way back to hell.

The body to the early churchmen and those later was considered only the housing of the soul, its prison no less, and as such was very vulnerable to temptation. Accordingly, the Devil and his fallen angels may flatter the body or he may oppress it with disease and discomfort. Although Man's spirit is not directly under his control, the Devil can work his influence upon it – and thereby affect Man's soul.

DEMONS OF NIGHT – AND OF DAY

Less corporeal, but equally frightening, was a genus of nightmare demons. Disturbed sleep patterns were ascribed to malevolent spirits, phantoms of the dark, as witness the incubi and succubi. The writings of many nations testify to belief in night demons, and large is the vocabulary invoked. The vampire story itself is related to this night demonology. The visions usually seen in nightmares were believed to be akin to the hallucinations of the insane, so many of the demons of nightmare were seen to be also demons of madness. These nightmare spirits were regarded not always as bad, but nearly always so, as instigators of terror or erotic visions – both equally bad in their own way in the eyes of the Church.

Nightmare demons tortured women more than men, and convents were among their favourite places. Accusations of sexual relations with devils were very frequently levelled at so-called witches, who as a result were condemned to death. Locking doors and windows was of no avail to these demons, who could enter through key-holes, even cracks in wainscots. Their progeny was always a witch or a monster.

The incubi and succubi always adopted a human or animal appearance when assailing their victims. Belief in night demons created a roaring trade in protective amulets and charms, of course, believed to ward off nightmares.

Demons in any case were generally thought to be most active at night, at least in the view of the medieval Church.

Activity by demons in the hours of daylight, however, is noticeable in the Bible. This is so especially in the New Testament, where demonic possession and deliverance from the demons by Christ (or his disciples) feature prominently. The Devil himself carries out, according to the Scriptures, many if not most of his depredations during the day. (This may have been because not many of the witnesses to the preternatural events were about at night – so this caveat must be entered. Nevertheless the phenomenon is noteworthy.)

Possession can, should be, temporary in the sense that it is not lifelong, although some cases detailed in the New Testament were clearly of long standing. Illness on the other hand could have been from birth, and sometimes was, whether physical and/or mental. Severe cases were always described in the Bible as, we gather, if not dating from birth, at least fated to be with the afflicted to the end.

Jesus, his disciples and the Jewish people recognized the difference between the two states: that of demon possession or obsession, and that of physical illness. Whether they always differentiated mental, emotional and psychic illness from possession cannot be stated with authority. Psychosomatic illness, of course, was a concept beyond their ken. They could, however, distinguish between ordinary madness and demonic possession. (*See* Matthew 4:24.) It has been claimed that the Jews were aware of the strange differences between cases of illness and other cases which exhibited the same symptoms, but, as Leahy puts it in *Satan Cast Out* (page 80), '[they] lacked the sinister aspect known only in the demoniac'. A sinister aspect of possession was the fact that it seemed not to be the demoniac who spoke or answered, but the possessing demon, who somewhat naturally had a completely different tone (and manner) of speaking, obvious to all.

WHY INHABIT MAN?

One puzzling question (among many!) is why powerful spirits like demons and their master the Devil should think it appropriate to enter into Man – day or night. Surely they have enough power to corrupt the human race without tying themselves up in human bodies for what in many cases was a long time? I have given stock answers such as: demonstrating their polymorphous abilities, their insulting of God thereby, and their ability to fight good.

One other answer lies in the manner of their fall, already adduced, when they were but half complete, without bodies. Not only were they jealous of Man, whom they sought to corrupt, but they also desired to enjoy the pleasures of material life – not only sex, as I have said, but bodily warmth (and love!) – and to enjoy the manifold activities of the human being. Hence, they sought human bodies to dwell in, preferably good people whom they could damage more grievously, but any person would do.

Much of the belief in demons was born of ignorance among the masses and deliberate fostering of the idea by clerics. Superstition engendered fear, and fear reinforced belief in evil spirits who could materialize at any moment or assail anyone with their diabolical powers. Great misfortune begot tall tales throughout the centuries, whether from physical or mental disease, enemies or malevolent natural phenomena, bad weather and so on; the tendency was to attribute all these to the agency of demons. Devils and demons, it was believed, dwelt in hell, where they roasted sinners and from where they arose to torment us, the living.

'Religion', says Graf (*Story of the Devil*, page 9), 'is the composite result of a multiplicity of causes, which cannot always, it is true, be traced and pointed out.' Belief in many gods, or one god, an antagonist Devil, angels or beneficent spirits or malevolent demons – and the entire panoply deified by churchmen, dogma and doctrine, theory and principles – therefore comprise religious belief. Demonology, like angelology, is, or was rather, an integral part of early belief systems – early in the sense that such belief dominated religious thinking from before Christ made Man until a couple of centuries ago, if indeed it has completely passed away even now.

Clear ideas regarding demons came to the Hebrews only after the period of the Babylonian captivity, but, as we have seen, were extant long before this time in other mythologies. For the Hebrews, the supreme god was Jehovah, who appeared oftentimes a vindictive god, jealous and savage. With such a god as this, what need was there for a demon? He could wreak as many evils as he wanted. No wonder their demonology was late, comparatively, in developing. An emerging Satan could later be blamed for misfortunes. Great as he was, Satan could not encompass all ills without the help of other beings – hence the concept of the demons. The divinities of the ancient civilizations were, as we stated, not wiped from the slate, but transformed into demons by Christianity, ready made. Infamous figures from past history are demonized and they join the horde of 'conventionally' created devils.

EVIL FORCES

It is useful to begin this section with a quotation from Olsen's book *Disguises of the Demonic*, because it is so profound and at the same time relevant to our study:

> *The deepest discovery of God as the lord of life will occur decisively only as he proves able to sustain in us the humane strengths of trust and love while the demonic is at work.*

I take this to mean that by God's grace we can avoid sin, the attacks – figurative or actual, according to one's belief – of the Devil. Having compassion for one's neighbour is an elemental doctrine of the Christian Church. Having compassion on one's own soul by holding out against temptation is equally doctrinal. Working in the service of God is the highest position to which Man can aspire. But, as Olsen says, this dimension of service begins only when one is willing to endure the impact of demonic enormities. By the latter we can understand the attacks on us of evil spirits, or of evil men. Perhaps these attacks are one and the same. Throughout history, demonic assault has been held responsible for much personal wickedness; maybe the wellspring of human wickedness lies not in the demons, and never did, but in the essential human psyche.

In this study, references to demon and demonic are suggestive of evil, though as I have said, demon could have referred, often did refer, to a benign force. In Shakespeare's *Hamlet* the word 'daemon' (or demon) is used in the sense of a guiding spirit, a good being. Demonic forces in our context are forces which assail people, which make them bad, through either temptation, obsession or possession.

For almost all of the era under consideration, demons were an absolute reality for the cleric and for the common man; demons could take bodily form and affright by their very appearance, until belief in the corporeality of these entities began to wane. This left behind a real concept of devils or demons as evil influences on the soul of Man. Ultimately it (belief) derives from the fear of early Man, who felt vulnerable, almost helpless, in the face of the unknown.

Men and women have from the beginning had a sense of what is right and what is wrong, which, by their lights, helped to make the world a better place, misguided though many of their beliefs and practices seem to us now. This sense, or trust even, was inculcated by tradition, handed down orally or in writing on the one hand and/or superimposed upon the tribe or nation by belief in some supernatural power accounting for good and certainly evil in their world – the gods existing somewhere in the earth or in the heavens.

However, Man was not completely helpless in the face of these forces, but could influence their instigators by propitiation or by sacrifice. The supernatural sources of evil, however, were aided by devils, or demons, who were intrinsically evil and whose malevolence could not be deflected once they had selected a victim except by the powers of religion – eventually.

THE DEMONIC TODAY

Experience of what we may call the demonic influence is visible around us in the world. It may be within ourselves, some form of guilt which we always suppress; or it may be external, in regimes and their rulers. Either way we tend to be conscious now and then of the demonic at work, an evil power that can motivate on occasion or all the time. This demonic power has outlived Satan.

Satan himself has become for most people a symbol, a metaphor of evil, while the demonic continues to exist, if not materially then as a disruptive force within the psyche. Modern Man is able by means and knowledge of psychology to try to repress this inner awareness of the demonic, but no such palliative was open to the early Christians.

It may be that cases of possession (or oppression) related in the Bible were a consequence of the Devil's fury in being rebuffed or combated in some spiritual manner, so that in a kind of last resort way the Devil tried (and usually succeeded) to control from within a person created in God's image. The argument is dependent, of course, on accepting the truth of scriptural word.

JESUS AND THE DEMONS

In the Scriptures, many sick and demon-possessed people were brought to Jesus to be healed, but the conditions were not synonymous: some were sick and some were possessed. The New Testament, particularly, makes this clear. The New Testament frequently uses the expression 'unclean spirit' as if to emphasize that spirits could be 'clean' – that is, good – but of course we do not hear much of them, just as good news is not as newsworthy as bad news. But it is clear that good spirits existed. Angels were some of them, but their influence and action tended to be external to Man. Demons in the New Testament seemed to have rather a tenuous grip on their victims compared with later exorcisms, where we are told that driving out demons may take an extensive time. Jesus naturally had to appear as the overwhelmingly superior power. By and large, He accomplished His expulsions with the utterance of a few authoritative words. He did not adjure or resort to formulaic word patterns. Matthew's Gospel (8:16) is typical: 'he cast out the spirits with a word'.

Other acts of Jesus mentioned in the New Testament were undoubtedly healing miracles as opposed to expulsions. For Him they were all manifestations of evil which oppressed mankind in the world. As such they had to be destroyed. Jesus recognized that a Principle of Evil was abroad and had to be opposed. Jesus exorcized in the name and through the power of the Father; Jesus' disciples exorcized through Jesus' name. Abundantly it is obvious that Jesus attached the greatest importance to the overcoming and casting out of demons, or unclean spirits. These spirits were the almost physical embodiment of evil in action and were of the greatest significance among men and women of the first millennium AD. As Christianity grew in importance and numbers, its adherents recognized one God and His Messiah, Jesus. During Jesus' lifetime it is supposed a plurality of gods was believed in, if only because at that time the Jews were under the domination of the Romans, who of course had many gods. Jesus recognized one kingdom of Satan; in His eyes demons were part of a larger whole, the Devil's dominion.

Much of Christ's teaching was allusive, and herein lies its difficulty for exegetes or interpreters. Jesus often spoke in parables, illustrating a truth by means of an allegory which by its very nature cannot be understood literally. Some of His utterances can be, but others cannot be. Often we have to look below the surface meaning of the words to discover their burden. The words of Jesus (Matthew 12:30): 'He who is not with me is against me, and he who does not gather with me scatters' has the deeper meaning of emphasis on the reality of a true personal commitment to Christ's teaching and a detestation of the Devil's snares.

In many of Christ's parables the abiding, underlying message is that there is a constant war to be waged between good and evil, but that ultimately – with certain stipulations – good will triumph. When it comes to a direct conflict between Christ and Satan, it is no contest because Satan is powerless before Him. And this also is the case with Satan's army of demons.

There is, however, a very interesting passage in Luke 24:26, where Jesus (through the words of Luke) indicates that demons are not always permanently and infallibly banished when he speaks of the possessing demon that vows to return with seven other spirits more evil than himself. The moral here is that without leaving something in place in Man's heart, something that would forbid the demon returning, in effect a state of grace, banishment of the demon force is but temporal. The vacuum left by evil (the demonic) must needs be filled by goodness – a person so delivered must be given something in return; which relates to the importance of 'aftercare' in modern deliverance ritual. Jesus' teaching is that now as then, a delivered person must be filled with the Holy Spirit if he or she is not to be left vulnerable again to demonic attack.

In summary, it is clear from the New Testament that demons were firmly believed in by Jesus as much as by the people; that they were held to be spiritual beings of great power and knowledge; that the battle between good and evil was fought out over and within mankind; that the tempting and possessing demons were under the orders of Satan. Jesus and his disciples truly believed that He had authority over Satan and his demons. The Holy Spirit was immensely superior to the evil spirit, whose final downfall was assured. Ultimately everything depended on the individual's genuine and loving relationship with his Maker.

CHAPTER THREE

THE PRINCE OF DARKNESS EVOLVES

D emons became more and more powerful, and were feared as well as worshipped. As Satan was increasingly referred to as the King of Demons, the greatest thinkers and theorists of the time, from St Augustine to Thomas Aquinas, were increasingly occupied with trying to resolve the issues surrounding demons, Satan and Christ, set against the early backcloth of confusion and persecution.

Christianity became stronger, all the while being subject to influences including those of the Apostolic Fathers, mysticism, scholasticism, scepticism and romanticism, and was increasingly threatened by deviant sects and cults. Among these cults were believed to be the witches and their sabbats, who brought every kind of harm to the populace. The Inquisition was instituted to discover heretics – women especially being unjustly persecuted – and those who practised sorcery and witchcraft.

PRINCE OF DARKNESS

The Christian prophet John in about AD 100 described his visions of a new heaven and earth in the book now known as Revelation (22:1–5), the last one of the New Testament:

> *Then God showed me the river of the water of life, bright as a crystal... on either side of the river, the tree of life... there shall no more be anything accursed... but the throne of God and of the Lamb shall be in it, and his servants shall worship him, they shall see his face, and his name shall be on their foreheads. And they shall reign for ever and ever.*

For persecuted Christians John's writing had great moment and much of what he had to say was a beacon of light for the embryo Church. His work gave hope in the dark days the struggling sect had to endure. He took care, however, to say that only the righteous would be saved, or alive (spiritually) to enjoy it as he foretold the glorious future. Later he spoke of the fate of the wicked 'who were not killed'; these people 'did not repent… nor gave up worshipping demons and idols…'.

From John's words it is clear that demons were not only feared but worshipped, probably as gods, remembering that Christians demonized all the false gods of the ancient and their own world. It was comparatively easy to turn the people away from this demon worship by means of Christian teaching and convert these demons into universal objects of loathing. Of course, it took some time to do this among wavering potential followers of the new religion.

The Prince of Darkness was another thing altogether. In writing of the binding of Satan, John envisions the Last Judgement (although he never refers to it in these words) when Satan is the first to be judged and condemned to the underworld. There he is to remain for 'a thousand years' while the souls of the martyrs are resurrected.

Later Satan is to be released, suggesting that the power of God over evil is so great that He can allow it with impunity to continue its existence. However, in the end Satan is destroyed for ever, before a Second Coming when all humanity is judged according to their record in the 'book of life'. The permanence of deep evil personified by Satan, the Devil, cannot, it is implied, be mitigated until the Last Judgement. The fact that evil continued to rear its ugly head implies that the binding was to occur sometime in the distant future. The significant omission of any reference to the binding of the demons also implies that while Satan is *hors de combat* evil spirits are free to carry on the Satanic work. The following passages from Revelation (20:1–11) had a significant influence on the developing Roman Catholic/Christian faith and coloured its attitude to the personification of the Devil for many centuries.

John wrote:

> *Then I saw an angel coming down from heaven, holding the key of the bottomless pit and a great chain. And he seized the dragon, that ancient serpent, the Devil and Satan, and bound him for a thousand years and threw him into the pit and shut it and sealed it over him that he should deceive the nations no more, till the thousand years were ended. After that he must be loosed for a little while. Also I saw the souls of those who had been beheaded… [who] came to life and reigned with Christ a thousand years. The rest of the dead did not come to life until the thousand years were ended. This is the first resurrection… Over such [the holy and blessed]… the second death has no power but they shall be priests of God… and when the thousand years are ended, Satan will be loosed from his prison and will come out to deceive the nations but [later] the devil was thrown into the lake of fire and sulphur… and [he] will be tormented for ever.*

Naturally, the Christian Church did not know when the Second Coming would be, so it conducted itself for centuries as if the Day of Judgement was at hand. This meant that its growing band of adherents had always to be in a state of readiness, a state of grace, and always to be circumspect regarding the wiles of the Devil, who grew in stature as the years went on.

As we have seen, it was the New Testament that created, from ancient stories, the eventual reality of the Devil in the minds of the early and medieval Church. It is therefore a truism to say that the concept of the Devil has been of the greatest moment for Christians for centuries and that it continued so until quite recently. For educated people, clerics and the like, Satan has been feared as a threat to the soul; but to uneducated people down the centuries (the great majority), he was terrifying. Satan was associated with every kind of sin, and brought about physical as well as moral evil.

This reality of belief concerning the Devil made for his dominance over Christian scholarship and teaching. Certainly up to the nineteenth century, Satan had been an objective reality. The overriding influence of Satan on the religious thought of the millennium and a half after the death of Christ is little short of incalculable, and it is this period we shall be concerned with in this section.

Any study of Satan in this period must encompass to a certain degree the attitude to demons, for Satan was increasingly referred to as the King of Demons. This in turn leads to such subjects as witchcraft, necromancy and magic, which we will not go into in any depth as these are vast subjects on their own. The Devil, demons, Christ and theology were some considerations which occupied the minds of the greatest thinkers of the age. A brief outline of their contentions is illustrative of the development of Christian thought.

DESERT TEACHING AND DEMONOLOGY

The first significant group of influential thinkers, who flourished about AD 100–200, are known as the Apostolic Fathers. Justin Martyr (about AD 100–165) discussed the problem of evil for the first time, and elaborated a cosmology that supported his beliefs. For him, demons were the offspring of the illicit union of fallen angels with human women. These demons dwelt in all things pagan, but are not gods as Satan would have us believe. Pagan gods were real entities, not figments of the imagination. We must remember that Justin was writing when Rome ruled, but he advocated passive resistance to the Romans, for violence is doing the work of the Devil.

Clement and Ignatius, also writers in this period, mention the Devil but not demons. The same is true of Polycarp and Barnabas, who stress that Satan and all his works and pomps are diligently to be abhorred. However, in some writing of this period reference is made to demons, and many moral evils are said to be due to their agency. One of the most notable writers, Irenaeus, emphasizes the efficacy of exorcism to combat the power of Satan. He is fully convinced of the reality of demons and the Devil, and describes as abominations the magic arts practised by some people aided by the Devil.

Demonology is treated far more fully by Tertullian, who seemed to be obsessed by notions of the demons. For Tertullian, demons were fallen angels who rushed from heaven lusting for the daughters of men. According to his belief, the Devil was created good, but because he had free will he chose wrongly and became corrupt. Demons (and angels), he alleges, can travel with amazing swiftness from place to place and this ability combined with their supreme intelligence and knowledge makes them formidable foes: foes hardly to be resisted. They are ubiquitous and ever watchful, and therefore 'are they very dangerous'.

Origen was probably the most original thinker of this period. The Devil and his 'angels' or demons, he agrees with Tertullian, were apostate angels who fell from heaven, but mainly from the sin of vanity rather than of envy or lust. Again the exercise of free will enters the argument, for Origen says that the Devil had the power of choosing good or evil. It was the same with Eve and Adam, who exercised free will in succumbing to the temptations of the serpent. The demons were created when they fell from paradise by the exercise of their free will. Demons are rational creatures not created malignant. They only became so when they departed God's presence. All demons by now are wicked, although demons were not originally thought of as being all wicked, especially among the Greeks, and it took some time before the name acquired a wholly evil connotation. In the writings of the early Christian era this transmogrification takes place, and demons are viewed as wholly evil. Without doubt, Origen believes, Satan and his demons are the cause and instigation of sin. Man's natural concupiscence is seized on and exploited.

The demons are not mere spirit: they have a body which is different from Man's and not usually visible – unless they want it to be. Origen says there are two ways by which demons attack men: one is by obsessing with, say, evil thoughts; another is by possession, whereby people appear to be out of their minds. Demons may also enter the bodies of animals to make them hostile, or more so, to man. Magic was also accomplished by the aid of demons. Origen believed sincerely in the importance and efficacy of exorcism, which needed specific ritual and the utterance of unvarying phraseology to be effective in expelling the demon.

Then came an influential group of theorists who lived from about the third century to the eighth. For them, doctrines concerning the Devil and demons loom large. Within the limits of this study we cannot go into the work of all of these writers except to say that their contributions to the subject of demonology, although quite extensive, do build on the ideas of their predecessors; much of what they have to say is consonant with accepted views regarding the origin and nature of demons. They tend to have more to say about the Devil.

We should, however, refer to Jerome, writing about AD 400. He is generally critical of far-fetched stories of encounters with hideous demons and so one might say he is in this regard at odds with the traditional view of the Church. It must nevertheless be stressed that Jerome deals quite extensively with demon phenomena and adduces several tales of notables assailed by evil spirits. By the time of Jerome and certainly of Augustine (died AD 430), belief in polymorphous demons who took various shapes was established. They could, and often did, manifest themselves as semi-human or as animals of weird form, possessing beetling brows from which protruded wicked horns, and with splayed, cloven feet. They were almost always hairy, if not actually shaggy. On several points he criticizes Origen; for instance, for the belief that a human being can under certain circumstances become a demon. He was firmly convinced of the reality of demon possession.

St Augustine is without doubt the most important thinker of this early period. Much of his accounting for the creation of the Devil and the demons is conventional, in so far as he tends to follow the arguments of his predecessors. This is not to say, however, that his scheme of demonology is not extensive or well thought out. It is, and he introduces some original ideas about the nature of demons and their habitations. It is the fact that he treats so thoroughly the whole question of the reality of demons that makes him so remarkable. He never doubts for a minute belief in demonic influence; this alone is significant because we are dealing with one of the greatest intellects of that or any age.

His writing on the cosmos reflects the contemporary Christian view in its construct, but advances the principle that the universe (as conceived at that time) exists in God's mind; it is eternal; but for humanity the world does have a beginning and an end. Like Aquinas later, Augustine was occupied with the problem of evil. Demons are permitted to afflict humans with suffering; evil is necessary in creation, but some may choose evil because they have the greatest good in creation: free will. It is in the area of discussion of free will that Augustine is eminent. In his writing on this subject, he is led to the conclusion that happenings are preordained: the theory of predestination, which was not the orthodox belief of the Roman Catholic Church. The propounding of this theory landed Augustine in the proverbial hot water *vis-à-vis* the Church.

MEDIEVAL WRITERS

A number of writers followed in the next few centuries who contributed to demon lore and evinced their wholehearted acceptance of demon reality. Among these, worthy of mention in our pages, are Peter Lombard (1100–64) and Albertus Magnus (1205–80), both of whom treated the subject of demonology in some depth. The main function of demons (because they hold power only under God) is to act as tempters of Man – for the benefit ultimately of Man, who has to be tried and tested for his worthiness to enter heaven.

This is where the free will of mankind comes in. The argument is: no person has to sin. The soul is inaccessible to the Devil. His influence on mankind is indirect, external in the sense that he disturbs material things, the body and the senses even when he is 'in possession'. Man's spiritual faculties are never truly acted on. By his actions the Devil seeks to produce what seem to the observer to be spiritual phenomena, although this is spurious under examination. The manifestation is one of disorder. If total confusion and disorder do result, it is because the victim has chosen it. The physical disturbances characteristic of possession lead us to believe that demonic influences are at work, but psychological and physiological phenomena are often the root cause of the display. Both writers believed implicitly in possession.

Of the medieval writers the greatest was Thomas Aquinas (about 1230–75), possibly the most erudite thinker on Christian theology, angelology and demonology. He discusses in detail the topics of the fall of the angels, the creation of the Devil and his demons, ransom and combat theories. In much detail, Aquinas discussed the questions of good and evil, but differed from some thinkers in that he did not teach that Satan was necessary to any study of moral evil. Nevertheless, he did take the existence of the Devil for granted.

Aquinas, of course, was typical of his time when everybody, including members of monastic orders, were simply obsessed by the thought of a hostile Satan and his minions, the demons. The latter were everywhere: they could be swarming about nunneries or monasteries, or might be in the birds in the skies or the flies on the windowsill. Holiness of places and of people was particularly the target of demons, which they abhorred. Even at the most solemn moments of devotions or of the Mass, demons would assail, and would especially rejoice if they could distract a celebrant. If unsuccessful in the lifetime of a person, demons would gather with renewed strength at the moment of expiration of a potential victim. Many pictures illustrate the crowding round the death bed of the demons, who are striving to carry off the dying person's soul. For Aquinas as for others, Satan has the power to control men and his supreme endeavour in this respect is his power to possess. The argument is that demonic influence on Man is permitted by God for His own, not always fathomable, ends. The explanation largely is that Man has been granted free will by God, so he can indeed choose between evil and good; by this is he measured.

CONCEPTS OF THE DEVIL

At the present time we ask if the concept of the Devil is just an example of an outmoded belief – albeit a belief that ruled men's minds for something like two thousand years. Maybe the Devil does not, and never did, exist outside men's minds, but his long history down the centuries must give us pause. As the Principle of Evil, Satan (or equivalent name) features in Christianity, Islam and the Hebrew religion. Traditional belief has been added to, changed and has evolved throughout the ages, so that it may with authority be stated that the beliefs of the first century AD are not the same as those of today. Historical tradition accounts for what we know about the Devil. It is fashionable to state that many old beliefs are superstition, often simply because they are old, but treading such ground can be dangerous. It is as arrogant to deny the quondam existence of a Devil that ruled lives for ages as it is to take up an inflexible atheistic position. We cannot know for certain, one way or the other.

Notable Writers

The writers mentioned were notable figures of their time; perhaps not exactly public, but certainly known as profound thinkers who exerted significant influence on the still young Church. Among the writers of the period from about 500 to 800 are several historically important names, who by their contributions to religious doctrine both reflected current thought and added to the Church's perspective. Among them are John Damascene, who elaborated on received Christian doctrine and diabology, and Gregory, who tackled all the major problems of faith comprehensively and was notable for his views on Satanic or demonic temptation, arising largely from the experiences (of others) of monasticism. Gregory sees the world as a battleground where we, soldiers of Christ, await attack in the front line. The Devil employs several strategies to breach our defences and if these do not succeed, he will finally confuse our understanding so that we do not even know we are being tempted. Eventually we give in to sin because we no longer believe we can win.

Hermits and Ascetics

In distinction, the hermits who withdrew to the deserts or retired from the world and its concerns under monastic discipline revealed in a practical way a life devoted to God. St Anthony was the first noteworthy hermit (died 356); it is to him and others of like mind that monastery life is attributed, where individuals could contemplate God undisturbed.

We learn, however, that the hermits were particularly vulnerable to attacks by demons, who hated their single-minded devotions. Apparently most of the hermits' lives were a constant struggle against the forces of evil, embodied (usually) by malignant demons. Often they appeared as beasts or huge figures breathing fire, with eyes like furnaces. They sometimes appeared to the tormented monks and hermits as good people, the better to deceive. The Devil himself on occasion tempted Anthony and suggested thoughts that were not themselves wicked, but were calculated to lead on to evil if pursued. He could raise doubts or try to instigate lewd thoughts; on occasion he would resort to physical means, and try to terrify. Satan was usually abetted by a crowd of demons appearing in frightening shapes. Monasticism in these early days had its perils. The hermits and ascetics were usually written about and lauded as exemplars, rather than propagators, of religious ideas in written form.

Scholasticism and Mysticism

An important movement, if so it can be called, was known as scholasticism, of which the greatest religious writers of the medieval era were representative. Aquinas was probably the most important.

Scholasticism endeavoured to separate concepts such as truth and error, mainstream belief and heresy. It adduced reason as a guiding principle in the contemplation of eternal verities. The scholastics discussed important questions such as when the Devil fell, and its relation in time to the creation. They stated that demons attack humans to hinder or prevent God's plan – nothing new here. They also added that every sinner is doing the Devil's work whether he (the sinner) knows it or not, and is aiding the Devil in his fight against God and humanity.

Mysticism is another portmanteau term for a type of philosophical religious view of the world, by which, put as succinctly as possible, mankind loves God for no other reason than love itself. The fourteenth and fifteenth centuries saw mysticism at its height, largely because many Christians perceived corruption in the institutional Church and sought guidance from contemplatives. Mystics believed that deep sensitivity to religious or spiritual experience might open up an intuition to powers of good and evil. They repeated the belief that the Devil had no real power over humanity and urged prayer when faced with the temptations of demons.

Deviant Sects and Cults

The growth of deviant sects and cults was considerable during the Middle Ages. Their activities were labelled as heretical by the medieval Church. Adherents of these sects were regarded as heretics who had to be extirpated. 'Heresy is a Christian theological view opposed to the teaching of the Christian community as a whole' (Russell, *Lucifer: The Devil in the Middle Ages*, page 184).

One sect that posed real problems for the orthodox Christian faith was the Bogomils, who appeared in the tenth century. Their central tenet was that Christ and the Devil were equal entities and that therefore dualism, not monotheism, was the correct belief. Far more serious, however, was their practice of worshipping Satan, repudiating the Mass and rejecting the ceremony of Baptism.

Another group known as the Cathars appeared in the mid-twelfth century, and revived the idea of dualism. They were mainly concerned theologically with the old problem of evil, and central to their concerns was the figure of Satan. Open conflict between the views of the Cathars and the Catholics led to angry exchanges and finally to the use of force. This was caused basically by a fundamental belief of the Cathars which had to do with the nature of evil: if evil does exist in the absolute, then it has a unique existence completely different from that of good.

St Anselm (1033–1109) in large measure further developed the thought of Augustine, and made additional advances in diabology possible because of the comparatively new application of reason to everything. Peter Lombard (1100–60) was another advocate of the movement, and his book *Sentences* was at the time very influential.

FREE WILL

Anselm discussed the question of what evil is (as did many religious thinkers). In a nutshell, Anselm said that evil was simply the lack of good; evil is nothingness, a deprivation of the good. Lucifer fell – but how could he do this? 'God gave Lucifer his will, so the will could not itself be evil', as Russell says in his book *Lucifer: The Devil in the Middle Ages* (page 165). Thereby, the free will of Lucifer introduced moral evil into the world. The story of Adam and Eve is his starting point from which to discuss the concept of free will. Original sin arose in the world out of Adam's choice not to obey the orders of his Creator. Anselm furthered the discussion about difficult religious doctrine and brought logical thinking to bear on the inconsistencies.

It can be seen that the early, but growing, Christian/Roman Catholic faith had many influences on it throughout this period, some beneficial, others detrimental. On the one hand, it had the mainly benign and supportive doctrinal approaches of the great thinkers and writers who contributed to the health and strength of the Church; but on the other hand, it had to contend with several breakaway forms of religion, cults and sects, which tried it sorely. Whatever the line, it may be said they all contributed to an examination and development of faith by the Church, and these influences of differing kinds, taken all round, can be no bad thing.

Before the earliest of these thinkers and writers, such as Ignatius (died about AD 150) and Polycarp (about AD 160), there were of course the Gospel writers Matthew, Mark, Luke and John and the author of the Epistles, Paul. They were evangelizing, endeavouring to spread Jesus' words in a hostile world. The first Christians had to endure the persecutions of the Romans and the enmity of the staunch Jews. Many Jews espoused the new faith – if they had not it is doubtful that Christianity would have taken root at all, or in any event, so quickly. More and more, however, as years went by, the Christian movement became composed of Gentiles, many of them former pagans. At this time, Christians were simply a minority sect within largely Jewish communities.

Christian preachers began to appeal increasingly to Gentiles who came from different parts of the Roman Empire. The trouble was that some of these converts still stuck to an extent to their old beliefs, so that the burgeoning faith had more than one source of irritation, to use a mild term, with which to contend. A salient doctrine of the early Church, which tended to disrupt, was the division of the supernatural into, on one side, a belief in one God and on the other a demonic realm, led by Satan. Naturally this demonization of their gods did not go down well with the overwhelming mass of pagan peoples. It tended to alienate and was something of a barrier to conversion.

BACKGROUND TO BELIEF

The backcloth therefore to the early Christian writers already mentioned, including Justin Martyr, Irenaeus, Tertullian and Origen, was one of confusion and persecution. It is important, though, to see the other side of the coin: Christianity was viewed by the Romans as a threat to the established order, and even in some ways sent the wrong message to the potential converts.

Many of the latter saw the teaching of Christianity as advocating societal, even nationalist, bonds as of little consequence in the perspective of eternal salvation to which only the new religion had the key. Indeed, not only are these bonds not to be regarded as important, but they are in essence devices to bind people to Roman rule and all its works and pomps which are in truth demonic – like the Romans gods.

Much, as we have seen, of the early Christian writing is concerned with devils. A passage of Origen (died about 254) sums up his (and others') position nicely, when he claims that the souls of those who die for the Christian faith 'destroy the power of the demons and frustrate their conspiracy against mankind' (*Contra Celsum*, 1:44). Origen concludes from this that demons sometimes refrain from attacking Christians for fear of bringing about their own destruction.

Deviations Branded as Heresies

Origen, like the other writers, was a persecuted Christian whose beliefs were very much at variance with those of the ruling power, but this did not mean that Christians were not good citizens. They might have courted controversy, but they certainly did not want to excite the enmity of the State.

In Origen's century and the following one, despite pagan persecution, Christianity flourished by following the precepts of the Bible, seeing itself as the ally of God. Far from being a seditious cult, Christianity established itself as a flourishing Church, with the Devil and his demons as arch-enemy. Unfortunately, its later development was accompanied by a pitiless fixation on such as heresy, its concomitant, witchcraft, and deluding, possessive demons. Any and all deviations from the official line were branded as heresies, even though the Church was itself struggling with inconsistencies and fresh thought might have served only to invigorate.

Heretics, so-called, quoted Scripture in order to substantiate their position, but this, as may be imagined, irritated the authorities greatly. Tertullian, writing about AD 200, adduced that heretics ought not to be allowed to appeal to the Scriptures since they have nothing to do with the Scriptures, and since they are heretics, 'they cannot be true Christians' (Tertullian, *Prescription*, Chapter 37).

In subsequent centuries, Christianity has anathematized the beliefs it has considered deviant, and has demonized individuals from the Roman persecutors to Martin Luther, from atheists to non-believers. The force of evil the Church construed as a species of demon attack and as such had at all times and with the utmost vigour to be resisted. This is still the position today, although not many churchmen will admit it!

THE SECOND COMING

These demon attacks, however, will not last for ever, we are told. The Jewish apocryphal literature (among others) makes this very clear. On the Day of Judgement, Satan and all his wicked spirits will be destroyed by being cast out into an abyss of fire. (See echoes of this in the passage quoted earlier on the binding of Satan from Revelation, page 54.) Until Judgement Day, the demons, it is said (in the Book of Enoch), are left free to torment. In this book there is a reference to a kind of purgatory, dark and painful, where the fallen angels are kept until, as it says, the great judgement. At this Second Coming, the evil spirits will be judged and found guilty, to be sentenced to everlasting torments, along with the unjust, and the great misleader of men, Satan himself. The Second Coming had, and has, the utmost significance for Christians after death, as it is the time when the righteous will be rewarded and the wicked condemned. The fateful last day is the first day of perpetual happiness for some with God and the ultimate overthrow of the Devil and his demons.

It is this belief in the Day of Judgement (or the Second Coming) which has been the mainstay of Christian faith for millennia. No matter the persecution or attacks by the Devil, the Second Coming has been a vast comfort. It denotes the ultimate triumph of good and the destruction of evil. Victory is assured. In many ways it was the final appeal to the faithful to remain on the straight and narrow. And it could come tomorrow! Or in thousands of years. Whatever, just reward would eventually certainly come. That was the clincher. In the meantime, the Church acknowledged, demons would be free to roam the world and some misguided souls would seek their protection, even ally themselves to these demons.

DEVIL WORSHIP

Some, inevitably, would worship the Devil. Homage to the Devil is an ancient practice, and showed itself in several offshoot sects of official Christianity. It is alive and well today but secretly so, in several obscure sects and cults. Devil worship in fact seems to come before worship of a benign God. As Paul Carus phrases it in *The History of the Devil* (page 6): 'Demonolatry or Devil worship, is the first stage in the evolution of religion, for we fear the bad, not the good.' It can, however, be the last stage!

Decline in religious belief generally in the twentieth century has been accompanied by growth in demonic sects and cults. It is as if something has to replace the void left by the demise of orthodox religious faith in Man's psyche. The Devil seems more overtly to produce results – of a worldly, material kind – so many people are persuaded of his power on earth. Of course most of these cults have undesirable undertones, apart from the explicit homage to the powers of darkness, such as sexual licence, abuse of various kinds, delusions of grandeur, control over others, and amassing wealth from gullible followers (notably for the cult leaders!). Ostensibly, worship of the Devil often means in reality worship of the founder. It is usually simply megalomania: the achieving of a spurious personal prominence.

Some of the deviant religious sects which troubled the early and the medieval Church practised worship of the Devil. For them, the Devil was of equal power to a God who had created evil, if He was the Creator of all things. These religions were dualist in nature, believing in two supreme beings. Naturally this was an heretical belief to the accepted orthodoxy of Christianity, to Catholicism at first, then later, after Luther, to Protestantism.

Worship of evil spirits arises out of fear of the unknown. To early Man, even early Christian Man, most phenomena in the world lacked an explanation. The natural thing to do was worship the being behind the phenomenon, propitiate it and by so doing hope to turn its wrath aside.

It seemed natural to presume that most happenings in the world were caused by a malicious agency, because it was unlucky or destructive events that bothered early Man most. In some ways unsophisticated peoples conceived of the good spirit as being the weaker of the two. Savages and civilizations alike have done homage from time immemorial to bad spirits.

Human and Animal Sacrifice

One only has to look at the concept of sacrifice, human as well as animal, common to primitive cultures as to more developed ones, in pagan and even Christian times. We can read in the Old Testament of the Israelites who offered their sons and daughters as a sacrifice to the demons. Jephtha believed that God required him to offer up his daughter 'as a burnt offering' (Judges 9:29-40).

The legends of Greece and Rome reveal many examples of propitiation of evil beings by immolation. Some of these practices stem from the belief that the cutting out of vital organs, such as the heart or brain, confers a special status on the perpetrator, while at the same time honouring the gods. Much of this idolatry is due to superstition, of course, and the lack of an alternative credo which can interpret, to some extent at least, the threatening world. Religion itself, like Devil worship, arises in the first place from fear: fear of evil and fear of the unknown. Devil and demon worship, however, did not reach its zenith until the witch craze came to its height in the fifteenth, sixteenth and seventeenth centuries. We shall consider this belief in the next chapter.

Adoration of Graven Images

An accompaniment of obeisance to evil spirits was the almost universal adoration of what the Bible calls 'graven images', or representations in the form of statues, of people and animals. Many of these idols or rituals have been taken over by the later (and present-day) churches: the burning of incense, holy pictures and statuettes, holy water, and the symbol of the cross. Most have their origin in heathen cultures. They were absorbed into Christian belief as they came to be regarded as powerful agencies in what was seen as a battle against the Devil and his demons.

Giants on Earth

There is a significant, if difficult, passage in the Bible (Genesis 6:4) which speaks of there being giants on earth 'in those days'. We have mentioned them before as being one explanation for the appearance of demons. The giants, as well as their offspring, came to be regarded as demons, because they were believed to envy Man and his works, which by comparison with their labours seemed far too easy.

These giants had the task of looking after and ensuring the continuance of natural features such as mountains, rivers, woods and the ground itself. Back in the mists of time, there was a consciousness among the common people of a period when Man was aided by superhuman beings in his great labours, such as the construction of some of the seven wonders of the ancient world. Also, many examples exist of natural formations the names of which suggest a supernatural connection, indeed have often been a focus for myth and legend: the Devil's Dyke in England, the Devil's Bridge in Wales and the Devil's Bit Mountains in Eire. In the USA there are the awesome rock formations of Devil's Postpile National Monument in California and Devil's Tower National Monument in Wyoming. There are many more around the world.

Unfortunately, these giants proved to be malevolent in their designs, although for a time appearing to be benign. It was to be expected that Man would abase himself faced with these formidable creatures. Sacrifice was one way of doing this.

THE INCARNATION

Surrounded by all these phobias and superstitions, medieval Man could nevertheless take comfort from the belief that he was destined, despite everything, to take his place in heaven – provided of course he lived a good life. This comfort derived from the belief that Christ was God incarnate, made flesh. It was the ransom theory that was mainly propagated by the Church: Jesus fought against the Devil and won by His death on the cross. By this fate, He atoned for all the sins of mankind, past, present and to come.

The opening battle between good and evil was begun with the Incarnation. The Son of God came down to earth as Jesus of Nazareth because no other was worthy to wipe away Man's sins. The doctrine of original sin, though by no means invalidated, could be believed in since now, after the Incarnation, Man could attain everlasting life despite the stain of the first sin on his soul. Hence the importance of the ceremony of Baptism very early in life, and at its end the ceremony of Extreme Unction when the dying person is *in extremis*. Nothing, however, was automatically guaranteed: a pious life was still needed if only as an earnest of good intention. It need hardly be emphasized that the doctrine of the Incarnation is absolutely fundamental to Christian theology. Without this belief Christianity would be just another sect.

Carus in *The History of the Devil* (page 261) states:

> *The Christian scheme of salvation may be called the vicarious atonement of man's sin through the blood of Christ. God's wrath upon the guilty human race is purified through the sufferings and death of the innocent god-man. Divine Justice is satisfied by the sacrifice of Divine Love.*

Alexander in *Demonic Possession in the New Testament* (page 249) states the position convincingly. He says that the Incarnation initiated the establishment of the kingdom of heaven upon earth, which determined a counter-movement among the powers of darkness. 'Genuine demonic possession was one of its manifestations.'

The Incarnation may have been instrumental in the final freeing of Man from sin, but this did not inhibit the diabolic forces, which continued the ultimate losing fight. Man still wished to attain the unattainable, as he still does; in this pursuit he turned to magic, sorcery and witchcraft, all of which were regarded as heresy by the ecclesiastical authorities. But more of these matters later.

Diabolic forces are power-driven by the Devil, of course, but many, if not most, Christians will not commit themselves to an outright confession of belief in the present existence of his eminence. Believed possession of a person by the Devil or a demon is attributed to a Principle of Evil, which cannot be defined. What is it? Who created it? For most people there are no answers even when exorcist clergy are convinced 'there is something there' in about five per cent of cases. I offer no definitive answers; I can only describe happenings in my own experience (*see* Chapter Seven).

No such embarrassment was experienced by the Desert Fathers and others of the time, who it seems daily encountered demons. Ecclesiastical literature is full of accounts of encounters with demons. Either we have belief in these accounts, or Scripture and subsequent relations by men and women of the cloth are lies, or at best are allegorical (so they could literally mean anything) – or demon (and Devil) activity was once appropriate and had meaning for poet and peasant alike, but now is not so, when science and rational thought can explain everything!

The commitment to a belief that the Devil, the essence of evil, is an equal adversary of God is thought by many to be an implicit acknowledgement of the aforesaid proposition – in any candid admission of his, or demons', existence. It is in all judgements essential to remember that Satan was (is) an angel, albeit fallen. Belief, it is thought, in angels itself is fading, or has faded, at least among laity, so there is a difficulty here. But for early Christians encounters with and experience of both angels and demons, psychically and actually, were not thought unusual. For them the invisible world was a reality. This belief in the reality of the supernatural was not peculiar to the monks and anchorites; it was a belief shared by their fellows. They spoke and wrote of demons as a matter of fact.

The Church itself laid down that demons were real and that they owed their being to no rival Principle of Evil, but were culpable spirits who fell from grace by their own volition: that is to say, they were created good, originally, by God. That is why it was not always a good idea in the art of the time to depict the Devil and his demons as terrifyingly ugly. As angels they could be pleasing to the sight – as they often were on manifesting themselves – and were occasionally so depicted.

The conception of Satan as an evil entity who permeated all things, all men and women, and was the sworn enemy of God, as we have seen, was not sudden but evolutionary. When fully into its stride, Satanism harassed, befogged and led clergy and people alike. Its zenith came in the sixteenth century, though it began virulently in the preceding century and continued its domination in the following. Obsession with Satan and his machinations was seen not only in people's behaviour but also in the art and literature of the time. On the other hand, the Incarnation, God made Man, it cannot be too strongly emphasized, was the central theme of Christianity; without this doctrine the embryonic Church would never have taken root.

THE PERSECUTION OF 'WITCHES' BEGINS

The behaviour of women came increasingly under scrutiny. As I have said earlier, women were regarded as much inferior to men. They were the original weak vessel who corrupted all mankind in the Garden and whose wiles had to be combated vigilantly lest they lead men into sin. They were easily influenced and easily persuaded.

As such, they were pre-eminently suitable targets for Satan and his followers. Fear of Satanism, manifested often and largely through women, was mainly responsible for the anti-feminism of the time, which translated itself into witchcraft persecution. Witches, though they could be male, were overwhelmingly female. Literature of this period, when it is about women, is concerned with their social position, especially conjugal, which is always denigrated, and women become, if not figures of fun, then types of ogress or temptress, immoral and trivial.

Other literature, that of demonology, contributed vastly to the perceived pomp and circumstance of the Devil. Certain authors discussed the subject in detail and with scholarship; others wrote chiefly to inflame the fires of Satanic oppression.

In this era particularly, the Church was obsessed with sorcery and heresy, of which it saw an enormous growth. Satanism and its accompaniment, witchcraft, were targets for oppression, and the Church relentlessly and ruthlessly hunted down their instances wherever they might be. People found guilty of these practices were marked for death as the only appropriate punishment for such heinous crimes.

The Hammer of Witchcraft

In 1486 was published the most infamous book of the persecution mania that swept the Continent and England: the *Malleus Maleficarum*, written by two Dominican monks, Sprenger and Kramer (sometimes called Institoris). In it they gave detailed instructions how to discover witches, to try and to punish them.

Reading it now – the hammer of witchcraft – it seems amazing that people believed its arrant nonsense. But such was the credulity of the times, such was the hold organized religion had over the people, such was the fear of evil and demons, that it became a second bible for inquisitors and witch-finders everywhere. It was enormously successful, largely because it had the imprimatur of no less a personage than Pope Innocent VIII, who himself had issued a papal bull in 1484 voicing his disquiet about prevalent Satanism and sorcery.

This book seemed to open the gates to many treatises on demonology and witchcraft in the following century or so. Most of these works supported the theory of witchcraft, but one or two brave voices pleaded the contrary opinion, of which the *De Praestigiis Daemonum*, 1564, by Johann Weyer (or Wier) was the most thorough (*see* p. 133 ff).

Confessions were extorted from the accused witches by means of the most cruel tortures, and all this was justified by selective quotations from the Bible and

SIGNIFICANT DATES: SATANISM OF THE LATE FIFTEENTH TO SEVENTEENTH CENTURIES

DEMONOLOGICAL LITERATURE	ECCLESIASTICAL MEASURES AGAINST SATANISM
1486 *Malleus Maleficarum* (Sprenger and Institoris. *Expositio… Preceptum* (Beetz)	1484 Bull 'Summis Desiderantes'
	1494 Bull 'Cum acceperimus'
	1536 1st Council of Cologne
	1548 Council of Trèves
1508 *Liber Octo Questionum* (Trithemius)	1550 1st Council of Cambrai and 2nd Council of Cologne
1510 *Quam Gravier* (van Hoogstraeten)	1565 2nd Council of Cambrai
	1570 1st Council of Malines
1564 *De Praestigiis Daemonum* (Wier)	1574 1st Council of Tournai
	1576 1st Council of Antwerp
1579 *Traicté ensignant en bref* (Benoist)	1580 1st Synod of Harderwijk
	1581 Synod of Arnheim
1580 *De la démonomanie* (Boguet)	1585 Bull 'Coeli et terrae'
1589 *Tractatus de Confessionibus* (Binsfeld)	1590 Order of the Bishop of Tournai concerning child sorcerers
1591 *Discours des sorciers* (Boguet)	Synod of Dordrecht
1595 *Disquisitionum Magicarum* (Del Rio)	1594 1st Synod of Montauban
	1595 2nd Synod of Harderwijk
1596 *Von Zauberei* (Agricola)	1597 Synod of Goes
	1598 2nd Synod of Montauban
	1600 2nd Council of Tournai
	1604 1st Council of Namur
	1607 2nd Council of Malines and Synod of La Rochelle
	1610 Council of Metz and 1st Synod of Assen
1612 *Tableau de l'inconstance* (De Lancre)	1612 2nd Synod of Assen
	1615 3rd Synod of Assen, Synod of Zwolle and 2nd Council of Anvers
	1616 4th Synod of Assen
	1618 5th Synod of Assen and 2nd Council of Liège
	1619 6th Synod of Assen
	1620 7th Synod of Assen and Synod of Kampa
	1623 Bull 'Omnipotentis Dei'
1626 *Universis Theologica* (Tanner)	
1631 *Cautio Criminalis* (Von Spee)	1631 3rd Council of Cambrai
	1637 Instructions of Urban VIII to ecclesiastical judges
	1639 2nd Council of Namur
	1643 3rd Council of Anvers and 3rd Council of Tournai
1675 *Plaidoyez* (Hautefeuille)	

	SORCERERS SENTENCED (COMTÉ DE NAMUR 1500–1650)					
CIVIL MEASURES AGAINST SATANISM		BURNINGS	BANISHMENTS	VARIOUS	SENTENCES UNKNOWN	ACQUITTALS	TOTAL

CIVIL MEASURES AGAINST SATANISM	Year	Burnings	Banishments	Various	Sentences Unknown	Acquittals	Total
	1500	–	–	–	–	–	–
	1505	3	–	–	–	–	3
1532 Nemesis Carolina	1510	1	1	–	3	1	6
	1515	3	–	–	4	3	10
1563 Ordinance by the Provincial Council	1520	7	1	–	3	5	16
of Luxemburg concerning the powers	1525	2	2	1	–	–	5
of local officials with regard to sorcery	1530	2	2	–	1	3	8
	1535	–	2	1	2	–	5
	1540	5	2	1	6	–	14
1591 Ordinance of the Provincial Council	1545	6	4	–	11	2	23
of Luxemburg concerning sorcery	1550	11	9	1	8	2	31
1592 1st Ordinance of Philip II on the	1555	4	6	–	13	–	23
same subject							
1595 2nd Ordinance of Philip II on the	1560	11	15	2	5	4	37
same subject	1565	3	2	–	6	2	13
	1570	5	2	2	–	1	10
1606 Archducal Ordinance on the same	1575	1	1	–	–	–	2
subject	1580	–	–	–	–	–	–
1608 Order of Ernest of Bavaria	1585	3	2	–	3	–	8
concerning the activities of sorcerers,	1590	7	1	–	–	3	11
and Ordinance of the Provincial							
Council of Flanders on the same	1595	8	1	–	3	3	15
subject	1600	15	2	–	8	3	28
1612 Archducal Ordinance concerning	1605	18	2	2	6	8	36
child sorcerers	1610	11	3	2	6	1	23
1623 1st Ordinance of the Provincial							
Council of Namur concerning judges	1615	2	5	3	10	6	26
experienced in cases of Satanism	1620	8	5	–	4	–	17
1630 2nd Ordinance of the same Council,	1625	4	8	–	1	1	14
on the same subject	1630	8	–	1	–	–	9
1660 Repetition of the Archducal							
Ordinance of 1606	1635	–	–	1	–	–	1
1682 Ordinance of Louis XIV on the	1640	1	–	1	2	1	5
suspension of proceedings against							
sorcerers	1645	–	–	–	1	–	1
	Totals	149	78	18	106	49	400

by the thunderous words of the clerics. The people who sat in judgement on the unfortunate people thus accused were creatures of their time who believed implicitly that what they had to do was right. Throughout the sixteenth century a succession of bulls and letters emanated from popes, governors and inquisitors, all aimed at destroying the curse of demonality and sorcery. The Holy See had become preoccupied with Satanism and its effects.

Sorcery and Heresy

Ecclesiastical Councils met throughout the sixteenth and seventeenth centuries to promulgate decisions relating to the practice, as they saw them, of sorcery, magic and soothsaying. All practitioners of these arts were to be condemned as heretics, and they were mainly women.

After the Reformation, which saw the establishment of the Protestant Church, fear of Satanism redoubled and witches were persecuted by the new Protestantism with all the old enthusiasm of Roman Catholicism. Not only were the ecclesiastical authorities determined to extirpate all heresy manifesting itself largely in sorcery, but lay or civil authorities regarded the practice with hatred. From the Middle Ages, the Common Law had fulminated against diabolic practices and set severe punishments for those found guilty of them.

State edicts (on the Continent) had revealed an attitude to Satanic rites and rituals as implacable as any the Church had shown. Kings, popes, jurists, governors were as convinced as any Roman Catholic cleric of the reality of Satan and the demons. Canon law and civil law both conspired to bring about the demented bloodshed in the illusory hunt after sorcery and witchcraft. Anti-Satanic legislation was justified on religious and social grounds, it was claimed.

The crime of sorcery came later, under the jurisdiction of lay tribunals, and offences of a purely religious nature came under the ecclesiastical courts or authorities. Attempts were made to distinguish between the two types of offence. Somewhat naturally this differentiation, often artificial, led to a degree of animosity between lay and spiritual power.

Sorcery itself was a crime punishable by death; as it was believed that ecclesiastical courts should not be involved with death sentences, practitioners, so called, of these black arts were usually handed over, after being found guilty, to the lay authorities for appropriate punishment. Inquisitors who attended these trials were sometimes themselves ignorant and uneducated (like the judges), but they maintained the position that theirs was an expert role, explaining legal niceties and giving guidance on procedures.

Europe was the focus of sorcery and Satanism, aided by superstition on the part of the people. In the eyes of the Church, sorcery was essentially evil, and so was harshly attacked wherever and whenever it occurred. But secular power also had much to answer for. (*See* chart of 'Significant Dates'.)

During this era it is no exaggeration to say that daily life in Europe lay under the influence of two opposing religions: Christianity and Satanism. Many practitioners of the occult worshipped demons, hoping to enlist their aid in doing evil to people they saw as enemies. The belief that demons stalked the earth undoubtedly led many to liaise in various ways with the Devil.

Satanism, although clearly a force for evil, had many adherents, to judge from the numbers executed for diabolism in this period. It must be said that much of this Devil or demon worship was actually fomented by unfrocked or renegade priests who remain forever anathema in orthodox religious eyes. Demonology (or Satanism) comprised advocacy of anarchy, sacrificial worship, copulation with demons, dabbling in the supernatural, sexual activities of an obscene or forbidden nature. Worship of Satan often seemed to centre around a domestic animal, especially on the occasion of the witches' sabbats.

'Satanist' is itself an umbrella term for a wide variety of sorcerers, wizards and the like. L'Estrange Ewen adduces that rigid adherence to the letter of scripture was the origin of much wrong-headed thinking, and I incline to think that he is right (*Witchcraft and Demonianism*, Introduction). Blind belief in demons (and witches) he attributes to nine causes: blind Biblical teaching; corrupt clergy; errors of the medical profession; intolerant and misguided statutes; lack of knowledge about mortality and death; confessions of demented (often tortured) persons; credence placed in the testimony of the mentally afflicted; the payment by results to witch-finders; and inflaming publications by the press – and authors.

Typical of the demonology literature of the age is the book, published in 1595, *Demonolatry* by Nicholas Remy, a Privy Councillor to the Duke of Lorraine in France. In actual fact he presided over many witchcraft 'trials' in his term of office, and, as he wrote in his Dedication (page vii):

> … *since my lot has been for so many years to conduct the trial of capital offences in Lorraine, it has seemed that there is no course left me but to publish the truth of all the prodigious tales that are told of witchcraft, particularly such as have come within my experience…*

In the academic world he was eminent, holding chairs in Law and Literature in several French universities. Nevertheless, his 140,000-word book is devoted to the reality of demon oppression and witchcraft malice. The contents are concerned with such topics as how the demons influence men, trick and delude them, and how witches ally themselves to these demons with the object of wreaking evil on other people and of garnering the advantages such liaisons bring.

Although Remy was illustrative of the sincere belief in the Devil and demons, there was an undercurrent (for such it was) of scepticism about the authenticity of the very existence of witches, to say nothing of their mysterious powers.

SCEPTICISM

Sometimes this latent disbelief did become overt (compare Weyer). The advent of the beliefs of Luther (1483–1546) on the world scene shook the foundations of established Christianity, for these beliefs criticized vehemently many of the ecclesiastical practices of the day, stipulating that only faith and the Bible were valid for religious thought.

It was not only Luther's fundamental objections to the courses of the Roman Catholic Church that made him an object of hatred by this establishment, but also the fact that some of his doctrines flew in the face of tradition acceptance. Doctrines such as predestination, which meant that Christ died not for everyman but only for the elect, could not possibly be ignored by the Roman Catholic Church.

The second greatest name in the van of the Protestant Reformation was that of Calvin, who came into contact with Luther's ideas in the 1520s and enthusiastically embraced them. By about 1600 a spirit of reform was abroad both in the Roman Catholic and in the new Protestant Churches.

In the late years of the sixteenth century great contemplatives such as John of the Cross and Teresa of Avila were leaders by example in the reform movement. This, however, must not be interpreted as an indication of a general disbelief in the Devil and his minions. Far from it! Luther himself was a wholehearted believer in the reality of demons and the Devil, and the witchcraft persecution continued for many years to come. The point is that there was a degree of scepticism especially about witchcraft and a much more overt rebellion by thinkers of the time against certain practices of the Church.

By about 1700, this scepticism had carried the day. Belief in witchcraft was minimal, as was belief in Satanism. Several influential philosophers (Hobbes, Descartes and Locke) by their writing hastened the demise of the belief that God and the Devil were constantly intervening in the world; it gradually became apparent to people that demons might be only symbols, metaphors, for the world's evil.

There still remained the question of possession, for many people seemed to exhibit the age-old telltale signs. Exorcism came to be regarded by the Protestant Church as an example of superstitious practice, while for the Roman Catholic Church it was more in favour than ever.

By the turn of the century (1800), the secularization of society had begun with the result that traditional belief in the Devil and demons as a reality, as living beings, had all but withered away under rational scrutiny. The clergy, particularly Roman Catholic, naturally continued to foster credence in supernatural evil spirits, and it is probable that the uneducated (still the great mass of people) and the selfsame clergy sincerely believed in it.

Prominent thinkers arose who did not: their ideas were influential and eventually trickled down to the masses. Not only this, but the political power of monarchies and aristocracies waned throughout the century – power which originally had been favourable to Christianity and moreover whose representatives were usually Christian, if only in name. Side by side with this development could be seen the growth of new powers and influences: those of industry and capitalism, all of which resulted in the decline of fearful religious belief, especially in demons and the Devil.

Romanticism, an early nineteenth-century way of looking at the world, notable particularly in the fields of art and literature, drove further nails into the coffin of traditional belief. Adherents of the movement tended to dislike the values of the Christian Churches, which is the plural term we should now use, and this was reciprocated. This antagonism gave rise to the feeling that Christianity itself was not good, but was in fact bad, and that therefore its opponents must be the good ones and the corollary followed that Satan must be good. How Christianity and its traditional beliefs have fared in modern times must be left to later chapters.

Scepticism among non-believers, generally confined to the intellectual, educated few (apart from the clergy), was often directed to main articles of faith of religion (Roman Catholicism) and gathered momentum with the spread of Protestantism. The ordinary people did not think deeply about these things, but accepted them as good Catholics should. Some of the rituals and ceremonies of the Church gave ammunition to its detractors unwittingly. Accusations of ritual unlawful killing and even of cannibalism were levelled. These accusations should be treated with the contempt they deserve, but are illustrative of the animosity generated by the Church among its opponents.

This may be illustrated from the example of the ceremony of the Holy Eucharist, that part of the Mass where Transubstantiation takes place; that is, the change of the wafer of bread into Christ's body and the wine into Christ's blood. This is the fundamental doctrine of the Holy Mass. Not to believe this negates the whole meaning and purpose of the sacrifice (as it is called) of the Mass. The belief originates from the Last Supper where Jesus said to his apostles, 'This is my body; this is my blood. Take ye and eat… in remembrance of me…' Note that the Lord did not say that this was a symbol or representation of his body and blood, but that it '*is*'. For Catholics therefore the doctrine is central to the Church's whole credo.

Mass, viewed as the reason for the coming together of the faithful in a congregation, is first spoken about in the initial Letter to the Corinthians by St Paul, where we read of a gathering in a church when provisions might be shared, especially loaves and wine. Already Christ's words were taken literally. Some early Christians might have been happy to see Jesus' words as a metaphor, but ecclesiastical authority saw it as a vital doctrine. So much so, that the distinguished Council of Trent meeting in the sixteenth century laid down that anyone denying the truth of Transubstantiation shall be 'anathema'. On this doctrine was based the charge of cannibalism directed at the Roman Catholic Church by its enemies.

This was not the only charge, though perhaps the most egregious one. Christianity down the centuries has been subject to harassment, both from outside forces and from within, if so we may call the divergent sects that have come and gone. Some of these breakaway religions have remained nominally Christian and by so doing have given the Church a bad name. Accounts of the activities of these Christian offshoots, if they are to be believed, can only bring the Faith into disrepute. One such account speaks of demon influence:

> *In the evening… they bring together… young girls whom they have initiated into their rites. Then they extinguish the candles… and throw themselves lasciviously on the girls, each one on whomever first falls into his hands, no matter whether she be his sister, his daughter or his mother. For they think that they are doing something that greatly pleases the demons by transgressing God's laws…*

These sects were accused of other infamies, of which there is some evidence, but little, it must be said, that involved promiscuous and incestuous orgies. However, orgiastic rites or ceremonies did seem to be the *raison d'être* for these meetings; presumably they were called to honour the Devil and to show him the devotion of the members, while at the same time to provide under the cloak of Devil and demon worship an opportunity for sexual licence.

Many of these gatherings, particularly those of witches, were presided over by the Devil himself or by a subordinate demon. This manifestation was the focus of attention and lewd homage was paid to it (or him) (more of this later in the chapter on witchcraft, *see* page 78). None of this, of course, did the reputation of Christianity any good, even though in its mainstream practices it kept to the straight and narrow.

THE INQUISITIONAL SYSTEM

We should now take note of the institutionalized system of discovering heretics, who were believed to practise sorcery by means of the power they derived from demons or the Devil. This legal procedure was from the first called inquisitorial, not accusatory, whereby charges against an individual lay with the authorities.

An individual had to be denounced before a judge could proceed to an investigation (inquisition). Action on a sufficient number of denunciations passed into the canon law as *de rigeur*. By the early thirteenth century, death was the standard penalty for heresy. The system of Benefit of the Clergy, as it was known, meant that clerics could be tried only in their own ecclesiastical courts; moreover, no cleric could be accused by one of lower status. The new inquisitorial procedure enabled the authorities to initiate proceedings against all clerics no matter what their rank. These official inquiries employed a procedure grossly unfair to the accused (of heresy). If allowed a 'defending' lawyer, the accused usually found the lawyer more occupied with trying to get a confession than defending him.

The so-called trials were held in camera, in secrecy, which allowed for abuse of the system. Torture was usually employed to extract a 'confession'. If an accused did not confess he could be imprisoned for life. If he did confess he had to repeat it all a few days later to affirm that the confession had not been extorted under torture. Judged on his words on the day, the accused could be forgiven, but had to perform some kind of penance, not by any means always light. But if he retracted his confession, he was regarded as a relapsed heretic and was handed over to the civil authorities to be burnt at the stake. It can readily be seen that it was a case of heads the judges win and tails the accused lost. It was a vicious procedure which had the full backing of the ecclesiastical authorities. And it went on for centuries.

The Inquisition must be placed in the context of the age. It was a time when the Devil and his demons were behind every evil or misfortune. The Church was paramount and its commandments based on the Holy Word of God. It was the fount of all wisdom and the one true way to reach heaven. Anyone who doubted this was a heretic and had to be destroyed for his own good and that of others who might also be led astray. Any means to this end was legitimate, including torture and death. This was the sincere belief of the clergy and the judiciary of the time, although it must be added there were subsidiary activities of a nefarious character, associated with the imprisonments and trials, of which more later (*see* pages 85 and 87 ff).

In moral problems (cases of heresy and sorcery), the power of evil, the Devil, was always present. The attitude of presiding judges can be encapsulated in St Paul's words in his Letter to the Ephesians (6:11–12), where he says:

> *You must wear all the weapons in God's armoury, if you would find strength to resist the cunning of the Devil. It is not against flesh and blood that we enter the lists; we have to do with Princedoms and Powers, with those who have mastery of the world in these dark days, with malign influence in an order higher than ours.*

It is clear from this that Satan was a person to be feared and combated.

The use of the masculine pronoun when speaking of a victim, an accused or a member of the public may give a wrong impression of early and medieval attitudes to the common people or those suspected of a crime. Most individuals who committed crimes or were arraigned on charges were in fact male (except in the case of witchcraft persecution), but this is nothing new and is paralleled in modern life. Females were in fact regarded for centuries with suspicion, even dislike, by the orthodox Church.

FEMALE WICKEDNESS OR VICTIMIZATION?

As already mentioned, this attitude to women arose from the story of the temptation of Eve by the serpent in the Garden. It is possible to interpret the episode as indicating that Eve had not only succumbed easily and without demur to the Devil's blandishments, but that she had actually become his friend! Women throughout Christian literature were associated with collaboration with the Devil, and with carnal allure whereby males could suffer perdition. Indeed, many accounts of demonic attacks on contemplatives feature the wiles of women, whose manifestations were usually of a lewd nature, encouraging males to sins of the flesh. It was preached that males became enslaved by Satan because of sensuality provoked by women.

In the Christian world there have indeed been more concrete instances of female wickedness, some would say victimization, down the ages. It is clear from the many histories of religious origin that have come down to us that there is an inference to be drawn that women often (usually?) allowed copulations with the Devil and sexual congress with the incubus demons over a period of time and might even have enjoyed them.

Not only this, but women had not seemed to the Church to have fulfilled the prophecy of God when He spoke to the serpent in the Garden after the sin of disobedience: 'She shall crush thy head and thou shalt lie in wait for her heel' (Genesis 3:15). Another one of the representatives of the first beings upon the earth was Lilith, the first female demon. She was a contemporary of Adam and Eve who apparently consorted with Adam after his breakup from Eve, producing a race of demonic figures.

Thus in conventional eyes, two of the most evil persons at the dawn of mankind were women. Eve and Lilith were the first to obey Satan. It is no wonder that women were held in such poor regard by the Church (despite notable female anchorites), and that the almost exclusive persecution of women as in league with the Devil – that is, as witches – began. The witches were not so much possessed by the Devil as affected by him – but voluntarily.

THE NATURE OF EVIL

In the New Testament there are about twenty references to Satanic or demonic effects on people. It was considered axiomatic that demons are instrumental in thwarting God's will for mankind: they wage combat, physical and mental, with believers; they slander God; they cause believers to doubt; they promote defection from true religion; and they make the choice of the good difficult. Ultimately, however, demons did not have the God-given power to back up their threats.

Sins which men fell into by their own choice were a different matter: the demons did have sway here. Demonic attack on men that involved possession or oppression was accepted, if viewed as a punishment or a testing of character.

A witch assuming an animal form
suggestively contacts Satan

Belief in demons had its difficulties in so far as one view prevailed: that men were at fault in some way whenever they sinned; but another view held that Man could not be blamed for his transgressions if he was being controlled by demons. Clearly, the jury was out in these years over the question of the power of the demon: was it real, and was it independent?

The Devil of the Middle Ages was both Jewish and Christian, for his domain was moral evil – a subject that had been of concern for a thousand years. The authority of the Church combined with the ignorance of the time about almost all things in nature produced a belief in Satan and demons that was implicit.

The prevalent view, however, was that evil was not an independent principle and this gave rise to the endless debate about the nature of evil – a question still unresolved. According to some theories, Satan himself was impotent against God and His Church, but later developments began to indicate that perhaps the evil was not so impotent as was thought. One problem was that in essence there were two conceptions of Satan: one of the cloisters; and one of the streets and fields. They often differed in the way they saw the power and influence of the Devil.

Sinning against the Commandments

As the later medieval period dawned, perceptions of the meaning of sin, atonement and penance began to change. A desire for identification with the sufferings of Christ and a closer adherence to the Commandments began for many people.

Consequently, witchcraft, for example, became less a matter of idolatry and more a matter of sinning against the Lord's Commandments, expressly the first. As the emphasis on living according to the Ten Commandments (the Decalogue) increased, 'old' conceptions were themselves increasingly seen as transgressions against specific commandments. Ironically, this tended to add to the belief in diabology and associated activities, such as witchcraft and sorcery.

Growing acceptance of the primacy of the Decalogue, however, led to a marked increase in scepticism about demons. Some writers on witchcraft saw it as a crime in societal terms with strong associations with sex and conjugal relations. Others saw it as a sin of idolatry and Devil worship.

We are now in a position to consider witchcraft and belief in it.

CHAPTER FOUR

A MANIA
FOR
WITCHCRAFT

W itchcraft, a powerful and terrifying phenomenon, is a subject related to our theme, in so far as witches were believed to exert their influence through the power of the Devil and, by association, with his satellites, the demons (or devils). We need to consider witchcraft phenomena, as witches (so called) were considered for centuries to be possessed by the Devil (or demons) – or at least to be controlled by them. It was through demon power that witches were able to perform all manner of extraordinary things, from bringing about plagues to causing the death of both Man and beast. Basically, it was believed that witches had voluntarily entered into a sort of bargain with the Devil by which supernatural powers were bestowed on them in return for giving up their souls.

The search was soon on for witches – anyone who practised maleficia. Victims were sought out by the inquisitors, and, if accused, were subject to Trial by Ordeal, until a confession was obtained, itself proof that she was a witch. Death was the only escape from a practice that became a form of big business.

BELIEF IN WITCHCRAFT INCREASES

The heyday of witchcraft straddled some three centuries, roughly from about 1400 to 1700, achieving its height in the seventeenth century. It was in the latter period when witchcraft persecution was at its most savage – and most thorough. Although these centuries figure in most people's mind as *the* years of witchcraft mania, the belief in the reality of witches has been with humanity since (and before) Biblical times.

There are very few references to instances of what may be interpreted as witchcraft in the Scriptures (*see* below), but one particular passage from the New

Testament is of great significance because in it, Paul, listing the iniquities of major transgressions of God's law, mentions witchcraft as among them. In his Letter to the Galatians (5: 20) he writes:

Now the works of the flesh are manifest, which are these: fornication, uncleanness, las-civiousness, idolatry, witchcraft, hatred, variance [strife], emulations [jealousies], wrath, sedition, heresies, and such like; of the which I tell you before… that they which do such things shall not inherit the kingdom of God.

The disciple Paul in old age must have been writing only about fifty years or so after Christ's death, but it is clear that witchcraft was prevalent even then. The sort of witchcraft Paul was writing about had more to do with sorcery than heresy, with the 'evil eye' rather than maleficia (malevolent actions), more to do with idol worship than Devil worship and with baleful influences rather than than the later Christian concept of a compact with the Devil, whereby witches (mostly) and wizards could wreak death and destruction. Nevertheless, the important fact is that Paul refers to a practice that must have been quite wide-spread in the first century AD – a practice that came to its deadly zenith some fifteen hundred years later. (Other allusions to witches or witchcraft occur in Exodus 22:18; Deuteronomy 18:10; Samuel 15:23; and Chronicles 33:6.)

So, direct references to witchcraft in the Scriptures are few. One important reference that bears scrutiny is that relating to the appearance of the spirit Samuel (in the Old Testament), called up by a medium (a witch?) who dwelt in a place called Endor. Saul wished to discover his fortune in the next day's battle and ordered his guards to seek out a woman 'that hath a familiar spirit'. She summoned up the spirit of the long-dead prophet Samuel to impart the information Saul desired. Much discussion of this episode has taken place. It should – because it is Scripture – be true. However, some writers have attributed the appearance of Samuel to an evil spirit who wished to influence and dishearten Saul with bad news.

There are other, more oblique references to what might be called witchcraft, perhaps rather necromancy, such as the story of Jacob and his sons when ordered to buy corn (Genesis) and of Jacob again in Genesis 31:8–12, which involved the feeding of Laban's flocks. The implication is that something out of the ordinary happened here, perhaps not witchcraft as such, but certainly magic or necromancy. In the story of Tobias we learn that by smoke and the help of St Raphael he defeats Asmodeus, a hideous demon, who from the narrative appears capable of sexual love. The story is basically an account of exorcism and the power of demons.

'The New Testament', says Montague Summers in *The History of Witchcraft and Demonology* (page 191), '… [is] evidence for the reality of magic and divination [which] cannot be disregarded by any who accept the Christian revelation.' And we may add, by those who do not!

Persecution for witchcraft was believed to be legitimized by Biblical references. Ecclesiastical and secular authorities justified the barbarities inficted on (innocent) people by quoting selected (and selective) passages from the Scriptures. The key one was that taken from Exodus 22:18: 'Thou shalt not suffer a witch to live'. Two comments must be made on this adjuration: firstly, the word 'witch' is a mistranslation of the original Hebrew, which meant a 'murderer', not a witch, as later accepted; and secondly, the Biblical witch was a very different concept from that of the later Christian Church. In fact, the Bible, Old or New Testaments, nowhere mentions the supposed various concomitants of the witch – pact, sabbat and so forth – for they were in reality creations, or rather suppositions of, the medieval churchmen.

The witchcraft delusion arose out of the concept of Christian demonology, itself a delusion. It is not straining language to say that witchcraft theory was fostered by the sort of mistranslation quoted, and by successive mistranslations by so-called scholars, clerics and demonologists. Where there is a preconceived point to be made, selective quoting and biased interpretation will always suffice. Reading meaning which is not there into something is commonplace: it is also a truism. Medieval authorities did it all the time, especially in respect of witchcraft and demonology.

The half dozen or so references in the Bible are largely of this kind; that is to say, they are mistranslations and subsequent misunderstandings of key terminology which purported to support the witchcraft belief. Relevant passages are: Leviticus 19:26, 31; 20:6 and 20:27; 2 Kings 9:22; 21:6; 23:24; and Isaiah 8:19. I cannot quote all of them. Two will suffice to give the flavour: 2 Kings (9:22): 'What peace, so long as the whoredoms of thy mother, Jezebel, and her witchcrafts are so many?'; and Samuel (1:15, 23): 'For rebellion is as the sin of witchcraft and stubbornness is as iniquity and idolatry'. Translate the Hebrew as 'witchcraft' instead of sorcery, foretelling the future or divination (in this context), and you have a perfect recipe for the absurdities and abominations of the witchcraft persecution.

It was unfortunately not only obscurantist clerics and benighted judges who nurtured and encouraged belief in witchcraft derived from erroneous interpretations and, let it be said, from their diligence in keeping their flocks on the straight and narrow. Some of the greatest thinkers of the Catholic Church, among them Thomas Aquinas and St Augustine, fostered the illusion of witchcraft. Formal belief in human association with the Devil was firmly held by them and was transmitted to the following scholarly and clerical generations. Evident corroboration of devilish influence on mankind by such eminent thinkers led naturally to the eventual concept of the witch and her agreement with the Devil. Aquinas staunchly believed that sexual relations with devils were possible; that demons could transport witches through the air; that demons could transform themselves and humans into other shapes; that devils could work disasters; and that the demons could affect married relations, interrupting or preventing intercourse. With such a demonic pedigree is it any wonder that belief in the power of witches to bring about all manner of misfortunes inevitably followed?

WITCHCRAFT THEORY

This belief was so widespread, at least in Europe, that some powerful force must have been motivating it, resulting as it did in a persecution so virulent as to be almost unbelievable. To try to understand the ideology, one must appreciate the context of the age: a belief in demons and the Devil as realities was paramount, which itself dictated the belief that witches motivated by the Devil were subversive agents bent on the destruction of the State, the social order and, above all, of the organized religion. Moreover, witches were purveyors of heresy and sorcery, aided by their alliance with the Devil, and as such were guilty of treason, for which the only fitting punishment was death – as gruesome a death as possible. Not only were the witches' crimes treasonable to the State, but they were treasonable to God, which was much, much worse.

This alliance with the Devil was known as a (voluntary) pact, whereby witches were granted supernatural powers in return for their allegiance. This conception of pact with Satan was implicitly believed in – and making the pact was unforgivable. In fact, witches (at least in England) were often arraigned more for their guilt (supposed) in making a pact with the Devil than for their actual evil deeds (maleficia). Witchcraft was therefore a crime of religion, emanating from an evil mind. In a society dominated by belief in witchcraft, the crime never lacked wicked motivation. All attempts at defining witchcraft made some reference to the ideas of pact. Del Rio, a Catholic writer, was typical of his age: witchcraft was 'an art by which by the power of a contract entered into with the Devil, some wonders are wrought which pass the common understanding of men' (*Disquisitionum Magicorum*, 1599).

I have mentioned that to theologian and judge alike, witchcraft was a Christian heresy; that is to say, it differed from 'simple' sorcery in so far as it was seen as a form of heretical religion. The craze itself was limited in time (although lasting three centuries) and place, whereas sorcery was/is not so limited. It was a mania, however, that sent many thousands of innocents to their deaths, a delusion fostered by both civil and ecclesiastical authorities, until the felony was removed from the criminal list as late as 1736.

THE INQUISITION

One of the chief agencies for the discovery and extirpation of witchcraft was the Inquisition, a sort of Holy Office, instituted by the then current papacy, by which certain members of the clergy, usually Dominicans and Franciscans, were authorized to go around Germany especially, searching out and examining suspects. It is worth noting here that the Inquisition was, of course, active in other countries as well, including Spain, the Netherlands and France. These teams of zealots, armed with their implicit belief in witchcraft and a determination to force (where they could not persuade) people to change their opinions, were above the law, and could in matters of heretical witchcraft overrule civil authorities. Consequently, there was no limit to the barbarism they employed. Intolerance was their trademark, promoted as it was by successive popes and rulers from the twelfth century onwards, an intolerance that increased with time.

Pope Lucius III, in 1184, is credited with establishing the idea of an inquisition or inquiry into the prevalence of heresy. The Inquisition organization was so highly successful in persecuting and killing people that at one period it looked as if the supply of victims, whose property would be confiscated, might dry up! It was not until the proclamation of Pope Pius XXII in 1320 that formal power was granted to the inquisitors to prosecute demon-worshippers who had entered into a pact with the Devil. The theory of witchcraft really dates from this era, when persecutions began with a vengeance.

This 'new' crime was witchcraft – heretical sorcery. Even to be the child of a witch was evidence of being a witch oneself. Clearly, it had to be a youngish woman to have a child (as distinct from a grown-up son or daughter)! Accusations of witchcraft could be directed at anyone, young or old, rich or poor, man or woman, commoner or peer. No one was immune. Just as there were many different kinds of demons and angels, so witches also had their names: lamias (blood-sucking night monsters), strix (nocturnal bird-like creatures), vir (or mulier) and sortilegi (magicians), some of which were soothsayers, divinators, enchanters or jugglers (not in the modern sense, of course). Witches were also categorized into astrologians, calculators, poisoners, conjurers, speculators or magicians – according to their diverse specialities. Above all, it was the latter attribute – magic – that underlay the belief in witchcraft before the crime of heresy – and before that, of sorcery.

It was not until 1432 that sorcerers were excommunicated and, with them, demon-inspired 'miracle' workers. Witchcraft itself was spread by the Inquisition, about which more later, and heresy replaced sorcery as a capital crime.

Catholicism was not the only home of the witchcraft delusion, however, for the new Protestantism embraced it just as enthusiastically (by about the middle of the sixteenth century). Essentially there was no difference in the attitude to witchcraft between the two faiths. By the sixteenth and seventeenth centuries witchcraft had moved on from its association with sorcery.

The idea of a pact was everything. As early as 1468, witchcraft was declared to be an exceptional crime in which usual and accepted rules of jurisprudence could be waived (in order to achieve justice). The delusion thereafter rose to its height; that is, after the Dark Ages, during the Renaissance period and the Reformation. The end of witchcraft came comparatively swiftly. Some dates of the last executions for witchcraft may help to clarify this point: in England 1684; in Scotland 1727; in France 1745; and in Germany 1775.

Well before the end of the fourteenth century, however, hundreds of people had been burned as heretics. In 1451, by order of Pope Nicholas V, the inquisitors' authority was extended to encompass all cases of suspected sorcery. Inquisitors began to write learned tomes on witchcraft asserting unquenchable belief in the phenomenon and usually detailing signs by which witches could be recognized with procedures for interrogation, torture and death.

The most famous, or rather infamous, book of all (mentioned earlier, on p. 67) was that written in 1486 by two German Dominican Inquisitors, Heinrich Kramer and James Sprenger. It was called the *Malleus Maleficarum* – hammer of witchcraft – and was enormously influential and successful. It continued as the 'bible' of the witch-hunters everywhere for centuries and went through many editions. The activities of these men and others like them were eased by the bull of Pope Innocent VIII in 1484 which commanded all secular authorities to cooperate fully with the inquisitors.

Thus it may be claimed that the idea of witchcraft emanated from above, the top of the Catholic tree. Ordinary people were not convinced, at least at first, of its reality and it was only after many years of insistence on the new doctrine that the populace itself began to believe it. As Robbins says in his *Encyclopedia of Witchcraft and Demonology* (Introduction, page 9):

> *Witchcraft was an intellectual aberration, devised by inquisitors with the exceptional powers of torture and confiscation and soon taken over and shared by civil authorities (who vaguely recognized that witchcraft was a method of government).*

The fact that it was 'an intellectual aberration' meant in the eyes of the inquisitors that accused persons had to prove themselves innocent; if they did not, it meant they were guilty – a procedure contrary to all concepts of justice. This procedure was itself held in secret; mere accusations by malicious persons were accepted without question; exact charges were themselves often concealed from the accused; informers' secrecy was maintained; torture was always used to extort 'confessions'.

Of course, no one was ever acquitted: once in the clutches of the Inquisition there was no hope. With such a system scores of thousands of innocent people met cruel deaths. It seemed not to have crossed the minds of these 'judges' that confessions under torture were meaningless. But the sad truth is that in many ways this facet was not really of moment. The procedure was not aimed at changing the person's mind or to give him a chance to prove himself innocent. It was to provide a victim, a symbol to others of like mind whose property could be confiscated by the actual judges, inquisitors, torturers or whatever, themselves – so there was a strong inducement!

Everyone profited from witch-burning: those directly involved in the barbarity, of course, and even the innkeepers who profited from the crowds who came to see the public executions. These included not only burnings at the stake, but a variety of methods used to entertain the groundlings: beheadings, hanging, and flogging to death, among others. Detailed records of inquiry and execution costings are extant which testify to the fact that everyone got in on the act. Most interesting and most repellent is a document, *Tariff for Torture*, authorized by the Archbishop of Cologne. Under some fifty headings are itemized the costs of each and every processs and implement involved in the torture and death of an accused person.

A devil summons witches to a sabbat

The Inquisition was in reality a Catholic Office or tribunal, the object of which was to expose and punish religious aberration. In 1184 the first episcopal inquiry was instituted by Pope Lucius III, who ordered bishops to discover any deviations from the one true faith. Some fifteen years later a bull of Pope Innocent III appointed the first real inquisitors who had the authority to overrule local administrators.

The Inquisition established itself about 1500 as a direct result of the growth of devisive doctrine, which itself arose from dissatisfaction with some of the practices of the Roman Catholic Church and the lifestyles of some clergy. One of the main features of the inquiry process, and it is worth repeating, was the presumption of guilt. Proving one's innocence was an impossible task under the circumstances. Torture ensured that the defendant confessed what the torturer wanted to hear. Having confessed, the accused had to repeat his confession 'freely and spontaneously' as the double-think jargon had it. In so doing he or she was considered to have admitted guilt *without* torture! Rich people might escape this by bribery, however. The lure of confiscation and opportunity for sadism was just as strong as religious zeal among the churchmen in perpetuating witch-hunts, which were themselves eventually taken over by the ecclesiastical and civil courts.

The Spanish Inquisition appears to have acquired an even more evil reputation than that of the Papal Inquisition. The Spanish version was not set up by the popes and so in this respect was independent. In fact, it did not descend to the depths of depravity characteristic of the northern European inquisitors and in some ways was actually a mitigating force, although as deeply involved as the European system in eradication of undesirables. There is, however, a deal of xenophobia about the reputation of the Spanish searches and trials, it must be said.

This persecution of the illusory witch was motivated by the fundamental belief that witchcraft was heresy. As Aquinas defined it (*Summa Theologiae*, section 'Faith'), heresy was 'religious error held in wilful and persistent opposition to the truth after it has been defined and declared by the Church in an authoritative manner'. Heresy was therefore a crime, not merely a sin. It was only when the world was no longer ruled from the cathedral and the pulpit that the spectre of witchcraft began to disappear.

CONFESSIONS: PROOF OF WITCHCRAFT

The 'confession' was of great importance and was read aloud at the public execution. By such means the people were eventually convinced of the fact of witchcraft; it was rule by terror and no one dared gainsay witchcraft's reality. Proof of guilt could be established only by confession and the latter could only be extorted by torture – such was the belief, the reasoning being that no one would voluntarily confess to a crime punishable by death.

These confessions always spoke of the appearance of the Devil, and a journey to a witches' gathering (sabbat) by demoniacal transportation, giving also details of intercourse with Satan in human or animal form. There seems to have been a deep and prurient interest in the sexual aspect of witch–devil relationships on the part of unmarried, celibate clerics! The process of getting the accused to confess was first oral questioning, the answers to which would prove guilt; second was inevitably the torture, the severest being reserved for cases where the names of accomplices (so called) were required. Naturally, under torture the accused would confess to anything, directly giving rise to the fantastic stories of witch activities which were believed by all and sundry.

One of the most nauseating aspects of the whole system was the posing by these monstrous judges as saviours of mankind and religion because of the efficiency they displayed in bringing malefactors to heel. Thus the judges grew in a sort of public esteem, mingled with fear.

This self-righteous behaviour was not all. In addition to confiscation of the victim's property, the expenses, if you please, of the inquisition and death had also to be met by the victim or his or her family. So in effect victimization had become big business and involved financial perks. It paid to have a constant supply of victims whose death was assured. Courts, secular and ecclesiastical, were self-financing through this blood money.

Hence the insistence on the naming of accomplices under torture (whom in many cases they hardly knew), to ensure the continuance of the lucrative system. The better off were naturally choice targets from this point of view. Accomplices worth liquidating were often suggested to the accused. Of course, people of considerable wealth and position could either buy themselves out of the clutches of the inquisitors or make enough fuss not to be accused, or tormented – this the inquisitors knew full well.

It is one of the prime misconceptions that witches were always aged hags, ill favoured and of malevolent nature, hostile to general society. Nothing could be further from the truth. Many of the accused were young, even children; many were of high social standing; and many more were male. It is true that the majority were female and some were indeed aged and antisocial. It was easier to deal with female victims anyway, and the pervasive misogyny of the age gave the witch-hunt greater credence. There were other aspects to the predominance of female victims which will be mentioned later (*see* page 87). Single females (or males) were not especially chosen as potential victims; spouses could be useful in providing the expenses incurred!

Of course, people on their own, those on the margin of society, particularly if they were cantankerous, were suitable victims because: (a) they were unlikely to have anyone to help them out or to make things difficult; and (b) the fiction spread by the courts (lay and clerical) that these people were malcontents and n'er-do-wells who would not be missed, would rebound to their (the judges') glory, as revealing a short way with such people, a commendable summary justice.

In view of the foregoing, it is clear that wealthy victims brought more in the way of returns – in expenses demanded, in confiscations – than the poor. It is a fiction reinforced by religious authorities through the ages that witches were invariably old baleful hags who in any case, besides siding with the Devil, were better off dead having been found legally guilty.

The corollary of this was naturally that people of importance, owning property and possessing wealth, were but rarely accused, as this would indicate that self-interest was indeed one of the main motivating factors in witch prosecutions. However, the prospect of loot *was* one of the chief reasons for the continuance of the witchcraft mania for so long. This was one strand; the other was the conviction that behind every witch was a demon who motivated her in her evil intents. The clergy led the way and condoned the suffering of blameless people, while learned laymen, judges (not always learned) and lawyers supported their misguided procedures. Witchcraft repression was the official policy of the Churches, Catholic up to the time of Luther, Roman Catholic and Protestant after. As Robbins so succinctly puts it (*Encyclopedia of Witchcraft and Demonology*, Introduction, page 17): 'Everything was sacrificed to a preconceived prejudice.' Because of this prejudice nothing was too extreme. Often victims died due to the severity of the torture or took their own lives. Demons were always blamed as aiders and abettors in the untimely suicide, if not for the actual killing of the accused.

The irony of all this, apart from its manifest idiocy, is the fact that the Catholic Church had itself in its early days (about AD 300) expressly forbidden belief in witchcraft, declaring it to be an illusion and that the belief was pagan, and as such was heretical. By the Middle Ages this doctrine had been turned on its head in order to fit the new circumstances and the doctrine was itself undermined by some of the greatest thinkers of the age. It had to be, otherwise it would not fit into the existing scheme of things devised by the demonologists of Church and State. One argument adduced was that this was a new and different sect of witches for which new laws had to be found. Doublethink had arrived long before George Orwell wrote about it!

THE DEVIL'S MARK

A sure sign of liaison with the Devil was believed to be the 'Devil's Mark' – a fantastic and illogical belief if ever there was one. As few human bodies are without some sort of mark or blemish, it can readily be imagined that very few passed this test. The Devil's Mark, put there by the Devil to signify that the witch was one of his own, was often found as a birthmark, for example, or a scar. This was different (at least in the early days) from the 'Witch's Mark', which was any kind of protuberance, such as a third nipple, a raised lump or even a prominent clitoris. The theory was that the witch's 'familiars' drew sustenance from these protuberances. Discovering these marks involved the stripping naked of the accused, usually in public, and the complete shaving of the body, including pubic hair. Occasionally the shavers were women. No part of the body was immune from the search and it involved close examination of the sexual and excretory organs. Special diviners were employed to seek out these marks (especially those bestowed by the Devil), who used long needles to pry into suspect blemishes, even in the private parts. These people were paid for their labours, and doubly so if they discovered a suspect in the first place by 'pricking' as it was called. The reasoning behind this practice was that witches were impervious to pain in areas of the Devil's Mark.

The pact was therefore the essence of witchcraft. By the pact the witch promised to dedicate herself to the Devil's service, to renounce God and forswear her Baptism. As the eminent demonologist Guazzo wrote in 1626 (*Compendium Maleficarum*, second edition 1626; Summers' translation 1929): 'The witches request the Devil that their name be struck out of the Book of Life and inscribed in the Book of Death.' The witches further promised to sacrifice children to the Devil and to abhor all the appurtenances of religion. Written pacts with Satan are extant which testify to a sort of quid pro quo agreement between the Devil and the embryonic witch. Subjection of self was always a vital part of personal dedication, and this was witnessed best by self-abasement, the Devil demanding the 'infamous kiss' upon his hindquarters or erect phallus. Indeed, phallus worship seemed to be a major ingredient in the Devil's acceptance of his new disciple. Pacts themselves could be of two kinds, according to the demonologists: the Private Pact and the Public Pact. In the first, a witch gave her allegiance via another witch; in the second, the allegiance was promised at a sabbat before other witches. In essence the idea of contract was paramount.

This theory is one of the reasons for the predominance of female victims: they were more 'interesting' to male examiners. There is no doubt that prurience played a part in the selection of females as witches, especially young females.

One only has to look at the many pictures of witches, especially in the centuries when the craze was at its height, to see that in most cases witches were depicted as young and nubile women. It was only later that the conception of the witch as hag began to take shape. (*See* Shakespeare's *Macbeth*, as one of the earliest examples.) Naked females placed in a terrifying location were very vulnerable – many were raped in the stripping and shaving process. 'Marks' could also be invisible, hidden away in all sorts of localities, such as in the eyelids or the inner recesses of the body. Pricking with the needle eventually led to the discovery of some insensitive area, such as a wart, corn or scar, and if it did not bleed, the accused was thereby condemned.

Witchcraft in its early form was thought of as evil-doing, a form of sorcery, directed at Man. Later the concept of the witch as a direct enemy of God was believed in by clergy and layman alike. Until about 1400, for example, few were put to death for alleged witchcraft, and punishments were relatively light. Trial was in an ecclesiastical court and the suspect was handed over to the secular arm for punishment.

WITCHCRAFT TRIALS IN BRITAIN

Witchcraft in England was without the extreme excesses which informed witchcraft trials on the Continent, notably Germany and France. In fact, the offence in England was comparatively late in coming on the scene – in the late sixteenth century. It was belief in the omnipresence of the Devil and his demons which lay behind the felony laws. Soon it became natural to label a malcontent as a witch and the anti-witchcraft proclamations made death the penalty for invoking evil spirits. This interdiction on suspected trafficking with the Devil grew, until the idea of making a pact or entering into a covenant with the Devil was accepted as the core of witchcraft accusation. The century from about 1560 to 1660 saw the witch-hunt at its height, at least in England. Areas of the country differed considerably in the number of witches tried, varying according to the energies and enthusiasms of local magistrates, judges and so on.

The extremes of torture and barbarity were never characteristic of English witchcraft trials; this cannot be said of trials in Scotland. Nor was the ultimate penalty of burning alive practised in England. Similarly, mass executions were never a feature of English trials – as happened frequently in France and Germany. The sabbat of witches was almost always mentioned by tormented souls on the Continent, whereas in England it featured not at all, or at least in a vastly reduced form. Of course interrogators always wanted to hear about the sexual exploits that the witch had had with the Devil or his demons, so that this aspect was commonplace in the 'confessions'. Even aged crones admitted to this type of activity – under torture, of course.

WITCHES' FAMILIARS

According to testimony, witches were always accompanied or aided in their nefarious practices by their 'familiars'. Familiars were demons in the guise of

Witches and their supposed familiars

small domestic or common animals, such as cats, dogs, birds, toads and the like, which were reputed to help the witch with her wicked schemes. As a result of this thinking, most common animals were viewed as having the potential to be morally wicked.

These familiars were cared for by their mistress, the witch, who apparently allowed them to suck nutrients from her body, particularly her blood, from her various protuberances, such as the nipples – another good reason for apprehending the female sex. This naturally tied in with the idea of the Witch's Mark, mentioned above. Sometimes, according to current testimony, young and old alike confessed to sexual congress with a dog or goat, being the Devil in disguise. These familiars, or imps, always had strange names which added, so it was thought, to their demonic status; Holt, Jamara, Vinegar Tom, Greedigut, Pyewackett and Sack are some.

Apart from sucking the vital essences of the witch, the imps were given choice foodstuffs as more solid nutriment. Accordingly, chicken, apples, cheese and oats might form part of their diet. The imps, it seems, particularly craved blood, and in the form of a cat or dog or other small animal visited their mistress sometimes in her sleep and, scratching her, sucked her blood. Frequently, too, the demon in diguise entered her private parts while she was asleep, seeking fluids, and producing, so we are told, a sensation of itching and sucking – but never enough to wake her up. These familiars were of course entirely different from the incubus demons who sought sexual intercourse with women (whether witches or no, nuns being especially choice victims).

Confessions of sexual relations with the Devil or his demons were always closely attended to by prurient or even libidinous inquisitors. This magical feat was implicitly believed in, and women and girls were expressly forbidden to have relations with the Devil. It was believed that even girls of six and seven could, and did, have sexual intercourse with the Prince of Darkness or one of his minions. Monstrous tales from the demented testimony of tortured victims were told of bestiality and sodomy. The accused spoke of the coldness of the semen (a usual attribution) and excessive girth of the penis which occasioned them hurt in penetration. Sometimes detailed descriptions of the act of intercourse and the appearance of the Devil's member are given by women who clearly believed they might as well be hanged for a wolf as for a sheep.

THE SABBAT

We may here say more about the sabbat (technically a sort of religious gathering of witches, not always local, where a type of blasphemous mass was celebrated). The name is without definite attribution, but may be a corruption of the Hebrew word for the seventh day, although it appears that sabbats took place any day, or rather night. The sabbat in the eyes of the demonologists represented the nadir of evil and Satanism, whose central activity was blasphemy against Christianity. It was, then, essentially an assembly of witches gathered together to honour the Devil. In about 1400 the idea of a coven of witches sprang up, although the infamous *Malleus Maleficarum* of 1486 makes no mention of the sabbat. By about 1500, however, the concept was widely accepted and considered as: (a) an assembly of witches; (b) who paid homage to the Devil; (c) who indulged in a nauseating banquet; (d) who enjoyed themselves in obscene festivities; and (e) who engaged in indiscriminate intercourse.

Satan, in the form of a goat, leads the witches' dance

Obeisance to Satan centred around the '*osculum infame*' – the obscene kiss on the hindquarters of the Devil or his current manifestation. The banquet, featured as the eating of certain loathsome items, was supposed to have the magical effect of rendering the witches impervious to pain under torture. Forms of forbidden intercourse, sodomy and incest featured largely and couplings took place among family members – according to sworn statements. One sixteen-year-old girl, in the writings of De Lancre, one of the most notable demonologists of the age, alleged that she had been deflowered by Satan and subsequently had had frequent intercourse with a close relative. She feared repeated intercourse with the Devil because, as she said, 'his member was scaly and caused pain'. Additionally, his semen was 'extremely cold, so cold that', as De Lancre writes, 'she had never become pregnant by him'.

Great attention, as we have remarked, was paid to these sexual confessions. In one, Sister Madelaine de Demandolx admitted to her inquisitor that she went every night to the sabbat:

> *Upon Sundays they pollute themselves by their filthy copulations with devils that are succubi and incubi. Upon Thursdays they contaminate themselves with sodomy; upon Saturdays they do prostitute themselves to abominable bestiality; upon other days they use the ordinary course which nature prompteth unto them.*

Guazzo, writing in 1626 (*Compendium Maleficarum*), tells of other forms of obeisance to the Devil. 'Sometimes they beg on bended knees; sometimes they fall down on their back; sometimes they kick their legs in the air and bend their head to the belly, always moving so that the chin points to the sky.'

Witchcraft was seen by some as a cult deriving from pre-Christian times. Pagan ceremonies usually involved worship of a goat-like god, nocturnal orgies and the practice of magic. Developments of this in the view of some led to witchcraft, regarded as a type of secret society bent on overthrowing the existing order of State and Church. The sabbat itself therefore became ritualized, characterized by the 'Black Mass' presided over by the Devil himself (or some man in disguise). A leading female present is a 'priestess', who in the absence of Satan sets up a figure of Satan, always horned and with a giant penis. She simulates copulation with the represented Devil and later allows her naked body to be used as an altar, on which a defrocked priest or debauched layman disguised as a demon makes sacrifice. However, this view of the sabbat (if it existed at all in any form) is derived from the fevered minds of tortured or demented creatures. Incest always occurred, frequently described, according to extorted testimony.

Sabbats were of two kinds, according to the demonologists of the day: Grand and Lesser. There was more discrimination in choosing the actual site of the former, while the Lesser might be held almost anywhere (provided it was rural), and in a place convenient for the local coven (a society of witches). Night, as has been said, was the usual time for sabbats and they commenced at the stroke of midnight, lasting till dawn or cock-crow. The witches travelled to them, according to current report, on foot or more usually by means of magic levitation, or being transported by a demon, often on horseback. A broomstick, it seems, was the favourite method of propulsion, smeared beforehand by some magic ointment (usually derived from dead bodies). The witches were almost always portrayed as naked and curvaceous as they flew, or were about to fly, through the air. It was a matter for serious debate among theologians whether witches, living at a distance, actually attended the sabbat or – by sceptics – whether it was hallucination and illusion (stimulated by torture) on the part of those accused. Guazzo certainly believed in the transportation of witches to the sabbat, as he reveals in his famous work *Compendium Maleficarum*.

WITCH TESTS – TRIAL BY ORDEAL

This section on witchcraft would be incomplete without some mention of the physical 'tests' for suspects, apart from all the other spurious indications already stated. These tests went under the heading of Trial by Ordeal. For instance, a popular device for infallibly discovering whether a person was a witch or not was the custom of 'swimming'. This involved tying the big toes to the opposite thumbs and then throwing the accused into deep water. If she sank she was innocent (because the natural element, water, had accepted her); if she floated, she was guilty on the premise that the water had refused to take her. Another test might involve walking on hot coals or heated iron or being forced to grasp a red-hot piece of metal. If the accused bore this with a degree of equanimity she was innocent! Not many passed these tests, of course.

Yet another was called Trial by Combat, not often resorted to in the case of women, whereby the accused was pitted against an experienced warrior, physically much superior. A proxy fighter was sometimes granted to accused persons whereby they did not have to fight themselves.

Occasionally a witch was weighed against a massive medieval Bible. The witch was naturally stripped naked, to help her pass the test of course! Clearly, in all these 'trials' the scales (sometimes literally) were weighted against defendants. It was in modern parlance a case of flipping the two-headed coin: heads the inquisitors won. In much of this chicanery the belief was that the Devil would come to the aid of his own, just as, untrammelled, by demonic power the witch could do supernatural feats. This belief was ages old already when demonic acts flourished in early Christian times. The old pagan beliefs died hard.

As the Church increased its power and influence, it levelled its attacks on practices it knew as 'witchcraft' – from about the thirteenth century on. As Lowe-Thompson summarizes in his book *The History of the Devil* (page 94): 'In brief, the major religions of the pre-Christians gave way to the ceremonies of the Church.'

I have almost always used the feminine gender to characterize the witch, and I have given some reasons why this was so. Did not St Augustine himself declare that 'woman represents the lower part of humanity and man the higher part, reason'? After all, woman was a sort of afterthought, created from the rib of a man, Adam. Anti-feminism of this kind held sway in religious minds for centuries. This attitude was reflected in the literature of the day, which fanned the flames of misogyny, which in turn led to witch persecution. Succeeding anti-Satanic legislation had women as its primary target. Sorcery itself was believed to be a crime peculiar in the main to women, who were more malicious than men. Women during the ages had called up demons to aid them with some problem. The blood-sucking demons who seduced men and killed babies were female; the instances of abhorrent sexual intercourse with the male devils involved women, mostly as witches. Witchcraft can succinctly be said to be demonization, a belief thundered in sermons and preached in homilies up and down the land, stressing the power of God as our/their aid in the struggle. No wonder people began to believe it – an invention of inquisitors and so-called scholars. This section can fittingly be concluded with an extract from J. B. Russell's *Lucifer: The Devil in the Middle Ages* (page 299):

> *Scholastic theology was the most important element in [the development of] witchcraft. Witchcraft was less a popular movement than an imposition of ideas by the intellectual elite upon the uneducated. The fundamental theological assumption... was rooted in the New Testament and farther. Just as the saved constitute the mystical body of Christ so the Devil's followers constitute the mystical body of Satan. All who oppose Christ's mission on earth, whether pagans, sinners, Jews, heretics and sorcerers are limbs of Satan. Christians are obliged to... eliminate them... and such was*

thought to be Lucifer's power to protect his followers that fire and sword were often deemed necessary…

– to combat maleficia, evil deeds.

MALEFICIA

Let us look at the notion of maleficia in more detail. The notion was indeed one of the main ways to define a witch: one who practises maleficia. The phenomenon of witchcraft originated in the earliest days of Man's development. Death soon became the penalty for lethal acts arising from 'witchcraft' or sorcery. Maleficia could produce effects other than death or sickness: alienation, fear and impotence being some. By the power of superstition alone, witches or sorcerers could bring about their intents. Marital difficulties were so induced, a favourite bane it seems, no doubt arising from envy as much as from sheer malevolence. Full intercourse or the ejaculation of semen could be prevented for example by means of 'spells' or the 'evil eye' – forms of bewitchment. In the Middle Ages such belief in the power of witches was deeply ingrained in the people. The incidence of maleficia became a matter of some public concern, and a backlash resulted in persecution.

The early Church regarded all 'magic' as pagan; paganism itself was identified with demon worship. The Church's attitude gradually influenced the lay authorities, so much so that in some countries laws were revised in line with Christian belief. Magic became a criminal offence. Church law and secular law became intertwined. Hence, in the Middle Ages lay authorities on occasion did concern themselves with magic as a religious fault. At this time it is clear there was no general wish to prosecute witches. Maleficia itself, however, became an offence in the eyes of both authorities. The dawn of witchcraft was at hand.

A practitioner of magic, it was believed, summoned up demons by name to aid him or her in some particular task. In Reginald Scott's *Discoverie of Witchcraft* (1584) we can read some of these names, which it was of the utmost importance to pronounce. It must be said that many of these acts through demonic contact did not necessarily harm other humans. Conjuring up demons, as it was called, for beneficial purposes, by early members of religious orders, had to involve a period of fasting and prayer and stern personal discipline – reminiscent of the modern-day exorcists' preparation, but for a different purpose. Later, summoning demons became a reprehensible practice, as it was, it was believed, an act of close collaboration with devils – usually for nefarious purposes. Magicians were now winning over demons by acts of adoration and homage, trying to bind demons to do their bidding, a heinous crime indeed in the eyes of the Church. The magicians themselves, however, did not see themselves as demon-worshippers, believing that their powers were only granted by God in any case.

Notable cases in this period (the fourteenth century) reported that people had kept private demons for appropriate consultation. Some even had demons for parents! Others, often people of some standing – notaries, clergy, magistrates and so on – were charged with invoking demons as an aid to successful seduction of women. Of course, under torture, victims would confess to all manner of maleficia: affliction, disease and congress with devils. In short order, a new crime had been invented: the offence of *'crimen magicae'*, the crime of magic.

Later still, in the fifteenth century the role of those associating with demons underwent a great change, encompassing the charge that disciples gave themselves up to serve their demons. Some neurotic or sexually frustrated women actually believed they had been to a sabbat or had been visited by the Devil and his demons. Such people (mostly women) sought to harm their neighbours for personal reasons, and malicious accusations became frequent. Accusations were often made between people who knew each other, either because they heartily disliked the other person or because they wished to break some sort of personal bond, maybe familial or financial. Midwives, as they had access to babies, were often accused of killing new-born babies as homage to Satan. In contrast, some females prided themselves on their power of doing good, 'white witches' as they were called, but even they in the view of the Church were guilty of sorcery. A witch was seen as the embodiment of evil and apostasy. Although anyone could be accused of being a witch, high born as well as low, it was rare to find a high-born person arrested – it came too near home! But there were always plenty to choose from. The frequency itself of witch trials depended to a certain degree on the zeal (or otherwise) of the local authorities, lay and ecclesiastical, and how open they were to other influences (apart from the clerical), such as the all-pervading climate in art and literature.

In fact, we should here briefly refer (there is fuller treatment on pages 133 ff) to the influential writings of such as Remy, Weyer, Sprenger and Kramer. Remy's book *Demonolatry*, of 1595, is a testament to the ubiquitous power of witches aided by demons. Weyer, on the contrary, although a committed believer in devils, in his tome of 1563, *De Praestigiis Daemonum*, attacked the belief in witches, a very brave thing to do in those days. Sprenger and Kramer showed in their *Malleus Maleficarum* (1486) an absolute belief in witchcraft and all its associated works and pomps.

Though it must be stressed that most of the witch mania was clergy driven, it must also be admitted that many of the so-called witches were undesirables, mental defectives, emotionally disturbed, schizophrenic and so on, who roamed the streets because there were then no secure institutions to care for them. Such people were vulnerable, shunned by neighbours, and so it is not surprising that they turned to animals for love and affection and, as is common, spoke to them, which action led to their being accused of communing with evil spirits in the guise of pets. How anyone could believe that people would devote themselves to a lifestyle so fraught with danger as witchcraft is a mystery. Many of these witches, who believed in it themselves, were undoubtedly mentally unstable. Many more were fakes, impostures who sought attention for one reason or another. That benefit of some sort would follow is one reason: increased income, prominence otherwise denied, more converts or communicants (for clergy) or whatever. Often, ministers of religion fostered and encouraged those of their flocks who were deluded by the thought of witchcraft, so as to draw attention to themselves (the ministers) and their parishes. Spurious 'deliverance' often followed, thus further enhancing their fame.

TORTURE PRACTICES

Distasteful as it may be, no account of the demented periods of witch persecution would be complete without some reference to the sufferings inflicted on innocent people by those who should have known better. It cannot be overemphasized that all confessions were accompanied by torture in various degrees of refinement in order to extract the truth as the torturers saw it and especially to implicate other innocents. If there is any defence at all, it is that all concerned believed the crime was so heinous that torture was justifiable, meet to the occasion. As an indication, the torture implements were blessed by a priest before being put to their deadly use!

Belief in the efficacy of torture was an intellectual conviction held by judges, clerics, torturers, jailers and the like. The Christian God was supreme and *any* means to aid recognition of the fact was justified. For the general good, a person such as a witch had to be killed. Trafficking with the Devil was the greatest sin of all. Torture, especially that instigated by the Inquisition, was appropriate and had proved a successful method for both Catholic and later Protestant persecutors.

Imprisonment was the mildest of all the punishments, although a diet of bread and water in perpetuity ended the lives of many prematurely. Confession to being a witch was the aim of the Preparatory Torture, which involved a preliminary viewing of the instruments and hearing the screams of prisoners in nearby cells. At this stage binding with tight ropes was the usual accompaniment. Stripping and shaving generally followed.

Final Torture, the aim of which was to elicit the names of accomplices, took many forms: thumbscrews, the rack, crushing of the legs, tying hands behind the back and hoisting up the victim, letting him or her drop to just short of the floor, often with weights attached to the feet. The latter, as may be imagined, had the effect of dislocating most of the joints of the body, especially when repeated.

The agonies of the victims, to which the torturers were urged to become impervious, can only be imagined with difficulty. Often the accused needed to be revived in readiness for more torture. Iron chairs under which a fire was lit, baths of scalding water, leg vises, or torture by forcing water down the throat were some of the methods employed. Tearing the flesh with red-hot pincers or chopping off a hand was the usual punishment for alleged desecration of the Sacrament. Burning was the ultimate punishment (though many died under torture), mercy being shown to some by strangulation before the fire was lit! Burning alive, though, was quite common – always before a throng of interested spectators and officials.

Some tortures of the Inquisition

The number of times someone could be tortured was unlimited – except by death. Applications of boiling water and lighted sulphur, generally under the armpits or in the loins when the victim was hanging, were favourite devices, as was subjecting the soles of the feet to fire. Sometimes boiling oil was poured over a victim; sometimes whipping to death was resorted to. Indeed, there were various ways of bringing about death apart from burning: hanging, beheading, disembowelling and flogging. Dismembering limbs and gouging out eyes were frequent. All this, remember, was done in the name of true religion according to the lights of the time. It is what fanaticism and extremism can lead to.

Other 'refinements' resorted to by the Inquisition included: suspension by the feet over a smoky fire until the accused choked to death; being roasted on a spit; having sharp implements inserted under fingernails and toenails; suspension by the middle from a tree until hunger or extreme discomfort claimed her; being hanged by one hand with weights attached to the feet; being attacked by men armed with swords and knives; and smothering in caves and holes in the ground. Some were taken on journeys and had a limb cut off at intervals, the limb being set on a stake. Pregnant women had their stomachs cut open and the babies ripped out and killed. Tying two witches together and seeing if they could both be run through in one thrust was regarded as a display of prowess. Bashing out brains with a hammer or axe; cutting throats; pulling off noses and breasts with red-hot pinchers; and tearing limb from limb by tying victims to four horses – all were resorted to in the name of dogma.

As I have said before, women proved to be choice victims for various reasons, some of which were undoubtedly sexual. These accused were interrogated nude, then torture was applied to their vulnerable bodies. Searching for the Devil's or Witch's Marks was often, no doubt, an excuse for mistreatment of a sexual nature. Variants on torture and death were more likely in the case of females: for instance, suspension of the naked witch by one leg, sometimes over a pond or river so that the head and breasts were in the water. Another form of this was again suspension by one leg and leaving the victim hanging until she died from starvation. The torturers or sentries who watched these poor creatures die were of course always men. The local populace could come and be entertained – there were no restrictions on sightseers.

CHAPTER FIVE

THE POWER
OF
POSSESSION

B elief in possession, stemming from the Bible, lasted throughout the centuries – and still holds sway at the present time. Demonic posses-sion means being under the control (or influence) of, physically and emotionally, perhaps mentally as well, some extraneous or supernatural force – usually meaning the Devil or demons.

Possession in Biblical times and in the Christian era can be considered in view of the words of Jesus, who cast out demons, and the accounts of scores of cases of demonic possession – sometimes voluntary, sometimes involuntary – and exorcism. Such a subject that has maintained its credibility for two thousand years, a subject that has been examined by some of history's greatest minds, must be, one may think, more than a mere ancient theory.

POSSESSION IN BIBLICAL TIMES

Great importance was given to belief in diabolical possession by the people of Biblical times, none more so than Jesus Christ Himself; it is impossible to read the Gospels in the New Testament books of the Bible without realizing this. Many instances are related of possession by 'unclean spirits', which apparently transformed the person. It is clear that Jesus and his disciples regarded it as one of their highest duties to expel these spirits.

In the early literature of the Church are to be found many descriptions of demoniacs and states of possession. It was taken very seriously indeed: had not Jesus Himself testified to its reality? It must be understood, however, that people of Biblical times realized there was a difference between diabolical possession and physical illness (Matthew 4:24):

And his fame went throughout Syria and they brought unto him all sick people that were taken with divers diseases and torments, and those which were possessed by devils and those which were lunatic and those which had the palsy; and he healed them.

This quotation is of great significance, because, by inference, it indicates a prevalent belief in the reality of possession: that is, the entering into, and domination of, a person by demons for evil purposes. Illness, sickness, physical malady was something separate – and different.

This state of possession has, since Biblical times, been distinguished from the state of obsession – a distinction which is maintained by the major Churches today. In obsession a person is assailed by the Devil from without the body. Both states nevertheless were, or are, held to exculpate the victim from what he or she did or said. It was early on supposed that virtuous people could not suffer from possession, only obsession, and the lives of many of the saints testify to this.

The most well-known instance is probably that of St Anthony, who it seems was tormented by the Devil and his demons; they took the shape of voluptuous women who attempted to beguile Anthony with their lascivious behaviour. 'Day and night the demons varied their snares' (biography of St Anthony by St Athanasius).

Demons, as we have seen, were often referred to in translations of the Bible as 'devils' and 'unclean spirits'. In the Book of Revelation of St John the Divine (16:13–14), written about AD 100 or somewhat earlier, it is clear that belief in possession of Man and beast by evil spirits had taken firm root among religious writers:

And I saw three unclean spirits of devils [demons] like frogs come out of the mouth of the dragon… and out of the mouth of the false prophet… For they are spirits of devils working miracles which go forth unto the kings of the earth and of the whole world to gather them to the battle of that great day of God Almighty.

We would understand by the word 'miracles' something more in the nature of 'signs'.

Roughly fifty or so years previously, in the Gospels according to Matthew, Mark and Luke, instances of demon possession abound. It is probable that the origin of the theory of possession arose from the inability of peoples to comprehend many manifestations of illness, physical as well as mental, especially, and emotional. Belief that these strange and often terrifying manifestations were due to the workings of evil spirits came as second nature to peoples whose religious culture was dominated by ancient beliefs in the spirit world – spirits who were usually malevolent.

Jesus Expels Demons

Casting out devils was, of course, a sure sign of the dominant power of Jesus, and this may be the reason why the Gospel writers wrote about it so much. This casting out demonstrated beyond dispute that Christ's power was greater than that of Satan, particularly when we read that Jesus *with a word* dismissed the evil spirit(s) from the possessed. Matthew (8:16) writes of the people who 'brought unto him many that were possessed with devils and he cast out the spirits with his word and healed all that were sick'. This is one more indication of the current realization of the difference between demon possession and being sick.

It may of course be imagined that the authors of the Synoptic Gospels (the first three, excluding John's) exaggerated these instances in their zeal for proselytizing – but it would be unthinkable to adduce that Jesus Himself dissembled before His disciples. It is just as clear that Christ Himself firmly believed in the fact of demon possession. No other interpretation is possible. One of the most remarkable of Jesus' expelling of demons is the famous episode of the Gadarene swine. Matthew (8:28–33) gives an account:

> And when he was come to the other side unto the country of the [Gadarenes] there met him two possessed with devils [demons] coming out of the tombs, exceeding fierce, so that no man might pass by that way. And behold they cried out saying 'What have we to do with thee, Jesus, thou Son of God? Art thou come hither to torment us before the time?' And there was a good way off from them an herd of many swine feeding. So the devils besought him saying 'If thou cast us out, suffer us to go away into the herd of swine.' And he said unto them 'Go'. And when they were come out they went into the herd of swine and behold the whole herd of swine ran violently down a steep place into the sea, and perished in the waters. And they that had kept them fled and went their ways unto the city and told everything that was befallen to them that were possessed of the devils.

It is evident from the above that: (a) the possibility of devil possession was taken for granted; (b) devil possession made the victim's behaviour unrecognizable from his normal state; (c) it was the demons themselves who spoke, not the men; (d) these demons recognized Jesus at once for what He was, the Son of God; (e) one word was sufficient to expel the evil spirits; and (f) this power of expulsion was attested to, and spread far, by the owners of the swine.

It may be that the words 'before due time' refer to the time of the Last Judgement or simply to when the demons felt they had caused enough evil and distress through their bodily habitation. The expression is open to conjecture. The demons' request to be allowed to transmigrate into the swine (an unclean and illegal beast in those times) might be interpreted as a sign that these demons had been 'instructed' (by their master) to possess bodies and would have failed in their mission or would simply dissipate if they were cast out to roam. Either way, it is certain that they desired bodily possession either of animals or of humans; corporeal possession was, it seems, the lot of certain kinds of demons. It is possible that the demons did not know what effect their entering the swine would have – or that they did know. Either way, destruction was their goal. It is assumed that the demons lived on, unlike the swine. The mention of a *herd* of swine indicates that many demons dwelt in the two men – another common conception being that of multiple possession.

Jesus' Words

As related in Mark (9:25), we have another aspect of Jesus' power to dismiss the evil spirit, this time with a form of words. This is the occasion when an afflicted and deaf-and-dumb child was brought to Jesus, who 'rebuked the foul spirit, saying unto him "Thou dumb and deaf spirit, I charge thee, come out of him and enter no more into him"'. It appears the disciples had tried in vain to cast out this 'foul spirit'. Jesus' reply is very significant: 'And he said to them, "This kind can come forth by nothing but by prayer and fasting"'. The inference is that the disciples' lack of success was due to their spiritual unpreparedness. It clearly has its echo in present-day acts of exorcism, where the officiating priest has to prepare himself beforehand by suitable prayers and a period of fasting. This itself indicates that Jesus saw these situations as cases of good pitting itself against evil beings which could only be removed by an exact spiritual preparation, namely being in a state of grace which was strong enough to combat the powers of the devils (or Devil).

Seen also in Mark (16:17), power over devils was delegated to the apostles by Christ when Jesus appeared to them after His crucifixion. Speaking to them, He said, 'In my name shall they [believers] cast out devils; they shall speak with new tongues.' Note that it may be construed Jesus was saying that His actual name (or God's) must be invoked in any attempt at exorcism; or at least, credit given, as it were, to divine power. Christ Himself was always quite unequivocal when He spoke about His power over inhabiting demons. When addressing some of the Pharisees who had gathered to question Him, He said to them, 'I cast out devils and I do cures today and tomorrow...' This also shows the distinction Jesus made constantly between demon possession and bodily ailment (Luke 13:32). Staying with Luke, we read of Mary Magdalene 'out of whom went seven devils', who was one of 'certain women which had been healed of evil spirits and infirmities' – indicating again the differentiation made between the two manifestations.

Important also to our theme is the passage where we read (Luke 4:40 ff): 'They that had any sick with divers diseases brought them unto him and he laid his hands on every one of them, and healed them.' It is important to notice here that: (a) once again disease is named as a separate entity (as distinct from demonic influence); and (b) Jesus actually touched the afflicted – which He by no means invariably did; on occasion He healed at a distance. Why Christ touched in this instance is not clear, although it seems that by and large actual physical contact was made in cases of physical illness.

But even this is not always the case. The very next passage speaks of another entity, that of 'devils' (as distinct from 'divers diseases'), where we read: 'And devils also came out of many crying out and saying "Thou art Christ the Son of God". And he rebuked them, suffered them not to speak' – for they knew

He was Christ! This passage confirms what we said earlier: that the demons knew, if Man did not, that Jesus was God made flesh. Again it was the devils who spoke, not the victims. Significantly, Jesus ordered the devils not to speak of His Godhead – demonstrated by his exorcist power – as at this stage He did not want people to know of His divine origin… in case it obstructed His planned mission on earth: His trial, suffering and death. At least, this is an interpretation.

It would, of course, be beyond the scope of this chapter to mention all the instances in the New Testament of the casting out of devils. The important thing to realize, however, is that there are many, and that the belief in possession both on Jesus' part and that of the people was implicit. Other passages that have to do with the casting out of evil spirits are to be found in Matthew (7:22; 8:13; 9:30; 10:1; 10:8; 12:43), Mark (1:34; 9:38) and Luke (8:36; 8:38; 10:17; 11:18). This list is not exhaustive, but is illustrative of the importance of demon possession to the people of Jesus' time. Note that He actually stated or implied that it was by power derived from God that He drove out spirits. The corollary of this is that the disciples also exercised this power by the use of the name of Jesus, and by so doing always gave acknowledgement to the fact that their power came from their leader, Jesus Christ.

THE CHRISTIAN ERA AND POSSESSION

The phenomenon of possession has been examined and refined down the ages, as it is still today, by various writers. Types of possession were discerned and the symptoms described by which they might be recognized. Underlying the belief in possession (as opposed to illness) was always the influence of demons, which was held to be responsible for such manifestations as facial and bodily contortions and changes in the voice. Somewhat naturally, the fact that spirits entered the body, which also contained the mind (and the soul), led to much speculation as to the invading being's *modus operandi*. Operating on the body could, it was felt, affect the mind, and, as we now know, things which affect the mind can affect the body. The diagnosis at that time was left unresolved.

Possession, Real or Feigned?

That the Devil could initiate possession off his own bat, as it were, was understood, but later, with the witchcraft craze, possession in people was considered to be caused by the maleficia (wickedness) of a witch. Cases of possession for a time, say notably in the sixteenth and seventeenth centuries, were frequent, especially it seems among the religious, nuns particularly, but it is reasonable to assume that many of these were spurious, being essentially stunts. Some, however, were not and it is with these that we are principally concerned.

The difficulty is weeding the grain from the chaff. Relation (not always contemporaneous) is all we have by writers who often were deliberately tendentious or simply propagandizers. Perhaps it would be too cynical to say that virginity, vows of celibacy among female religious on the one side and on the other possession manifesting itself often in lewd gesture or posture went hand in hand. Perhaps it would; nevertheless, there does seem to be a link, to judge by the reported cases. Maybe a look at some of these instances would be of interest. There are scores of them, but I can mention two or three as illustrative of the theme (of possession, real or feigned).

In Cologne, 1565, the convent of Nazareth had a particularly bad reputation as a place where, it seems, far from virtuous nuns lived. Apparently it was quite usual for the nunnery to admit male 'admirers' (in reality, lovers) of the inmates. When the scandal broke, and the nuns were accused of immorality, they maintained that devils in the guise of dogs had abused them. Needless to say, such was the belief that demons could indeed perform such acts, the nuns were let off!

Dogs did seem to be a common shape for the lascivious devils to adopt, as nuns at Oderheim on Rhone in 1572 complained of nightly visitations from canine-like incubus devils. In 1595, at Milan, some thirty-odd nuns were believed to be possessed, adopting lewd actions and speech. Often the phenomenon in nunneries or other communities was started by a single self-publicist who spread the infection throughout the sisterhood.

Mass Hysteria and Scapegoats

Loudon, 1634, was the scene of one of the most celebrated cases of possession. The mania, it seems, was started by the Mother Superior herself, who from all accounts appears to have been something of a nymphomaniac. Perhaps in order to cover her tracks, she took to displaying the symptoms of possession. The convent confessor, one Father Urbain Grandier, was accused of bewitching the nuns and was ultimately burned as a witch. This was a classic case of mass hysteria involving a scapegoat, the unfortunate Grandier.

Similar to the above in general outline was America's famous Salem episode where once again an innocent was persecuted to absolve the throng of the demented, supposed possessed. Most of these instances involved females who were dominated by a religious overlord, usually the parish priest or father confessor. Often the unfortunate man became the focus for unhealthy sexual desire in a world ostensibly free from sex or from opportunities for sexual relations. One cannot escape the notion that many of these nuns were attracted to the life behind walls because they had lesbian tendencies or simply because they wished to escape the outside world for reasons best known to themselves. As I have mentioned, sometimes the leaders of these communities were themselves as bad as or worse than their underlings.

In 1583, in Vienna, a teenage girl suddenly developed a form of debilitating cramp which was attributed to demon attack. Many devils were expelled from her. Her seventy-year-old grandmother was diagnosed as the prime mover behind the illness, and was tortured into confessing acts including intercourse with Beelzebub himself. She was burned alive – an act of justice praised by the clergy of the day.

Another young woman found herself pregnant and tried to claim that she was possessed – as a form of diversion from her plight. A Jesuit priest was authorized to exorcize her of the invading devils, but he was only partially successful. According to the woman, one of the devils took up residence in her private parts, refusing to depart. This of course would explain the enlarged lower abdomen and, with a bit of luck, the pregnancy itself. Eventually she was unmasked as nature took its course, but in the meantime she successfully diverted attention. The priest involved was himself accused of sexual intercourse with the girl; that is, he was accused of being the father, and only narrowly escaped the charge.

'Voluntary' or 'Involuntary' Possession

It may with some confidence be alleged that these cases involved people who were mentally disturbed and by no means really 'possessed'. But according to the beliefs of the age there was indeed an element (or two) of credibility in some of the instances. Some of the protagonists escaped the charges, while others met their deaths. This fact speaks for itself.

The state of possession could be 'voluntary' or 'involuntary'. That is to say, in the first case, the 'witch' (not the 'victim') invited, as it were, the devil or demon into him or her in order to wreak havoc upon other people; in the second, the 'victim' (this time) was entered by the demon against her will in order to disorientate and destroy the inhabited person and hopefully those around her. That there were also induced trance-like states is evident, but these were, to people of the time, hard to diagnose, especially to say with any confidence that this one was an involuntary case or that one was voluntary.

Indications of True Possession

To aid investigators into these strange phenomena, some indications were proffered that purported to show true possession. These included such items as the leading of an antisocial, perhaps criminal life; the vomiting of strange objects (great store was set by this); blaspheming; having made a pact with the Devil (in the opinion of the judges, of course); distortion of the face; and violent and animal-like behaviour. It was taken for granted that a person would exhibit signs of being troubled by spirits.

Other signs that would, it was believed, definitely confirm a state of demonic possession were: speaking in tongues, as the phrase has it; unusual strength; imparting information that the person could not possibly know normally; above all, an aversion to sacred objects; uttering obscenities, usually of a sexual kind, very puzzling coming from the mouths of young girls or nuns, which they often did; relating activities at a sabbat; and general lewd behaviour. Absence of any knowledge of the fits or trances later by the victim was also an infallible sign. If all these signs were manifested, the person was indeed possessed and exorcism was required. However, whether the exorcism would be successful, especially on the first occasion, was a moot point.

Deliverance

It may be appropriate to say a word about exorcism at this juncture, although fuller treatment is given in a later chapter (*see* pages 120 ff). The ritual was more commonly practised in the Roman Catholic Church than in the Protestant Churches – this remains the position today. In theory, the Church of England or Anglican Church has little belief in the ability of devils to take possession of human bodies, but in fact there is still a good deal of 'deliverance' – which could be a rose by any other name. It must be emphasized, however, that the above remark relates largely to the *form* or ritual of the exorcist 'ceremony' rather than to the modern-day practice of praying in the presence of the victim. It was always believed that there was, as was said by Cotton Mather (1662–1728), the notable pro-witchcraft fanatic in *Memorable Providences* (quoted by Robbins, *Encyclopedia of Witchcraft and Demonology*, page 397), a 'near affinity between witchcraft and possession'.

Bewitchment of the person, and corporeal possession by a devil together, was indicated in a handbook of 1627:

a *when a healthy body overnight becomes changed for the worse;*
b *when secret or arcane knowledge is shown by the possessed;*
c *when things are done and said and afterwards the person remembers nothing of it;*
d *when superhuman strength is displayed;*
e *when strange sights are seen by the afflicted;*
f *when objects are strangely vomited.*

Later, particularly in the writings of enlightened authors opposed to the witchcraft persecution mania, such as Johann Weyer (or Wier), of whom more anon, a distinction was made between witchcraft and possession, the essence of which was that in the former the person was the willing instrument of the Devil, while in the latter the possessed person was taken against her will. Belief in the reality of corporeal possession by devils, as supposed by the credulous (almost everybody) in the sixteenth and seventeenth centuries, declined *pari passu* with growing disbelief in witchcraft.

As one of the major writers of this century on the subject, Oesterreich, states in his book *Possession* (page 378), when the Age of Enlightenment replaced the Age of Obscurantism, a world ruled by religious dogma, 'possession begins to disappear amongst civilised races as soon as belief in spirits loses its power'. Oesterreich's book emphasizes that possessed people do give the impression of being invaded by another soul to the extent that the true physical personality is transformed into something alien. This new personality can be the opposite of the normal personality. Often the possessed person loses consciousness – at least of his true personality.

Oesterreich states that this loss of consciousness is an essential characteristic of demon possession. Present-day medical knowledge can, however, account for these states – I say can, not invariably does – with our understanding of epilepsy and hysteria, for example. There are important differences between the two, however, but between them they could account for many of the alleged cases of possession. Nevertheless, there is a core which defies the easy solution of physical or emotional disturbance about which I shall say more later.

In many cases a patient himself becomes convinced that an evil spirit is directing his actions and possessing his emotions. It may be that such people are more in need of a psychiatrist than a priest. According to Jean Lhermitte in his article 'Pseudo-Possession' (*Satan*, ed. Moeller, page 298), patients react against the invading influence and it is precisely by these disguises that 'many… unwittingly create a second favourable personality which is opposed to the evil influence… keeping the [afflicted] in a state of painful struggle…' Often the basis of the pathology lies in a sexual disorder where, for example, fear of overwhelming carnal desire becomes dominant. Such people are obsessed with sin and consequently associate the Devil with their guilty feelings. This itself leads to 'a pathological interpretation of things' (Lhermitte, *idem*, page 299), which in turn leads us to conclude that 'there exist genuine psychopathic states whose chief symptom is the notion that the moral or physical personality, or perhaps the entire personality, is possessed by the devil'.

Genuine Possession?

However, as has been said, among the immense number of recorded cases of possession many, it must be admitted, are spurious and are mere attention seeking. Others may be attributed to hysteria, disease or sickness (such as epilepsy), and as with witchcraft some cases were fomented by clergy who wanted to appear to be in control, which itself imparted a sort of fame to them. Instances of initial obsession can be followed by possession (and vice versa). In severe and prolonged cases, expulsion of evil spirits was always thought necessary. From innumerable examples we can select a couple as exhibiting the sort of problem facing the family of the afflicted, the relatives and the potential exorcist himself, where there is a belief that they have before them a genuine case of demon possession.

The first one is a case that happened in 1815 in the county of Worcestershire. The 'victim' was a young married woman who was afflicted by a mystery illness. It seems that a local young man had become fixated on her; when he was rejected he had recourse to the help of a well-known local 'wizard' in order to wreak some misfortune on her. Whether coincidentally or not, the young woman complained of evil spirits who plagued her constantly. Sprinkling with holy water produced only maniacal cries. Eventually some calm was attained, only for this to be followed by violent agitation. A priest experienced in exorcism was summoned; he came before the contorted and writhing woman, who had to be held down. The priest was convinced she was possessed. It transpired in conversation that she had never been baptized and so the priest immediately performed the ceremony. A rapid improvement followed and a permanent healthy state was attained. Baptism as a form of exorcism appeared to have 'cured' her.

The case of Hélène Poirier of Coullons in the Loire Valley excited considerable interest when it occurred in 1850. Apparently, as a girl and young woman she was noted for her diligence and piety. However, one night she was awakened by the sound of blows as if struck on the walls of her room. No reason could be found for the noise after thorough searching by her parents. Months later Hélène began to fall to the ground, but epilepsy was not diagnosed as the cause. Disorders, both physical and mental, followed – these plagued her for the rest of her life (some sixty years). These were believed to be diabolic attacks, and other ailments were attributed to a supernatural origin. At one stage (in 1865) Hélène was admitted into a convent retreat where she was examined by a doctor, whose conclusion was that she was quite mad. She was dismissed from the convent and returned home, where she was somewhat naturally regarded by local people as a person to avoid. She was at first believed to be obsessed, then possessed, but was freed by an exorcism in 1869.

Months of peace followed a visit to Lourdes in 1875 which appeared to deliver her from recurrent affliction. However, she continued to suffer despite the regular ministrations of clergy. It was very difficult for those around her to understand why she had been originally persecuted by the Devil.

In the late 1860s she had apparently written infamous blasphemies against God and signed a pact with her own blood to serve Satan. She recovered from this episode after a struggle. About the same time she fell into convulsions in which she spoke with a deep, unnatural voice – in Latin, a tongue in which she had never been schooled. She fell into rages at the sight or mention of sacred objects. She also in lucid moments spoke of Satanists who gathered to worship the Devil and commit profanities and indecencies. She mentioned three towns as being places where Satanism was particularly active, and subsequent investigation proved her right. How could she have known this?

Later Hélène was examined by experienced clergy, but she constantly displayed fearsome behaviour, howling and spasms. Questioned in Latin and Greek she answered fluently – proof positive, some might adduce, that she was under supernatural control. Exorcism was again resorted to, repeatedly; all the while, Hélène writhed, blaspheming and cursing, and becoming very violent indeed. Some sexual activity accompanied her ravings, such as removing her clothes and masturbating in full view.

Eventually a period of relaxation came and she seemed refreshed as from sleep. Unfortunately, this recovery did not last and the symptoms returned with greater ferocity. She had to undergo exorcism again. This itself was only a qualified success and she continued to suffer physical and mental miseries. Eventually she was finally 'delivered' on a visit to another sacred shrine and, although constantly troubled, made a good Christian end in her eightieth year.

Were these cases of genuine possession? If not, they are certainly very puzzling even today. At the time everybody was convinced they were in the presence of diabolical forces. Perhaps in our more sophisticated age we can explain them – perhaps.

Possession – Fully Conscious

I have mentioned earlier that one of the indications for possession was, according to the writers of the age, the fact that there was no recall of the episode on the part of the sufferer. Not strictly true, says T. K. Oesterreich in his influential book *Possession* (page 40). There are two distinct manifestations of possession: in one type the episode is indeed not recalled, but there is another type where the 'patient' 'remains fully conscious of what is happening; he is the passive spectator of what takes place within him'. Oesterreich goes on to relate many instances of possessed persons writing or talking about their state of possession.

One of the most compelling is the story of a Spanish abbess, Doña Teresa, in an episode occurring about 1630:

> *I felt within me movements so extraordinary… that the cause could not be natural… several times I begged the prior to exorcize me… at length the prior… asked God to reveal to me whether the demon was in my body… after the exorcism I fell into a sort of swooning and delirium, doing and saying things of which the idea had never occurred to me in my life… accordingly it could not but be regarded as a supernatural being that… I committed follies of which I had never before been capable. The demon Peregrino would say 'Is Doña Teresa with the visitors?' I felt inwardly an inexpressible uneasiness [and] felt the presence of the demon who was in my body… myself muttering 'Lord Peregrino calls me'; so I came where the demon was…*

The foregoing shows how a person can be filled with psychic activity against her will and be conscious of certain unnatural changes such as strange sensations, actions, modes of thought which lead to her conclusion that she is possessed.

Possessed against One's Will – Not Conscious

Being possessed against one's will and not being conscious of it is something very different again. One of the most famous cases of possession is that of Surin, a French mystic and exorcist who was one of the protagonists in the celebrated 'Devils of Loudun' episode. It is rewarding to look at this because Surin wrote in some detail of his experience at the time:

> *I have been in combat with four of the most potent and malicious devils in hell… for the last [few] months I have never been without a devil at work upon me… I cannot explain to you what happens within me during that time and how this spirit unites with mine without depriving me either of consciousness or liberty of soul, nevertheless making himself like another me and as if I had two souls, one of which is dispossessed of its body and the use of its organs and stands aside watching the actions of the other which has entered into them…*

However, for one who cannot explain, Surin does a pretty good job of describing his feelings, reactions and thoughts when he was 'possessed', or rather invaded. It is clear, though, from his account that Surin does not regard himself as possessed, in the usual sense, but rather as sick in mind – another variation on a theme.

We can see from the cases cited that the possessed can talk with (or believe they have talked with) the indwelling spirit, either as an interior monologue or as an audible conversation. Everything appears to be heightened, including speech real or imagined, so that it is not so much a dual personality that makes utterance, but rather two persons seeming to express themselves through the same body. An exorcist attempts to converse with, or to elicit information from, the possessing demon. He (the exorcist) is conscious of there being two wills in the victim and his will makes a third. On one side there is the demon, who wishes to break the victim's body; on the other, the victim, who wishes to be delivered. There are some narratives which give the actual conversation of the demon with the possessed and clearly indicate the two personalities in one person.

TRUE POSSESSION?

What therefore is true possession? One definition of possession is when a person is conscious of a feeling of division in his psyche. But as we now know, schizophrenics sometimes feel this way. The crucial point is that in the case of possession a person can be aware that he is being directed, controlled by – what?

Declining belief in the Devil results in fewer cases today of possession. Not that instances of alleged possession are few (they may be fewer), but they may be put down to overpowering Principles of Evil. It does seem as if we may postulate that resistance to invading forces is proportional to the individual's strength of character. Some people do seem to be more susceptible to invading demonic influence (real or feigned) than others. We have seen this among religious persons, who appear to be disposed to influences of a desired superhuman agency. Often, as with the nuns cited, there is a basic, though hidden, longing for sexual activity manifested in fixations on the only males they could legitimately have contact with – their unfortunate confessors or parish priests.

In many of the older instances of possession it can be seen that a conviction on the person's part set in train subsequent events; that is, they believed themselves to be possessed and were determined to get others to believe them. Epidemics of possession usually follow on from the sight and company of a possessed person, as witness the instances presented earlier. Would-be demoniacs sometimes hallucinated and thereby convinced themselves. The religious who claimed to be possessed largely did so out of a desire to lay claim to a spurious spiritual ecstasy; the lesser educated claimed more out of their ingrained belief in the Devil. Autosuggestion played a part in both. To sum up, true possession occurs when a person is genuinely dominated by a spirit that has come into the body from 'outside'. But the question remains: how accurate is the diagnosis?

Possession Today

It would be foolish to deny that there is a great difference between most cases of possession now and those in earlier times. Possession at the present day is manifest more in the speaking of the spirits of the dead, rather than that of the Devil of, say, the Middle Ages. For the Roman Catholic Church especially, belief in accredited cases of demonic possession still holds sway: that is to say, where all indications are that something supernatural is at work. To a lesser extent this is true of the present Church of England. Belief in the spirit world is as old as mankind itself; the concept of the Devil and his demons will not easily die a total death; many people believe in them either as manifesting themselves today as personifications of the dark side of the human psyche, or as principles (with or without a capital 'P') of an evil they see all around them.

Present-day attitudes to the phenomena are all too often to be summed up in the words of Oesterreich in *Possession* (page 376):

> *The dominant conception… is that no psychic life supervenes except in the presence of a material vehicle and that no spirit either pure or possessed only of an ethereal body, exists in the world.*

He does not claim to share this sentiment, however. Do we? Possession – is it 'an impossible concept or merely an unfashionable one today?' This question, posed by Richards in *But Deliver Us from Evil* (page 92), is, to say the least, an interesting one. There is a third alternative: it is both possible and fashionable!

Research into psychosomatic disorders has gone some way towards shedding light on suspected cases of possession which are thought to have epilepsy as their origin. But as Wilkinson trenchantly says in a well-argued article (quoted by Richards, page 103):

> *If demon possession is a fact there seems no reason why it could not be the cause of some cases of epilepsy. We do not know enough about the spirit world to disprove demon possession nor enough about epilepsy to deny that it may be caused by such possession.*

In fact, it is true to say that the interaction as we now know it between mind, body and spirit (and, some would add, the soul) is barely understood. Diagnosis between the two, or more, states is difficult, therefore. The comparatively modern sciences of psychology and psychiatry have had a considerable influence on inquiry into states of possession, particularly pseudo-possession.

The already quoted French neurologist Lhermitte's view is apposite. Nothing could be more catagorical than his position, an opinion that must be respected (quoted by Richards, page 110):

> *There are many genuinely possessed people. The critical and scientific approach has dispelled many clouds and broken down many myths, but even so, the number of people demonically possessed in our modern world is considerable.*

His conclusion was based on personal experience of a *medical* nature over many years.

We may examine another quotation (Lewis Maclachlan, *Miracles of Healing*, quoted by Richards, page 114), not consonant indeed with the above view, but very germane to the considerations of this chapter. It adduces an aspect already mentioned, that of the place of such as schizophrenia and hysteria in cases of suspected spirit invasion:

> *[In] several cases… in which Christian ministers have used an act of exorcism to give relief to patients… who believed themselves to be possessed by evil spirits… this kind of prayer was used not so much because the ministers believed in demonic possession, but because the patients did…*

SELLING THE SOUL

Self belief in (demon) possession is a concept worthy of some mention. As I have stated, 'invasion' can be voluntary or, as happens today mostly, but not by any means exclusively, involuntary. Voluntary cases largely involved the idea of 'inviting' the Devil in on a reciprocal basis whereby the soul was given up to Satan in return for magical gifts or temporal power, wealth or sexual gratification.

The idea of 'selling one's soul' is a very ancient one, which from all accounts persists today. Throughout the ages there are stories of bargains struck between mortals and the Devil for mutual advantage. Faust and Mephistopheles are probably the best known. The heresy of pact was born, which was at the core of witchcraft belief. Notable scholars who epitomized this belief in selling the soul are the influential German bishop Peter Binsfeld, writing in the sixteenth century, and Francesco Guazzo, instanced earlier, writing in the seventeenth century. To the latter we owe an impressive list of allegiances made by the would-be demoniac to Satan:

1 *I deny the Creator of heaven and earth… and my baptism…*
2 *I submit to re-baptisment in the Devil's name.*
3 *I surrender to Satan a piece of my clothing as a token.*
4 *I swear allegiance to the Devil within this magic circle.*
5 *I promise to sacrifice children to Satan.*
6 *I request my name to be put in the Book of Death.*
7 *I mark with the Devil's mark parts of my body, especially the anus [in men]… the genitals and breasts [in women].*
8 *I promise to abhor anything holy.*
9 *I promise to keep silent this exchange.*

This declaration was made before Satan, represented by a black goat and what is presumed to be a man made up to look like the Devil. The sign of the cross was made with the left hand, and as a token of submission the backside of the goat was kissed, as were the testicles of the man-Devil.

The essence of the contract 'selling the soul' involved concessions on the Devil's part, of course. From a source of the seventeenth century, we are informed that the sellers undertook to commit the Devil to bestowing certain favours of which the following are typical: making available a substantial sum of money; preserving from illness or injury; causing people, especially those of the opposite sex, to love him or her; aiding in all endeavours of life; giving useful information; endowing with intelligence and knowledge; offering protection when needed; appearing when desired in an agreeable form; ensuring that people obey whatever is commanded; and keeping secret the agreement. This contract might last for life (if the Devil could be persuaded) or more usually for a finite term of years at the end of which Satan would possess the bargainer's soul. More later about this classic Faust–Mephistopheles syndrome.

SIGNS OF POSSESSION

It may be hackneyed to state that each of us has a latent devil within us to which the majority do not, thankfully, succumb. This may be Man's fundamental and indeed normal nature, the legacy of the original sin. Man is naturally concupiscent, finding the slippery slope the easiest – to descend, that is. Some believe this; some do not. Mainstream religious doctrine has always maintained the former belief. Possession, voluntary or involuntary, is always of the Devil. Diabolic invasion can be demonstrated by visible signs, as we know: face, voice and body are transformed, the whole marked by uninhibition, by flagrant behaviour and speech. Those who believe themselves possessed think of demons, small enough to enter them through their orifices (there are many illustrations of small, black devils driven out by exorcism and floating away). The possessed complain of coldness, which is often experienced by the ministering attendants. We have met this phenomenon of coldness before in respect of testimony to the Devil's ejaculate. Coldness is associated with frigidity and loss of sensibility to pain – all of which has an echo of previous chapters.

In addition to these physical symptoms there are the mental, some of which have been mentioned: recondite or esoteric knowledge; thought reading; and above all, I believe, is the phenomenon of speaking in tongues. I have yet to hear of a satisfactory explanation – there are some, but they are not convincing. Perhaps it is something we are not at a high enough stage of development to understand. But this can be offered as a explanation of anything! Sometimes what is uttered is true and can be verified; but mostly a possessed person lies, prompted by the demon, and bears false testimony, however seemingly impressive, in order to confuse the witnesses.

Obsession we have already mentioned. Often feelings of guilt are at the bottom of it; a feeling that suffering for a past fault is the only expiation. This is frequently exacerbated by a sense of solitude, by being cut off from mainstream society, by a feeling of being different in a detrimental manner. Feelings of inferiority often accompany unnatural states, which turn into an obsession, which itself leads on to a state of possession. The guilt feeling becoming an obsession is illustrated by the confessions of the prioress at Loudun, the other main mover in the Surin saga (*see* page 104). Sister Jeanne des Anges analyses her emotions, writing that she was 'nearly always suffering from remorse of conscience'. At times she was able to resist the urges of the devils; while at others she admitted to taking pleasure in his wiles: 'The Devil often tricked me by a little feeling of pleasure that I had in the disturbances…' Both Surin and Jeanne des Anges were obsessed by guilt feelings, an ambivalent attitude to sin, suffering and pleasure, and an aggression directed at the norms of the age. Their devils, if devils they had, were invited in, not intruders, but to act as foci for their hosts' uncertainty.

Is it possible to prove, or rather to adduce proof, which is not the same thing, in the existence of genuine demonic possession? It may be alleged that diagnosis is a subjective thing; that is, it differs with the individual observer, despite there being overt signs in the victim. Interpretation of the signs, mental, affective, as well as physical, taking into account all background circumstances, is this what it comes down to in the end? Helping us in the inquiry are the 'rules' of W. M. Alexander, in his comprehensive study *Demonic Possession in the New Testament* (pages 147, 163 and 172):

1 *Whatever is explicable on the principles of modern science is to be regarded as natural.*
2 *Whatever is inexplicable on the principles of modern science is supernatural.*

Accordingly, says Alexander, two classes of the possessed emerge:

1 *cases simply natural and not genuinely demonic;*
2 *cases truly supernatural and genuinely demonic.*

On this basis, the instances in the Bible of Jesus' exorcism are genuinely demonic. Alexander goes on to point out, after examining cases in the Scriptures, what he calls two distinctive characteristics of genuine demonic possession:

1 *insanity of some sort, forming the natural element;*
2 *the confession or testimony to Jesus as Messiah (by demons), forming the supernatural element.*

Further study of Bible cases leads to a two-fold classification of the possessed:

1 *cases self-attested and clearly supernatural;*
2 *cases not self-attested and simply natural.*

These two classes, he says, must have been very conspicuous to the contemporaries of Jesus. The first was absolutely novel and unique. The second class was commonplace. On this reasoning, the depravity of the Biblical possessed is an integral part of their sickness and Jesus did not condemn demoniacs as responsible for their condition, nor did He 'ascribe to possessing spirits moral influence over the possessed'.

A Unique Spiritual Environment

What must strike anyone reading the Gospels is the great number of instances of apparent demon possession cited, which seems to bear little relation to activity of the present day. So much so that the question has been asked – was the environment peculiar in the time of Christ? One answer has been that at that time the demons were at the stage of abandoning their old oracles, shrines and godheads, and instead taking up abode in mankind. Like many elements in the realm of faith and belief, this thesis is incapable of proof. Physically the environment was not unique.

What was unique was the ethical, or rather spiritual, environment. What made it unique lay in that element of the Bible where the devils or demons recognized Jesus as the Messiah and where at the time Jesus suppressed this demon testimony or recognition. Jesus had to fulfil His destiny, started by the Incarnation. The powers of evil fought back against this Redeemer. And this took the form of genuine demonic possession. It is instructive to read alongside this argument the sentence from Revelation 12:12 as explanatory of demonic activity: 'Satan is come down to you, having great wrath, because he knoweth that he hath but a short time'.

This was Biblical time. Then the states told of were always of evil spirits that invaded the person, but, as William Sargant (*The Mind Possessed*, page 44) says, possession has very often been

> *deliberately induced, to give a human being the most direct... experience of a deity, by becoming its living vessel... and acting as a channel of communication between gods... and their worshippers.*

The Power of Suggestion

People differ in their susceptibility to another's influence. Suggestibility too varies. There are cases even today of a person's being made to believe, by suggestion alone, that he or she is possessed by demons, where there are no controlled demonic forces. In these cases knowledge of, and upbringing in, Biblical and religious history can play no small a part. Autosuggestion can be a powerful force. Some people exhibit signs of possession when they suffer from the disorder known as multiple personality syndrome. These people experience at differing times controlling personalities, now murderous and threatening, now kindly or even beneficent, but most often cold and sullen, which they might attribute to a demon (possession).

People with a strict religious background are often the most susceptible to influences. Often such people are compelled to blaspheme and curse God among other infamous manifestations, but today we tend not to blame them on demons. Perhaps, some would say, we should?

The Gift of Clairvoyance

Research has added to our recognition knowledge: the lists given earlier of 'signs' of possession. Increased intelligence we have mentioned, but akin to this is an apparent gift of clairvoyance, believed by the Church to be either divinely bestowed or the result of demonic possession, and related is the facility of the possessed to predict the future occurrence of demonic attacks; and what appear to be selective sensory defects, such as temporary deafness and aphasia whereby a victim cannot hear, or hear only some people; seeing at times, at others not seeing; and sometimes capable of speech, sometimes not.

Thus, possessed people could see themselves as controlled by an indwelling, invading agency that at a variety of times created in them other personalities, different from their normal nature. Accordingly, even disruptive, eccentric and strange behaviour was usually adduced in past centuries as being due to demonic possession. Therefore, people (who by no means wanted the label) of, shall we say, idiosyncratic mannerisms were branded as possessed on the one hand, while on the other were those people who defined themselves as demoniacs, deriving satisfaction from being in a state of dependency for social and physical needs, from the accompanying rise in social status, achieving thereby a degree of prominence from the sympathetic attention to their every transgression, foible or mood swing, which were attributed to Satanic influence – not to the persons themselves.

In addition, the so-called possessed could revel in the awe they generated by giving rein to arcane knowledge, prophecies and the like, exhibitions of great strength, which were expected and thus largely (if not totally) in the minds of the beholders. Of course, many demoniacs believed sincerely that they were genuinely possessed by devils.

Belief in demonic possession persisted up to the eighteenth century, and even in the twentieth century there were people who believed that some diseases were caused partly by demonic forces and partly by natural causes. Growing knowledge of emotional states has led much medical opinion to opine that hysteria is very often the true diagnosis of 'possession'.

Summing up this section appositely is a passage from an article on demonic possession and hysteria entitled 'Witchcraft, Magic and Possession' by Spanos and Gottlieb in Levack, Vol. 9, *Possession and Exorcism* (page 277). They write that the social role theory (of professed demoniacs) was

> *shaped to fit Judeo-Christian conceptions of demons and demonic activity. The role was maintained because the status of demoniac became associated with a number of important social functions. The demoniac notion provided a culturally consistent explanation for various physical disorders and for otherwise inexplicable violations of propriety norms… the role provide a means of reintegrating deviants into the social community…*

and in various ways supported the religious and moral values of the community. The role also provided… some expressions of social and personal dissatisfaction. Finally the role was exploited as a means for controlling personal, political or ideological enemies by having the demoniac label them as witches.

PROVING DEMONIZATION

Adducing demonization of a person is one thing, proving it is another. Attempts to prove demon presence depend to a large extent on the beliefs, faith and attitude of the reader to the whole concept. Like many, if not most, facets of religion, belief is a matter of faith – faith which is not capable of proof. We know the 'signs' for recognition, but we can do more, as in the preliminary stages of exorcism, when for example the demon can be confronted by means of challenging questions which may bring about a change in the possessed (because of the demon's discomfiture). It must be emphasized that everything is done in God's name. Whatever is done must be done with sincere conviction that one is faced with genuine possession.

One can fairly easily be mistaken, even duped. There have been cases, says Dickason in *Demon Possession and the Christian* (page 175), that on face value give all the appearances of possession, but 'have turned out to be physical or psychological problems, not demonization'. In twenty-five years' experience of encountering possessed persons, Dickason admits to having dealt with some impostures or spurious cases. But out of hundreds of cases in that time, many, he states, have been truly demonized.

It would be fitting, I think, to conclude this chapter on possession by relating a famous case which illustrates vividly the syndrome we have been discussing.

A Famous Case

Anna Maria Uz, a Lutheran peasant woman, was born in 1799. She led a normal, happily married life, and was the mother of three children. She was religious but not overly so. When she was thirty-one, she suddenly experienced uncontrollable seizures, with wild movements of the limbs. This went on for months until one night the voice of a demon began to speak through her mouth, saying it was the ghost of a neighbour. Anna Maria appeared not to be conscious of this voice and remembered nothing of it afterwards. Intermittently, this ghost, or demon, would take her over, cursing and hitting out. After about a year when only prayer seemed to offer any relief, she decided to visit a local Catholic priest with the object of being exorcized. The demon raged terribly and convulsed her as she travelled. On arrival at the church, the priest would not perform the ceremony as Anna was not a Roman Catholic. He allowed her to pray there, however, in spite of furious protestations from the possessing spirit. During this time Anna was expecting another child and for a time after the birth the demon left her in peace. Then he was back again.

Medical attempts to restore her failed, so she resorted to prayer again before the altar. One day she fell down, lying motionless. Hopes grew that this time she might be liberated, but instead after a couple of days two demons began speaking through her mouth, cursing more than ever. Her family took her to a 'magician' who treated her, trying to get rid of the demons by prayer and communication. Some time later she experienced apparent labour pains and in a spasm one of the demons burst out. Unfortunately, the magician could not continue, and when Anna was taken home the remaining demon began again his torments. She was taken to be seen by a well-known physician, who saw before him an emaciated, pain-riddled woman. He was unable to diagnose any mental problem, but witnessed her sudden attacks in which the demon spoke. Apparently the ghost was that of a man who had committed suicide by hanging. During the attacks obscenities flowed copiously. The demon would not permit her to eat or drink properly; obstructed her attempts at praying; and distorted her face into a Satanic grin. After the attacks Anna felt headaches and pains in her limbs. Spoken to in Latin, a tongue she did not know, she (or the demon) answered fluently. She was also able to recite prayers and hymns, which ordinarily she would not have known. She underwent a form of hypnosis which induced a calm state, but frequently the demon became active, clearly hating the kindly hypnotist. On occasion Anna seemed to be recovering, standing as if blowing out something, then falling back insensible. It was obvious that hypnotism, though helpful, was not the answer.

Exorcism was again resorted to, and initially seemed to have a calming effect, even on the language of the demon, which became less abusive. The demon, it seems, asked for more time if he had to leave, saying that it was horrible outside.

The next day Anna reported feeling better, but that the demon was still inside her. He said he would leave that day and specified a time. They (Anna and her helpers) would have to assist him in departing and they would have to write down the confessions he would make. This confession was a litany of sinful acts of all kinds which led up to his suicide. Anna Maria herself had convulsions during which she screamed, then fainted. It appeared the demon had gone. A few days later, however, her affliction started again and she became possessed by, it was believed, another demon. The physician who had treated her realized that care afterwards was necessary and he arranged for her to come under the protection of an experienced and religious man, who was among other things a herbalist and clairvoyant, claiming to be in contact with the spirit world. He was successful in freeing the miserable woman from the demons and was able to protect her against future possessions. Anna Maria was freed for good and never again experienced demonic attacks. She returned to the contented life she had known before the affliction mysteriously began.

This well-documented story is typical of many where a possessed person has finally won through after much suffering and after exorcism has been performed. It illustrates also the vital importance of faith on the part of the victim and the necessity for a form of aftercare to prevent any reoccurrence.

It also raises many questions of which perhaps the most important is: why? Why was the particular person chosen? Cases adduced in serious studies are well authenticated and well documented, witnessed by several people. There can be no question of deception *about the testimony* itself. If there is any deception it must lie in the victim herself. Hardly credible from clearly suffering people. How can uneducated people talk in languages of which they know nothing? How can they know about far-off happenings or of the future? A myriad questions spring to mind. Either it is true or a monstrous fraud has been perpetrated. We are unable to *prove* it one way or the other. It may come down to only one question: that of faith and belief.

CHAPTER SIX

EXORCISM – EXPELLING DEMONS

T he ages-old Roman Catholic formula for discovering the indications of true possession, and the ritual of exorcism – when the Devil is ordered to leave the body of the afflicted person or a place – and the practicalities of performing an exorcism, are, remarkably, often just as relevant today as they were hundreds of years ago.

The greatest of all exorcists was Jesus. This much is clear from the New Testament accounts of His healing ministry. But exorcism was not a new thing in Biblical times. Exorcism had existed from the times of the earliest civilizations, among all races, and still exists today. To require exorcism, a person must be possessed demonically – a state that completely transforms him or her, except perhaps for short intervals. To restore normality a religious type of ceremony is performed, the purpose of which is to drive out the possessing devil.

THEORY OF EXORCISM

It is with Christian exorcism and the Christian invading devil that we are mainly concerned. The exorcists' power over demons was derived from their acknowledgement that the demons were subject to a higher authority: that of the Christian God. Usually the possessing spirits were malevolent, entering the body by their own power or by being invited to take possession of someone through the agency of a witch. The latter were cases of bewitchment. Many indications by which this could be recognized were given by contemporary writers. If these 'indications' were convincing, an exorcism was required.

A certain ritual had to be followed, as had a form of words initially to ascertain several points: the name of the demon (great store was set by this); why he had taken up abode in the victim; when exactly he had entered; and how long he intended staying. Often several demons could inhabit a body at the same time, or one followed another in taking up residence. Many handbooks were written on exorcism rituals, especially in the sixteenth and seventeenth centuries, concerning the removal of spirits from animals and places as well as people. These manuals all stressed the seriousness of the rite and the need for a holy and experienced cleric to administer it. This still obtains, particularly in the Roman Catholic Church, although it is far from a dead letter in the Protestant Churches today.

No attempt at solemn exorcism must, however, be made in either Church without the express permission of the diocesan bishop. The ritual itself (at least for the Roman Catholic Church) is laid down in the Roman Catholic clerics' manual of exorcism, the famous *Rituale Romanum*. Based on an original of the early seventeenth century, it was updated in the 1940s and 1970s and is undergoing a revision to date. A shortened version of the ceremony is given in Appendix 1. The Rite of the Ordination of Exorcists is given in Appendix 2. (The office of exorcist itself is or was one of the orders conferred on the tyro or novice priest.)

There is no denying the conflict in present-day attitudes to possession and exorcism. Three main views prevail. One is that exorcism involves the casting out of an objective power of evil through an authority given to the ministry by Christ, and may involve belief in demons or evil spirits, or belief in a Principle of Evil. A second view is that exorcism is effective psychologically in restoring to normality those who believe themselves possessed. A third opinion is that 'possession' is explainable in social and psychological terms. Those who hold this view emphasize that as their belief in demons is very tenuous, or non-existent, pastoral care is all that is needed, backed up by assurance as to God's love and concern.

Exorcism and Remedy

Exorcism can be administered in two forms: Ordinary or Simple, as in the ceremony of Baptism, which can be conducted by any priest; and Solemn or Long, for use in such serious cases that a bishop's permission is needed. The latter can be a dangerous procedure and cautious, deliberate approaches must be made. The adversarial demon can be a nasty customer!

An exorcist has to diagnose first – and then apply a remedy. This has to be done before witnesses, which itself testifies to the subjective nature of the proceedings. Most important initially is to approach the 'case' with a healthy degree of scepticism, or at least caution. Inquiries into the victim's background must be thorough; then the problem must be discussed with peers.

It is perhaps natural to think of demon possession when confronted with someone normally polite and docile who exhibits lewd behaviour and utters foul language. But this is not always the case. The exorcist knows that he is faced with 'signs' that can be misleading and that it is very important to distinguish between those which indicate the abnormal and those which testify to the supernatural. It is not easy, though, and mistakes can be, and are, made. Illness, mental and physical, can undoubtedly confuse the issue, hence the importance of consultation with a medical doctor and/or psychiatrist. Above all, the exorcist must believe in himself and his competence attested by his experience, training, background and personal life.

The *Rituale Romanum* lists, among others, three main indications of diabolic possession: use of an unknown tongue; hidden knowledge; and physical power much above the expected. We have met these signs before. All three are difficult to explain away, although attempts to do this have been made, adducing the following: thought transference, telepathy, knowledge in the (remote) past of a language by an ancestor which surfaces; utilizing parts of the brain and of the body which are not normally used; and tapping into sources of muscular strength that in the course of everyday life are never called for.

However, the question remains: how or why is the person able to do this? If some of these phenomena are thought to be inexplicable, what *is* the diagnosis? We may be left with the supernatural or at least with the preternatural. 'Conversation' with the victim can be enlightening. Does the conversation seem to be with the subject or with the possessing devil? Answers or rejoinders need to be carefully analysed as an aid to arriving at the truth of the situation.

F. X. Maquart, in an article 'Exorcism and Diabolical Manifestation' (*Satan*, ed. Moeller, page 199), sums up the position as he sees it:

> In genuine possession the action of the demon doubtless dominates the body, seizes on its organs and uses them as if they were his own, actuates the nervous system and produces movements and gesticulations in the limbs, speaking for example through the patient's mouth…

EXORCISM AND DELIVERANCE

John Cornwell relates in his book *Powers of Darkness: Powers of Light* (page 347) that he interviewed an Italian priest about exorcism. The priest made a distinction between exorcism and deliverance:

> In exorcism we address the Devil in person to force him to leave;… in deliverance we call upon God to order the evil to depart… deliverance is much more common… exorcism is very rare…'

In the conversation the priest also distinguished between possession and oppression (as we have done). 'Possession involves a person's will; the possessed person has invited the evil spirit in… and is brought about by the deliberate courting of the powers of darkness…'

When asked about the characteristics of possession, the priest replied, 'Any of the symptoms of oppression or possession may just be the result of psychosis, depression or auto-suggestion…' He then went on to give a list of symptoms. He concluded, 'When all these things come together in a unique circumstance and when medical help has repeatedly failed, we would be advised to consider deliverance, and then exorcism.'

Clearly, this Italian priest believed in demon possession and explained things as he saw them from his viewpoint. Belief by the person that he *is* possessed presents the exorcist with as great a problem as if the person were genuinely possessed. Sometimes psychological projection is the key to what is occurring, by which is meant that the psychological disorder is the result 'of a disturbed group or family projecting their negative or wicked attributes on to an individual, whom they make their scapegoat…' (M. Perry, *Deliverance*, page 71). It is through this process of projection, says Perry, that people actually may become controlled by others. Perry, in the above book, enumerates guidelines for exorcists and counsellors and it is therefore important reading. He gives some of the signs by which one may come to a right conclusion regarding false and true possession. With regard to investigation into a person's circumstances, the background may reveal, for example: a sinful life; practice of the occult; deliberate subjection to Satanism; self-centred materialism; family interest in the occult; and an overwhelming desire for something.

Exorcizing Places

Places can be reputed to be haunted by ghosts or evil spirits to the extent that some mischief always seems to befall people who live or visit there. Accordingly, exorcisms of places loom large in current practice, and often these places are houses or rectories or even stretches of road, crossroads, stretches of sea such as the so-called Bermuda Triangle; or Scotland's Loch Ness of monster fame.

As with persons, careful investigation is needed. The exorcist (of places) must first inspect the place then exorcize at once without allowing any interruption. The exorcist never works alone, and throughout, the 'team' backing the protagonist must maintain a prayerful mien. After the pronouncement, the place is blessed and holy water sprinkled. Condemnation by all present of all things Satanic or occult follows, and everything is destroyed that has been connected in any way with the disturbance or the diabolic. Anyone seemingly associated with the manifestations must be baptized anew if he has renounced his baptism, and the person must be helped to integrate himself within a Christian, caring community. Finally, a detailed report is sent to the authorizing diocesan bishop.

Performing Deliverance

Perry lays down certain instructions for performing deliverance or a minor exorcism. Emphasis is placed on the following: proper preparation by prayer; importantly, the involvement of a team of committed Christians, of which at least one should be a woman; a state of grace on the part of the exorcist; the need to elicit as much information as possible from the victim; and the need to consult the bishop if a major exorcism is thought necessary.

The 'team' should consist of clerical and lay members who are approached for advice by the parish priest to whose attention the case has been brought. This group should include a psychiatrist. The team should meet several times a year to review matters and should undergo training. The potential officiating ministers should visit the person in question in his own home, after which a provision-al diagnosis is made. It is essential that there is collaboration between the priest and the doctor, and consultation must take place.

The reality of the need for casting out devils is unequivocally seen in the New Testament, where a large part of Jesus' ministry was concerned with exorcism. The practice has continued to the present day; although its forms have varied down the years, essentially it has been deemed necessary, especially, it may be thought, among non-Christian people. The two main Christian Churches, the Roman Catholic and Protestant, by no means have a monopoly on the rite, which indicates a well-nigh universal belief in demon possession.

Exorcism can be performed by a lay person, but should be confined to the minor rite. Baptism is a form of major exorcism where the candidate (usually a baby) is prayed over to ensure deliverance from original sin. Water, blessed, plays an important part and is reminiscent of John the Baptist's activities in the River Jordan.

Non-Christian exorcism, to take up that point, refers to occult groups and those allied with them, who also make use of the ritual. Christian exorcism is undertaken in the name of Christ. The non-Christian form is also frequently practised as a therapy for internal conflict. In emergencies even non-Christians can administer a form of simple exorcism, or deliverance rather. The main-stream Christian Churches have laid down very careful criteria for proposals to exorcize and for principles on which to base potential work. As the *York Report* on exorcism and deliverance in the Church of England (study group on the Christian Ministry of Healing, 1974) states: 'Proposals must be consonant with sound philosophical, psychological, theological and liturgical principles.'

Regarding the essence of deliverance, Richards, in his pamphlet *Exorcism, Deliverance and Healing* (page 18), states that he does

> *not see the service as primarily concerned with driving away evil. Whether it is con-cerned with a troubled person or a disturbed place, I see it as the Church active in bring-ing into a distorted situation through its ministry the grace of our Lord Jesus Christ, the love of God and the fellowship of the Holy Spirit. It proclaims through word and action God's rule and invites those who can hear and see it to acknowledge it, and – as far as they are able – to respond to the living God.*

The Specific Rubrics to be observed, as laid down in the *York Report*, are as fol-lows: (a) extreme care in preparation (to exorcize); (b) encouragement of the suf-ferer to undertake spiritual preparation (if possible); (c) support from a prayer group; (d) the ceremony should be in church; (e) traditional vesture; (f) pious assistants; (g) unbelievers or the curious should not be present, as neither should animals or young children; (h) hands should not be laid on the sufferer until after the deliverance; (i) any item of an occult or evil connotation should be removed; (j) flexibility, spontaneity and authority are required on the part of the minister; and (k) careful follow-up is essential.

There are recommendations for the patient as well: providing absolute privacy; placing him where he cannot damage himself or objects; keeping warm water, towels, drinks (non-alcoholic) to hand; providing a comfortable chair; and giving an explanation as to what is to be done. The assistants must be Christians; must be capable of restraining the sufferer; and they must be spiritually and mentally prepared.

No set rite is stipulated by the Church of England and so the Anglican exorcist is at liberty to devise his own. The Roman Catholic exorcist must follow the set rites of his Church. Whatever the procedure, the service must include: a command to the demon to go away; a command that the demon hurts no one; a command that it never returns; a command to depart at once, in the name of Christ. The patient's reactions, apart from the abnormal behaviour manifest in these cases, are likely to be dictated by the demon, who clearly will not want any exorcism to occur in the first place. He will try to resist by concealing his presence for as long as possible and by attempting to create discord and disharmony between the patient and the exorcist and to dishearten the minister himself. Often there is a strong atmosphere of evil pervading the room or place; Christian symbols will always be attacked and desecrated, with, as Howell-Everson says in his *Handbook for Christian Exorcists* (page 163), the sufferers

> *being unable... to make any specific Christian act such as praying, Bible reading or meditation. Those under attack will observe unaccountable and hostile happening[s]... display[s] of outbursts of rage... manifestations of spite and envy... there can be the threat of injury and even death... in such an atmosphere of strain severe mental illness will not be uncommon.*

GOD'S PERMISSION?

It may with justification be asked, in view of the foregoing, why God permits this tyrannization of Man. That the Devil wishes to enter human bodies and thereby to desecrate them and their surroundings – this much is abundantly clear. He wishes to speak through the 'temple of Christ', particularly when he had to desert his former dwelling places, idols and shrines. In destroying God's image, Man, the Devil comes as close as he can to taking revenge for ancient hurts. At the time of Christ's arrival on earth, God permitted people to be possessed so that His Son might all the better demonstrate his supreme power. By a similar token, God allows them to exist at the present time to show the power His ministers have and to confound the critics (of the reality of exorcism). Seeing a demoniac is also salutary for us all as an earnest or indication of what living with Satan is likely to be like.

Exorcism was always a type of healing, especially in the time of Christ and before in pagan religions. Certainly Christ saw Himself in His public ministry as engaged in healing, physical as well as mental. Among the Hebrews the basic notion was accepted that evil spirits could influence men and women and could cause detrimental physical effects. The possibility of possession therefore led to the possibility of exorcism, reflected in Jewish writing of a later era. Christ Himself was born into a world where exorcism was common – by all sorts and conditions of men. The unique power of the Messiah was reflected in His exorcisms. Christ, it seems, was well aware that only a few illnesses were caused by demonic possession – but that some *were*. Exorcisms were a radical form of treatment, dependent on a change of attitude in the sufferer. As Baker says (*Binding the Devil*, page 26), 'the ultimate Christian message remains unchanged; exorcism in this context is not the triumph of ritual over superstition, but that of good over evil realized in the most positive way'.

A FAMOUS FILM

It may be that the film *The Exorcist* demonstrated this with terrifying force when it was released in 1973. Sensationalism accompanied the showing of the film and exorcism became synonymous with the horrific. In the film a twelve-year-old girl develops abnormal behaviour and subsequent medical investigation can throw no light on the condition. Eventually an exorcist is called in to confront the screaming, distorted creature. The exorcism ritual makes up most of the film, during the course of which one priest dies of a heart attack and another throws himself to his death from the bedroom window. Emphasis throughout is on a physical cause which may not be so; the climax is represented more as the triumph of a ritual over superstition.

There is little realization that what we have been watching is deliverance by the Holy Spirit and that the struggle is concerned with good and evil. For most people, seeing the demented antics of the girl was the attraction: screaming obscenities, urinating, masturbating, grabbing the testicles of one of the helpers. Eventually she was 'cured' by exorcism.

The film was adapted from the book by William Peter Blatty based on an actual case of demonic possession which occurred in 1949. In reality the possessed was a fourteen-year-old boy, who was exorcized with the result that the possessing spirit departed, but not before identifying itself as one of the Biblical fallen angels. The film itself can be criticized as not really being a true reflection of the seriousness of the ceremony of exorcism, but it did have the merit of awakening people's consciousness to such elements as good and evil, the Devil, demonic possession.

Close members of the girl's family were pictured as non-believers, which heightened the tension between opposing forces in the scenario. We may believe that the film and attendant publicity did no service to a Christian ritual of great import. But it certainly updated the idea of demons and their ability to possess human beings. On the other hand, the film had some propaganda element for the Christian cause.

POSSESSION OR MENTAL DISORDER?

It has been believed since Biblical times that demons caused mental illness, but that the act of casting them out showed great power, as is the case today. Demons could be replaced by souls of the dead, or demons could transmute themselves into the spirits of once living persons come back, as it were, to plague the living – who it seemed had some connection with the dead person, however tenuous. Whatever the invading spirit, the phenomenon has always to be understood as a real (or figurative) struggle between good and evil. There are eminent thinkers in the Catholic Church, however, who criticize the whole idea of demonic possession, adducing that exorcism *per se* was, and is, not an example of casting out devils, but more a cure (of disease).

'Possession' may be caused by various factors: excessive religiosity, abuse in childhood, susceptibility to occult phenomena, Tourette's Syndrome (a type of nervous disease marked by incoordination, speech disorders and possible convulsions), and all the other items already mentioned, but this would not explain away the ability of some victims to read minds or to speak foreign languages. It may be that there are unknown forces we cannot at present understand. As Underwood says, the Church recognizes 'that we know little and are indeed not meant to know much perhaps in this world about the affairs of the next' (*Exorcism!*, Introduction, page 19)

Notable too is the fact that the ritual of exorcism does not always work, or is effective only for a limited time; sometimes, however, it seems to be completely effective. Why this should be so no one knows. It may reside in an incomplete preparation or state of readiness on the part of those officiating; it may reside in a less than complete acceptance by the patient; or it may be accounted for by the tenacity of the dead or evil spirit.

By and large, though, exorcism is, always has been, accepted as able to remove demons by means of threats and commands, and the use of holy water. It was believed that evil spirits could not live in bodies made holy and sanctified by blessed water, and hence the importance of the sacrament of Baptism, a symbol of new life and purification from sin.

The sceptical position alluded to is neatly summed up by Underwood in his book *Exorcism!* (page 87):

> *Psychologists believe that cases of possession have nothing to do with spirits of any kind, but that the answer lies in greatly increased brain activity, often the result of emotional excitement or upheaval. Meanwhile, the student of the paranormal points to: the relative ease with which apparent possession is achieved, the spontaneous appearance of possession in many diverse individuals, and the evidence of anthropologists whose researches show that states of possession are achieved in primitive societies in ways that vary from rhythmic drumming to excessive sexual excitation. It seems likely that ninety-nine per cent of cases of possession have an emotional basis.*

Clerics, however, trained in the procedures of Christian exorcism often have another view. For them, evil is an actual force, not an abstraction; in exorcism, therefore, the priest has to accept the power and guidance conferred on him by the Holy Spirit. They believe they are carrying out the command of Jesus: 'preach the Gospel, heal the sick and cast out demons'.

EXORCISMS IN PRACTICE

It may be that exorcism can only fully succeed when those who feel that they are, or appear to be, suffering from the effects of evil forces are able to discover a wider and deeper meaning to life than the mundane existence we all know.

If they are unable to discover it – this leads on to the most infamous example of an exorcism gone wrong (or rather not fully thought through) in recent history. It is the cautionary story of Michael Taylor, whose strange and irrational behaviour in 1975 led to his being exorcized by two inexperienced clergymen. One of the exorcisms lasted all night, at the end of which the exorcists claimed to have driven out scores of demons from Taylor's body. They believed they had succeeded totally in freeing Taylor and had restored him to normality. In a mistaken euphoria they left Taylor alone with his wife. That night, or early morning, he attacked his wife with such ferocity that she choked on her own blood. He gouged out her eyes, tore out her tongue and ripped the flesh from her face. Later Taylor was deemed to be insane. Exorcism and exorcists acquired a bad name, not surprisingly. There was a general feeling that it was the exorcism itself that had triggered off the hideous murder. Was Taylor possessed or just a clinical maniac?

I have mentioned that places as well as people can be exorcized. One of the most well known of haunted places is (or was) Borley Rectory in Essex, which was built in 1863 and inhabited by the large family of the then rector and by subsequent vicars. All testified to hearing strange noises and seeing strange sights. Among the apparitions were the figures of a nun, a man and a girl. Noises included the sound of whispering, horses' hooves, music and various rappings. Messages appeared on the walls, appealing for Mass or prayers. In the 1930s several attempts at exorcism were made. On one occasion the bells in the kitchen all rang at once although no one could possibly have caused the occurrence.

Signs of the cross and blessings in every room had some temporary success in quieting the manifestations. The well-known feeling of coldness was experienced. Exorcism was tried again with some success. The exorcists left confident they had liberated the rectory from the unquiet spirits that were haunting it.

A couple of years later the remains of what was believed to be the nun were found and reinterred. About five years after that a family visiting the rectory experienced some very peculiar happenings indeed: movement of objects, bell ringing and a hail of stones. Even with the destruction of the rectory by fire in 1939, the site was regarded as haunted. In 1946 the site itself had a form of exorcism performed over it – to little avail. Incidents continued to be reported. Was the rectory possessed? What is the explanation for the strange events?

Cured by Exorcism

Marc Alexander has written about the famous exorcist the Reverend Donald Omand. In his book *The Devil Hunter* (pages 57–8), he writes of an exorcism that

Omand described to him (the patient had been attacking people to suck, vampire-like, their blood):

First I blessed the salt and water… the patient watched… but did not move. He said nothing throughout the preliminaries… but on coming to the final exorcism there was a sudden outburst. With a bound the young man was upon me… his intention was murder, not blood sucking… no doubt his possessor knew that if I was liquidated none of the others present could expel him. He was eventually overcome by the two fit male nurses. An argument ensued between the doctors and myself [regarding whether] the patient should be sedated… I felt that the power of the Holy Spirit should provide whatever restraint was necessary… however I was outnumbered and the patient slumped drugged in his chair. When I came to the last four words, 'Give place to Christ' I knew that the work of the spirit had triumphed… and a blessed weakness came over me. Next day I was reassured by one of the doctors that they believed the patient was cured. I went to see the young man who appeared to have grown younger and more vital… his attitude was one of friendliness. He refused samples of human and animal blood. In his own best interests it was agreed that he should undergo a degree of restraint for a period… the young man's family were delighted with the news; eventually he was pronounced completely cured.

Dr Omand has some interesting words to say on the subject of exorcism. Sometimes, he says, an operation goes wrong. Would anyone say that therefore all surgery should be banned? In the same way an exorcism can go wrong. Individual churchmen can do what they like as the Church of England has no official attitude to exorcism. However, one commonly held fallacy is that no special gift is needed in the practitioner. Special gifts *may* be needed.

Dr Omand speaks about blessing the salt and water used in the exorcism – this is in reality the exorcism of the elements themselves. There is a prayer, or ceremony, to this end of which the essentials are as follows; the priest says aloud:

I exorcise thee, O creature of salt, by the living God… that thou mayest by this exorcism be made beneficial to the faithful… and that in whatsoever place thou shalt be sprinkled, all illusions… of Satan may be chased away…

I exorcise thee, O creature of water, in the name of God the Father Almighty… that thou mayest by this exorcism have power to chase away all the strength of the enemy, and put him to flight…

Let this mixture of salt and water be made in the name of the Father, the Son and the Holy Ghost.

EXORCISM PAST AND PRESENT

It is not fair, as Omand and others have pointed out, to use modern-day criteria to explain the understanding of people in former centuries. A definition is needed that would have been understood by people of that time. Graham Twelftree writing in his book *Jesus the Exorcist* (page 19) gives us one:

> *Exorcism was a form of healing used when demons or evil spirits were thought to have entered a person and to be responsible for sickness and was the attempt to control and cast out or expel evil spiritual beings or demons from people.*

Deriving from the picture of exorcism in the New Testament, there was, says Twelftree, the notion that demons and the exorcist must, sometimes willingly, confront each other; that the exorcist, often only in general terms, was believed to need to address or abuse the demon; that the personal force of the exorcist was thought to be sufficient to effect success without mechanical or physical aids; that the conversation between demon and exorcist and the conversion of the sufferer were also elements of the exorcism. He goes on to say that data shows that exorcisms were thought successful as a result of the interplay of three factors: (1) the exorcist; (2) a source of power-authority; and (3) the ritual or form of application of that power-authority against the offending spiritual being.

Consequently, it was of great importance to know the identity of the demon the exorcist was confronting, and to know that what he was about to do had the backing of a supreme Power. Often these exorcisms used the Power-authority (God or Christ) to impose a sort of restraint or restriction on the demon. Speaking special words or performing some special activity often accompanied the exorcism; sometimes diagrams, charms or amulets were employed. It may be claimed, however, that the greatest exorcist who ever lived did not employ any of these methods. He was unique, though in many ways a child, as He had to be, of His time. Twelftree says:

> *Jesus was the first one to link the relatively common phenomenon of exorcism with eschatology [the doctrine, as I understand it, of final future states]. Though Jesus is not unique in combining the role of teacher and exorcist, he stands out in his era as one who not only relied on his own resources for success in exorcism, but at the same time claimed that in them God himself was in action and that that action was the coming of God's eschatological kingdom.*

There is a contrast between the form of exorcism seen in the New Testament and that often practised today. In the Bible it is not a dramatic ceremony. Present-day Christian exorcism is mainly in the domain of the 'minor' when it concerns individuals, or more commonly now, it may be claimed, concerns places.

According to Dom Robert Petitpierre (*Exorcism*, page 35): 'Fundamentally Christian exorcism is no more and no less than a miracle performed by Jesus to clean up the mess in the world about us.' Minor exorcism, he says, consists of nothing more than a simple prayer while the use of blessed oil, used to anoint the forehead of the troubled person, can be of much efficacy. Exorcism itself should be regarded by Christians as an act of faith in the life, victory and power of Christ. As the act of exorcism is an assertion of faith it follows that the exorcist also has to act in faith.

Petitpierre, who had much experience of the exorcism of places, mentions that many 'haunted' places are the abodes of earthbound spirits endeavouring to attract attention to secure release from their condition. Sometimes the 'ghosts' are of sinners 'who get stuck on the other side' and cannot move on, but are filled with remorse for wrongdoing while alive. Some specially mischievous spirits are the poltergeists, whose name comes from the German verb *poltern*, which means to crash about, be noisy. These do not appear to be especially receptive to rites of exorcism – but only because they are of a different order from other spirits, ghosts or evil entities. Poltergeist activity is believed to be generated by human thoughts and by human activity, perhaps by electrical impulse from the brain, perhaps by the awesome power of the untapped regions of the human mind. It is not responsive to exorcism, which is directed at external influences, diabolic oppression and possession. Exorcism can deal only with non-human spirits.

Dr Robert Petitpierre takes us through an exorcist rite as he experiences it as a Catholic priest. It is interesting to see the elements of this and its stages, all the while remembering that the ritual is ages old, instituted to combat the evil spirits who had taken possession of one of God's people or places.

At the place or in the room, the exorcist should lead the prayers, which include the Lord's Prayer, a confession and absolution, a short reading from the Gospels with a request to our Lord for His help and an invocation of the Holy Spirit. The exorcist ought then to pronounce the form of exorcism, which may consist of only about three sentences. The sign of the cross is next made and the exorcist again says about three sentences of appeal, as it were, to God's help. Sprinkling and blessing next follow around the entire building, with the opening of all doors and cupboards. Pause for prayer is at all times important. Blessing of the house or building concludes this stage. The whole procedure, sprinkling and blessing is now gone through again. The whole group, including any members of the household, meet for a short prayer.

When the exorcism concerns a person a minor ceremony is often all that is required, but, as we have seen, if the person is believed possessed, then a major exorcism is needed which may take a long time or may even need to be repeated over a period of months. During this time the officiant will try to get the sufferer to make a confession and to become attached to a Christian church. The ceremony itself must always involve two priests, several attendants/helpers, and at least one person of the same gender as the victim – all of whom must be sympathetic to the deliverance ministry. No one unknown to the priest is allowed to attend, nor are children or animals. A church is the desirable venue. Wherever it is, the venue must be secure. The sufferer must never be left alone. People capable of restraining should be present. Finally, the exorcist should consider giving Holy Communion.

The people present should group around the patient, then the procedure as outlined above follows. All present must be committed Christians to lessen the danger of the evil spirit transferring to another.

The Exorcism Itself

'Binding' the devil is customary whereby in the Lord's name he is commanded not to injure anyone else. Then the exorcism itself follows. After the adjuration, again which should be only two or three sentences, the exorcist should exhale deeply or sprinkle holy water on the sufferer. There might be violent physical reactions. A final prayer is made and baptismal vows renewed. A final blessing is given while the officiant's hands are placed on the sufferer's head. The ultimate act may be the administration of Holy Unction – the anointing with holy oil – and the receiving of Holy Communion.

Human Christian contact is necessary afterwards in a caring atmosphere. Aftercare is very important, so that the victim is not left to sink or swim on his or her own.

This casting out of demons 'is the work of God through his church and a sign of the coming of his kingdom, the doing of his will and the deliverance from evil for which every member so faithfully prays; it is God's action, not ours, because the Kingdom, the Power and the Glory belong to him not to us' (Richards, *But Deliver Us from Evil*, page 161). Richards gives a formidable list of what exorcism is *not* (*see* the chapter 'Exorcism', section 'Christian Exorcism'). What it *is*, is a demonstration in power and love of the Lordship of Christ over His world. Many of the accounts of exorcisms follow a pattern of the exposing of the demons by the Spirit of Christ, their panic-stricken reaction causing physical manifestations, their reaction to the name of Jesus, and the final deliverance by the binding and driving out of the demons.

That failures of exorcism do occur has been mentioned, but in many cases neither the officiating cleric nor the patient have been ready; that is to say, they have not been adequately prepared for the ordeal. It is so easy to take the circumstance out of the context of deliverance and by so doing to make things worse. Speaking with the authority of Christ is essential if the duel is to be won – but it is far from simple. Diligent preparation of *all* involved is necessary.

We know that Catholic priests have to follow the guidelines laid down in the *Rituale Romanum*, but there are no such rules, except the one about reference to a bishop, for Anglican clergy; consequently, they have to draw on the experience of the diocesan team, or 'local exorcist' minister, as a first step. Perhaps a definite policy is now required. There is a danger of relying on a 'qualified' exorcist who will have to shoulder the burden. Compassion for the sufferer and authority for the exorcist are needed if the rite is to be successful. The authority comes from a feeling that God is with the exorcist. He must feel himself invulnerable to anything the possessing demon can throw at him.

THE CATHOLIC RITUAL

The *Rituale Romanum* or Roman Catholic Ritual, originally written in Latin and dating back centuries, lays down the procedures for most ceremonies of the Church. It is updated from time to time, each time tending to place less emphasis on the reality of demons and possession. Nevertheless, it still embodies the elements of rituals and procedures which have obtained since the first edition in the papacy of Pope Paul V (1605–21), and major reissues under Pope Benedict XIV (1740–58).

The 'rules' for exorcism are contained in '*Titulus X*' (Section Ten), '*Caput I*' (Chapter or Heading One), 'Concerning the Exorcizing of Possessing Demons' (roughly translated). It is very thorough, at approximately 7,000 words plus, and for reasons of space we cannot go into detail here. (For a more complete translation of the exorcism section refer to Leonard Ashley's book *The Complete Book of Devils and Demons*, the section entitled 'Dealing with the Devil'.)

Here are the main stages in the ritual:

1. *The Litany;*
2. *Psalm 54;*
3. *Adjuration (calling on God's aid);*
4. *Gospel readings;*
5. *Preparatory prayer;*
6. *First exorcism;*
7. *Prayer for success;*
8. *Second exorcism (a lengthy process of commands to the evil spirit);*
9. *Another prayer for success;*
10. *Third and final exorcism (similar procedure to 8);*
11. *Final prayers.*

The exorcizing of a house or place has a slightly different form of words. Clearly such a 'Handbook' has immense value for Roman Catholic clergy who perform exorcisms.

INFLUENTIAL LITERATURE

Clearly, the very existence of the Roman Ritual implicitly acknowledges the need for written procedures regarding exorcism. Equally clear is that there is no 'modern' dilution in the traditional belief in the power and reality of demon oppression. Just as much concerned with the reality of belief in demons is the treatise of Johann Weyer, one of the few voices speaking out against the prevailing witchcraft mania. His book is an impressive volume of some 350,000 words in Latin published in 1583, entitled *De Praestigiis Daemonum* (Concerning the Deceptions of Demons). Weyer, though believing implicitly in the existence of demons, nevertheless attacked the idea of witches *per se*. Indeed, he refers to the persecuted as 'innocent women'. It was in some measure due to Weyer and others like him that the belief in witchcraft was eventually undermined. The book itself exhibits an encyclopedic knowledge of several disciplines and treats its subject in great depth. Some of the headings are: the Devil, his origins; magicians; lamiae (a type of female demon); their afflictions and the afflicted; and the punishment of magicians. Within these main headings is a myriad of detail. The book is a most interesting insight into an educated mind of the day on a subject of abiding interest. The full text can be read in the edition of 1991, published by the Centre for Medieval Texts, New York, under the general editorship of George Mora, foreword by John Weber.

On the other hand, there is the equally influential tome of Nicholas Remy of 1595, titled *Demonolatry*, which, apart from showing the utmost conviction in the reality of demons, links witches irrevocably with them. For Remy witchcraft and diabolism go hand in hand. As a judge in many witch trials, Remy thought it about time that he spoke out against these evil people. The book, he says, draws on the capital trials of some 900 persons who within the last fifteen years have in Lorraine paid the penalty of death for the crime of witchcraft. He, like thousands of others, had not the slightest doubt of the rightness of their cause. It is a terrifying book to read knowing that innocent people were mercilessly put to death for a mistaken ideology. Details of an edition are given in the Bibliography.

The *Malleus Maleficarum* (the Hammer of Witchcraft) of 1486 by the two Dominicans Kramer and Sprenger is fascinating for its blind allegiance to the concept of witches being in league with the Devil or demons. It is a thoroughly evil book in its recommendations for the apprehension, torture and killing of accused persons, mainly women, merely on the say-so of what was often a jealous rival or simply malicious neighbour. The tragedy was that it dictated practice for hundreds of years. Clerics who should have been models of compassion were instead murderous monsters who believed in what they were doing out of religious zeal. It is a salutary lesson in the evil, extremism and bigotry that dogma can lead to. Details of an obtainable edition are also given later. (*See also* the Appendices for the exorcism ceremony; the ceremony for exorcist ordinands; guidelines for exorcism counsellors.)

Most of the writings on the subject during the witchcraft era were wholeheartedly in favour of extirpating the evil that was believed to be everywhere and enthusiastically espoused the cause of hunting down and killing witches on the flimsiest of evidence. Only a few brave souls attempted the contrary view. I have mentioned one, Weyer. As time went by – slowly – the idea of demonic persons as guilty of heinous and sacrilegious crime gave way to the belief that expelling evil spirits (i.e. exorcism) was the right way forward.

CHAPTER SEVEN

THE EXORCIST AND THE POSSESSED

I n the face of often extraordinary situations, rare attributes are required in an exorcist, strong and unwavering qualities which will strengthen the chances of success in the fearsome battle against so great an evil. Among this preparation are spiritual fortification and, as Jesus said, fasting and prayer. The reason that some exorcisms do not work may be that proper preparations have not been made.

Often the causes of so-called infestation can be identified. However, in a disturbing five per cent of cases there is no rational explanation. In these instances the Solemn Exorcism is required. Examples of personal experience of exorcisms highlight the dangers that may await the exorcist.

It is unclear why some people are attacked, for it can happen to anyone. However, good-living people seem to be of most interest to the Devil, for there he can do the most harm in destroying the victim's spirit, as well as weakening the faith of all those involved.

A SUITABLE EXORCIST

Some exorcisms are successful, but, as we have seen, some are not. Well-known exorcists naturally emphasize their 'successes' and play down their failures – if any. Reading the literature about exorcism (or deliverance) suggests that most cases of exorcism 'gone wrong' or ending inconclusively are done by relatively unknown people, clerics that is to say. Why should there be any failure, especially where the exorcists are 'trained' or ordained in the Office of Exorcism? And why do some have a good track record in this difficult field? Generally, failure is attributed to 'one of those things', which may mean the demon is too strong or that the exorcist lacks something, perhaps conviction or experience or whatever.

Essential Preparation

I believe that lack of proper preparation is indeed one of the main causes of failure, but I would go further: nearly all unsuccessful exorcisms have their root in the personality or nature of the exorcist, which is not adequate to the task. This is, mainly, the reason why the demon triumphs in appearing to be the stronger party. The fact is that many attempting exorcism are not spiritually fortified – sufficient to combat and overthrow the formidable forces of evil they are facing. The exorcist, we have learned, needs to have special qualities – there is a whole litany of them – before he is chosen to attempt the task. But these *by themselves* are not enough. As Jesus Himself said to His Apostles, when they had to confess to failure in their attempts at a particular exorcism: 'This kind comes out only by prayer and fasting.' We may add that Jesus was, on this occasion particularly, stressing the importance of prayer and fasting. It is, however, clear from reading the Scriptures that a period of prayer and fasting was *always* necessary for casting out evil spirits.

Christ and His disciples, to whom he gave the power of casting out spirits, were mostly ordinary men, artisans and fishermen in the main, only Matthew, a tax-gatherer, perhaps being the exception, and not even he if his role was more of an enforcer, to use modern parlance. As followers of Jesus they were bound to devote themselves to a main tenet of His – that is, the need for prayer at all times to give direction to their lives – while frugal fare, it is to be supposed, was usual with them.

Fasting in the Biblical sense is not necessarily synonymous with the complete abstinence from food and drink, which itself would render the exorcist physically inadequate to the task. Whatever the interpretation, the point is that the followers of Christ were much better prepared to undertake the confrontation and overthrow of possessing demons than we are today. By 'we' I mean the clergy, both Protestant and Catholic, who undertake the daunting job. The words of Jesus to his followers, emphasizing the importance of prayer and fasting as related in the Gospel of Matthew (6:19–35), are apposite:

> *Do not lay up for yourselves treasure on earth… but lay up for yourselves treasure in heaven… for where your treasure is, there will be your heart also. No one can serve two masters, for either he will hate the one and love the other… You cannot serve God and mammon. Therefore I tell you do not be anxious about your life, what you shall eat, what you shall drink, not about your body, what you shall put on. Is not life more than food and the body more than clothing? And which of you by being anxious can add one cubit to his span of life… Consider the lilies of the field… Therefore do not be anxious… your heavenly Father knows that you need all these things. But seek first His kingdom and His righteousness and all these things shall be yours as well.*

The context of modern life is largely to blame. We have become used to the comforts of society, and we find it difficult to give them up, even in such a cause as freeing someone from evil influences. How many of us throw away our worldly goods and follow Him, as Christ said was necessary? On another occasion He said that it was easier for a camel to go through the eye of a needle than for a rich man to enter heaven. We may of course regard many of Christ's utterances as allegorical, but the innate meaning is clear. Simplicity in behaviour, frugality in manner, lack of ostentation and of any kind of excess was His rule. His disciples manifested these qualities and in this respect were much more suited to confront evil in possession of Man than we are today. How many of us can claim to live up to the rule or vow, at least in the Roman Catholic Church, of voluntary poverty and scrupulous adherence to absolute obedience? It is precisely in these areas that many clergy of today are lacking. Days of prayer and fasting are regarded as too onerous and as a result lip service only is often given to the solemn occasion. We are not sufficiently prepared, with our desirable houses, cars, house-keepers, secretaries, money in the bank or schemes for making money, ambitions or whatever, for the enormous task of casting out the devil.

And the Devil knows this. He knows that underneath the show of bravado there is a soft underbelly, a weakness, a vulnerability which he can exploit. As a result he knows he it is who will emerge the victor. The unfortunate sufferer remains unchanged in all this – if he is lucky. Often he is left worse off than before.

THE FIVE PER CENT

I am talking now about the five per cent of cases which have no rational explanation: in psychological, physical or emotional terms – cases in which we must pause and reflect that we are dealing with the unexplainable. Because it does occur. In these cases the major form of exorcism, the Solemn Exorcism, is needed. There are people who believe they are in need of exorcism when they are not. Usually the minor exorcism does the trick – psychologically.

Most often these days it is the exorcism of places that is called for. No doubt people's imaginations can run riot regarding a place in a way that they cannot if the focus is a person. Places are alleged to be haunted by 'ghosts' or plagued by poltergeists always accompanied by strange noises. Insubstantial figures may be seen by several witnesses.

Often the reason, if it can be called this, can be traced back and dealt with – or nothing seems to do any good. Occasionally, one is forced to the conclusion that there is genuine demonic influence at work. What then? Cases I have been involved in may provide some answers.

Thorough investigation into referrals where angels fear to tread is vitally necessary beforehand. Sometimes the basic problem is made clear in a short time; others may take longer. One of the simplest to diagnose is the projection syndrome, which has been mentioned earlier, in which the sufferer is, in reality, the focus of a group's attention, family or other, who project their own fears and/or inadequacies on to a scapegoat – the sufferer as victim. The help and advice of a professional team, including a medically qualified person, is invaluable at all times, and especially at these times.

Also invaluable is any knowledge of psychology, especially that pertaining to behaviour, and of psychiatry, which will help the exorcist to arrive at a correct diagnosis. There have been many cases where a wrongly diagnosed case of possession has to all intents and purposes turned an obsessed person into one possessed. Investigation of places can be less intimidating than investigation of an individual, in so far as the phenomena cited may not (and usually do not) manifest themselves. The most tiring part of place exorcism is the interviewing of all concerned, getting worthwhile answers and trying to prevent collusion, which is always to be suspected! Trickery is sometimes revealed, but not often. People are usually genuinely frightened.

I have always been surprised at how frequently people associated in some way with reputed possession (of persons, of places) have believed implicitly that the cause is demon infestation. Naturally not everyone believes this, but even in the late twentieth century I would say that *most* do. Even non-believers admit there is a Principle of Evil (note the capital letters) which does affect humanity, but for others the Devil or his demons are alive and well. If people have been eye-witnesses to mysterious movements of objects and have heard strange sounds, if the atmosphere becomes chill and foreboding, if shadowy figures are seen, and if strong odours are detected, who may gainsay them? I can only say that in my experience, though I have been unaccountably conscious of something not right, nothing I have personally experienced in places has been of this order *except* in the case of poltergeist disturbance at the time of the exorcism ceremony proper.

Exorcism, or as it is increasingly called the deliverance ministry, is in my view one aspect of the struggle, here on earth in this day, between good and evil, and it is given us as a weapon with which the better to fight this war. It is a healing ministry which strives to bring sick souls back into the Christian fold and for them to gain peace once more. While believing this wholeheartedly, I have to say that, after the initial feeling of fatigue and weakness subsequent on a presumed successful exorcism, there is experienced a euphoria bordering on the sin of pride! As a former Roman Catholic cleric, I freely confess it. As an ex-cleric I can write about it.

LET THE EXORCIST BEWARE – PERSONAL EXPERIENCES

An aspect of the healing ministry that has unfortunately come more and more to prominence is the incidence of suspected abuse in early life, physical and/or sexual, which has caused many people to believe that they are possessed when the memories, repressed for years, come eventually to the surface. Whether these victims or their abusers were possessed, I am not sure!

The fashion for 'proving' False Memory Syndrome has not helped the exorcist trying to find his way in an already well-nigh impenetrable jungle of human emotions. The women involved were supposed to recall childhood traumas, often prompted by so-called therapists who believed that existing problems could be explained by revealing early-life abuse (usually sexual) hidden in the subconscious. It would be superficial to deny that in some instances this was the truth, but it is equally to be suspected that these 'memories' were deliberately implanted and fostered by 'professionals' who wished to make a name for themselves. This whole area is, or can be, tied into ritual or Satanic abuse, which appears to be becoming prevalent – at least to judge from the headline cases in the newspapers of recent years. Whether this is really so of course is open to debate. By far the majority were and are females who had been born into Satanism or sexual aberrancy, and had therefore been 'introduced' to the practices their families espoused. False, or Repressed, Memory Syndrome, however, has been taken very seriously and a deal of research has been done on it.

One piece of research has made some cogent recommendations applicable to agencies concerned and those dealing with the clergy, and these are particularly apposite. The proposal is that all clergy and trainee clergy should be educated about ritual abuse and dissociative disorders, and the Church should be prepared to work with other disciplines, set up a network of information, educate the parishes and establish spiritual advisers on the paranormal. I wholeheartedly endorse this.

Wise words on the subject of possession versus induced dementia have been spoken by Kevin Logan (*Satanism and the Occult*, page 196) in relation to the question: what can be said to those who think the Devil and evil spirits are myths?

> *Many have experienced the power of Satan and it occasionally produces the logic: 'If an unholy spirit exists then maybe it's worth looking for the opposite'.*
>
> *Just as there are millions who can testify to experiencing a real holy spirit as they come into a personal living relationship with Jesus, there are also increasing numbers who can testify to the reality of an unholy spirit.*
>
> *When you see the effects of the Devil in people's lives, lingering doubts about the existence of an evil personality disappear. When you see occult victims released from their obvious bondages, the doubts fly out of the window.*

Firstly, possession can be genuine, of this I have no doubt. But, secondly, it can also be self-induced, as has been noted. The state can be self-induced. Thirdly, as happened more often in former times, though it still occurs today, possession can be induced by others for their own ends – in susceptible people. As a former practising exorcist, it was vital that I could discriminate between the three states. I do not claim to have always succeeded; occasionally, I have been duped or led up the garden path. But I would like to claim that in the great majority the outcome has been satisfactory.

Manifestations of possession seem to be constant through the ages, the only difference being that greater mention was made of demons and devils in earlier accounts, clearly indicating the ubiquitous beliefs of the time. I find nothing over the top in Kerner's records of states of possession, written decades ago. (Kerner was a German physician with much experience of treating the possessed.) Speaking of a woman disturbed by diabolic influence, among other things, he records that:

During five months all the resources of medicine were tried on her in vain… On the contrary two demons now spoke in her, who… barked like dogs or mewed like cats…

Old accounts of possession can be compared with a recent example. The famous Loudun case (Sargant, *The Mind Possessed*, page 48) had one of the nuns possessed by the demon Asmodeus:

Asmodeus was not long in manifesting his supreme rage, shaking the girl backwards and forwards a number of times and making her strike like a hammer with such rapidity that her teeth rattled and sounds were forced out of her throat. That between these movements her face became completely unrecognisable, her glance furious, her tongue prodigiously large, long, and hanging down out of her mouth, livid and dry…

A phenomenon which I have often observed is an uncritical acceptance by a sufferer of beliefs which normally would not have been accepted without an examination reasonable in normal circumstances. Thus, it is possible for a patient to hear something which she immediately adopts as an integral part of her belief system, even, I would say, of her very nature. Sometimes these adoptions are ridiculous, such as believing oneself to be a fox or goat, or whatever. Often the imagination can run riot, as in this not so untypical tale related by a female patient who claimed to have seen the Devil and who subsequently had to be admitted into a hospital:

He [the Devil] was tall with scales and legs ending in claws; he stretched out his arms as if to seize me; he had red hair and his body ended in a great tail, like a lion's, with hair at the end; he grimaced, laughed and seemed to say: 'I shall have her!'

She herself was convinced of the reality of her diabolic invasion. We, as exorcists, were not so sure!

Hysteria, schizophrenia and Multiple Personality Disorder are illnesses of the nervous system; many present-day patients are aware of this (provided they are still to a degree *compos mentis*), and in contrast to the above they blame their own nervous systems which have let then down for their state – rather than attributing their malady to diabolic influence, as would have been axiomatic years ago. Unfortunately, such cases are not the usual run. Sargant in his *The Mind Possessed* (page 57) encapsulates this idea nicely:

The fact that many disturbed people nowadays accept explanation of their troubles which differ from those customary in the past should not obscure the fundamental identity of the mental processes at work.

It does seem as if more people are interested in the occult nowadays, ouija boards, black magic, spiritualism, even witchcraft (or witch activities – some claim to be 'good witches' doing 'white magic') and the like. These *outré* interests can lead on to mental or spiritual disturbance, in my experience. They basically all call on the aid of beings in the 'other world' – spirits of some kind. The original subject of Blatty's book *The Exorcist,* on which the notorious film was based, was involved by his aunt, a practising spiritualist, in the ouija board, which fact was thought by many to have triggered off Douglas Deen's (the real name) possession syndrome. Some of the activities alleged to have taken place in the course of Deen's sufferings I have met with in other cases, other circumstances.

Places, as I have said, have not been so dramatic, but people – that is another thing. Manifestations of possession, such as raging, blasphemy, contortion, obvious lying, vomiting, shaking and screaming, are not of themselves *proof* of genuine demonic possession – though they are unnerving and scary, which of course must not show in the exorcist. I have experienced all of these; they seem to be par for the course. What, as I confessed already, I was never able to understand, though 'explanations' are given, was the ability shown by *some* to speak and apparently understand (by replying) languages they had never studied. Equally, I was always mystified by the seeming ability of some energumens (diabolically possessed) to read private thoughts, even to the extent of speaking about incidents in one's life that no outsider could possibly have known. Trying to ignore such revelations when confronted with them is very difficult indeed! A show of great strength (when the sufferer had with great difficulty to be held down) was also unnerving, but is more capable of credible explanation in the light of anecdotes that have testified to supernormal feats when a loved one's life has been at risk – the lifting of a car by a woman, for example. This *can* be a case of mind over matter. But the other two – ?

A Dangerous Ministry

It can be a dangerous ministry as well. In *The Exorcist* one priest drops dead and the other falls to his death from the window. Obviously these occurrences were intended to heighten the dramatic tension in the film, but unfortunately they are not flights of fancy. Deaths have happened. Why is not clear. It may be due to unbearable tension; it may be due to the demon, enraged, transferring into the body of the hated exorcist. It may be purely natural causes. There are many less dramatic stories, such as the minister himself becoming possessed or at least exhibiting the same symptoms as the person he is trying to help.

In nearly all the cases I have known, the patient (a word preferable to 'victim', 'sufferer' or 'client') has spoken in an unnatural voice, perhaps a deep male voice issuing from a normally softly spoken female, but this can be faked, although I personally found a masquerade hard to believe. It did always seem as if a personality different from the patient's was speaking. Given the torrent of blasphemy and foul language, it was hard to decide otherwise. But, as I say, these things can be faked, difficult though it may be. The word 'Jesus' always produced a violent reaction, violent in a spoken sense, from the 'other' voice. Conversations, if so we may call them, were, it seemed, with the possessing entity, who replied as if speaking for the patient or more likely ignoring the existence of the possessed. On occasion the demon, if so it was, would use the plural pronoun 'we'; on others it would be the singular 'I'. It was difficult to discern a pattern. Every circumstance was different. An exorcist's predicament can be and usually is morally difficult; I do not mean from the aspect of being unworthy, but because it is fundamental to a religious person to accept that *whatever* is done in this world, particularly in the field of possession, is done by God's permission. To be confronted by what appears to be evil incarnate is almost to be lured into the belief that two Principles exist in the universe: a Principle of Good and a Principle of Evil. But of course this cannot be so: belief in dualism, two equal and opposing forces, is heretical. Belief in one God, the Creator and Origin of all, is absolutely vital throughout the exorcism ritual – or risk failure! Lack of absolute confidence is a main reason for the ineffectiveness (or worse) of some exorcisms.

WHY ARE SOME PEOPLE ATTACKED?

The fundamental question is: why are some people attacked and not others? The answer, or one of them, it seems to me, is that the assailed have had some point of weakness in them or their background, a blemish in which they were vulnerable, and that this obtained in apparently good-living, righteous people. It might be adduced that it is precisely this type of person the Devil *would* attack as demonstrating his power all the more. Of course, possession or obsession or invasion, call it what you like, is no respecter of people. It just as frequently occurs in 'ordinary' people, the unassuming, those lacking in education, as in others. Maybe these latter are more responsive to suggestion, to put it at its mildest. Whatever the choice, the purpose is the same: to bring about the destruction of the victim's soul or spirit and to weaken the faith (or trust) of all those in any way involved.

In some cases I discerned that the 'possession' was not of a diabolical origin, but was rather more in the nature of a 'haunting' by dead spirits, relations or at least people who had had some connection with the afflicted person in life. I judged this by what the possessed person said or what was said by the possessor. These cases did not seem to me to be particularly malevolent – though they certainly were not benevolent!

'Possession' by, from all accounts, living persons was in my judgement always a sort of *cri de coeur*, a cry for help, on the part of the patient, who in some way became obsessed (in the normal meaning) with another human being, generally as a potential lover or potential enemy, with all stations in between. The minor exorcism, also called the Simple or Ordinary Exorcism, was all that was needed in these cases. Apart from prayers, blessings and asperges (sprinkling with holy water), reassurance that someone or some group *cares* usually accomplishes the mission.

All exorcisms, certainly major exorcisms, also known as the Solemn or Long Exorcism, must command, not entreat or cajole, the domineering spirit to come out in the name of God or Christ; in coming out to harm no one (which means not to infest anyone around); and to go elsewhere, which may mean hell, anywhere where its master dwells. I personally did not enquire of the demon his name, although this procedure is approved of by the Roman Catholic Church. I never could see the reason for it – or its efficacy. After all, in the Scriptures Christ did not always ask for the demon's name. I am willing to own, however, that the eliciting of a name has a long and seemingly effective pedigree – but might not the outcome have been the same anyway? Who can say?

Another controversial subject is the laying on of hands – and when precisely? Christ Himself rarely touched demented people. The Church's encouragement of the procedure is not, therefore, so much from Biblical authority (though there is a little), as from the fact that the laying on of hands is symbolic of healing, and as such is thought to bring comfort to the sufferer. It is also a form of blessing: the idea that a consecrated person's (such as a priest's) hands may have a curative effect by unseen and unheard intercession with the Almighty. Touching, according to clerical thinking, may have the danger of contamination by bodily transference of the evil spirit from the possessed to the minister, especially while the act of exorcism is still taking place. For this reason, and because I thought it more suitable, I always performed this act towards the end of the ritual. But I *did* perform it. I thought it essential. Deliverance when it did come was sometimes patent – accompanied by a moan or a groan, simply by a beatific facial expression, or by a sudden resumption of physical normality. Often, however, the deliverance (or exorcism) was accompanied by – nothing that could be discerned! Great faith on the exorcist's part is needed on these occasions: faith that the task has been achieved.

Which leads me on to the need to repeat exorcism rites. This happens, of course, because it is seen that the first ministration has not succeeded. It does happen, but should not necessarily be taken as a sign of failure. Exorcism to be successful needs not only a suitable minister in all respects, but a receptive subject as well. The person must be ready for the ceremony and/or be basically willing to be 'cured', which often involves renunciation of the sin or flaw which occasioned the dementia in the first place. He or she may not be prepared the first time, but may be on subsequent occasions. This not infrequently is the case.

Over a period of time practising this ministry, it is possible, on the one hand, to become just a little bit blasé, a little over-confident, if one's record has been good, *or*, on the other, somewhat despondent over evil manifesting itself in one's fellow men and women. Either way, it is very likely that encounters with wicked forces, powers for evil, over a long period can result, may result, in personal undesirable mental and emotional states. More than a few exorcists have had mental, emotional or nervous breakdowns attributable to their lurid and often horrific experiences. It is a great and holy calling, but it is very demanding – for some, too demanding.

Even then the exorcist has not finished. In some ways the real test is beginning: the aftercare. A delivered person needs to be looked after, never forgotten, nurtured in the ways of the Church, befriended by Christian carers, prayed for continuously – and as such is a constant drain on nervous energy, no matter how willingly it is given.

EXORCISM OF PLACES

Treating 'haunted' places, as I have said, has always been less traumatic for me. I think people, that is to say, those who discharge the ministry, do differ in their receptivity to phenomena and, by corollary, in their capacity to experience, some might say imagine, preternatural happenings. Maybe I am not naturally credulous (I don't want this to sound as if I am implying that others are), and do not have, at least as regards places, the gift, as it is sometimes called, of discernment. I always felt a little 'flat' after an attempted exorcism of a place, knowing that disturbances, though stopping for a time, may start up again later, possibly after years. It is a long time to wait after so much effort!

Also, in my experience, most of the reported strange happenings were nothing more than projections in the minds of people in some way connected with the scene; by infection these stories impregnated the minds of others who did not have necessarily any true contact with the area. I must assert, however, that it would be the height of arrogance to ignore or dismiss others' assertions just because they do not fit in with mine, or my experience. I trust I have never done this.

Causes of the Infestation

Causes of the infestation of places are variously interpreted as 'ghosts' (that is, souls of the dead), human sin, place memories and demonic influence, which

Infesting demons confronted by goodness

includes poltergeists. Ghosts are manifestations of people who, because of their excessive attachment to things of this world, linger on after death; human sin often involves tragic lives and deaths; place memories are often encountered in situations where items are especially associated with a dead person and their ways when alive.

Probably, in my estimation, the most frequent occurrences of disturbances in places are on the sites of former practices which were at least occult and generally Satanic. It seems as if malignant spirits are bent on wrecking anything smacking of good intent on their erstwhile patch. These places may call for exorcism as a 'cure'. Often it is possible to sense that things are not right, that there is an evil presence. One *can* rely on one's instinct – but, if it leads one astray, it is hard to justify the action taken. Human sin, as I said earlier, usually encompasses tragedy of some sort, but the place may be simply where a human vice was practised, such as sexual misbehaviour, deviance or abuse. Sites also where centuries ago pagan rites were held, involving human sacrifice, worship of false gods, cruel rituals, can get a bad reputation.

John Richards in *But Deliver Us from Evil* (page 212) has a fitting summary:

> *There would seem to be three different types of force which may be operating… 1) the impersonal: place memories…; 2) the demonic: invited either deliberately or accidentally… 3) human influence: poltergeists,… and the whole spectrum of sin and greed and domination to which humans are so prone.*

THE CONCEPT OF BLAME

Just as the denial of free will (see page 60) can mean that individuals are not to blame for their own actions, so it often seemed to me that some people described themselves as possessed in order to escape the consequences of their actions: a sort of evasion of responsibility. Related to this concept is the case of the abused (youngish) person who claims to be possessed by a demon who in their eyes suffered the abuse – and therefore to get rid of the demon was to rid themselves of the guilt, which rightly or mostly wrongly they felt. Blaming a demon is often a type of coping mechanism for such people, who are convinced they are in need of exorcism or some form of deliverance.

For many people, afflicted in some way or not, illness is equated with sin: the theory that sinners are punished in this world by the Devil. Some Christian groups subscribe to this belief; getting involved with them, as is frequently the case in the deliverance ministry, is usually a hindrance to effective and permanent healing. It cannot be helpful to disturbed people to be encouraged in the belief that they are possessed. When, or if, these disturbed people are 'healed', it is hailed by all who know them as a latter-day miracle. This reaction is undesirable and over the top. The last thing a healing minister wants is to be regarded as some sort of a freak – or genius. He knows, and wants others to know, that without God's power he is nothing.

Psychiatric patients loom large in the exorcist's case work. These are people who do need medical help, but in some instances refer themselves, or are referred, to the Church in the first place. Some people I have seen have undoubtedly been mad or demented, and I could do nothing for them. They were not receptive to the healing ministry of the Church; they were incapable of it. Basically they did not believe themselves to be possessed. What they did believe was impossible to fathom. On the other hand, I do believe there are some patients in mental hospitals who could benefit from Christian deliverance.

Many illnesses, initially mental which in turn may affect the body, are known to be stress related. If an individual is tormented by demons, real or imaginary, warring inside him, seeking control, is it surprising that this same individual is going to suffer stress? Some people I have ministered to, have been so 'distressed' that they have been incapable of normal everyday tasks. Some were senile and it was difficult to help them, especially when they refused to acknowledge age as being responsible, but preferred to blame a possessing spirit. There is the belief on the part of some groups of Christians that disease can be brought about by demon possession. With due deference to the effects of stress, I personally have never believed it. But of course in this sphere can anyone claim to have a monopoly on truth? What one *has* to believe is that help is possible, and that such help is evidence of Christ's power.

SOME SPECIAL PROBLEMS

Ministering to the aged has its own peculiar problems, but perhaps the greatest problems are presented by pubescent girls and young women generally. It seems as if the female gender is either more attuned to the supernatural than the male, or more naturally inclined to suppose the existence of strange phenomena. I think it is a bit of both. Certainly, the greater part of my efforts have been expended on individual females or on places that have had predominantly women as their main players. Females can be harder to deal with in any case, in my experience exhibiting much more frequently than men the symptoms of hysteria and hallucination. Also, the sexual aspect can be a problem, where some women have resorted, consciously or unconsciously, to sexual stratagems either as a status-enhancing role (the seduction of a priest) or as a diverting and time-wasting device. Sometimes it has been the exhibition of lewd movements or postures which could be due to a possessing evil spirit. The occasions when physical restraint or rather calming is called for, as in the case of female protagonists in disturbed houses and the like, can be hazardous, especially when the lower limbs or body of a female are seemingly affected, perhaps in a convulsive state.

On occasion I have been called in to investigate troubles at the home of a family, especially affecting the husband and wife. Often they would adduce a type of poltergeist disturbance or strange sights and sounds. In most cases the calling in of the priest was, I believe, a substitute for a marriage counsellor; it was clearly thought that recourse to the consolations of religion was the lesser of two evils! Some of these situations could be tricky, as I often found marital or sexual difficulties to be at the bottom of the trouble. I never found the need for deliverance in these cases – perhaps healing of a kind would be more appropriate.

In cases where I did think there might be a diabolic influence, where a ceremony would be called for, I had in theory the choice of a minor or major exorcism. In practice most of my exorcisms were of the short form, or Ordinary Exorcism, though in what I considered the serious cases I did employ the long form or Solemn Exorcism. Although the Roman Ritual lays down the form of exorcism in some detail, an individual exorcist is allowed some latitude in adaptation and omission. Generally speaking, one comes to the conclusion there is a spirit of evil by sensing an atmosphere of evil, of unnatural cold, of stench. When there is a constant babel of voices issuing from the human mouth trying to put off the minister, you may conclude that you have before you a genuine case of possession in which the devil must be silenced, then challenged. Tests for true demonic presence have been handed down through the centuries; they are by no means all manifested in any particular case. But they are always in the forefront of the exorcist's mind when face to face with a sufferer. Some of them are: fleeing or turning askance at the sight of a holy object, a sacred motion, such as the sign of the cross; jeering at or in any way poking fun at the Church or its clergy; trying to excite despair in onlookers; refusing discussion of the problem; and appearing unnaturally dejected or tormented. Add to this those extraordinary abilities mentioned earlier, and I believed an instance of true possession was before me. These symptoms do not belong to any medical condition.

It is taken for granted by all Christian exorcists that possession is not normally voluntary; voluntary possession combined with a disinclination to be freed is a task of another order of magnitude, but it can occur. The Long or Solemn Exorcism rite is then required. Occasionally I have had to repeat it.

Sometimes the simple laying on of hands (on a person's head), combined with prayers and blessings (and orders to the demon to come out), is sufficient in individual cases. However, I have known instances where I have tried to put my hands on a person's head and, as it were, met with some unseen and unknown force. I have exerted strength, but something seemed to resist. There was something there that did not want a priest's hands touching the head of one the Devil had claimed. This was the conclusion I was forced to accept. I have never been able to account for this phenomenon and neither have any of my fellow priests.

Working in this field entails close collaboration with medical men, colleagues and other exorcists. The 'team' has always been invaluable, especially for moral support – although strictly speaking this should not be necessary, but we are all human, with human frailties.

To conclude this section a quotation is apt. It is a description of demoniacal possession in a young person that, though it happened some time ago, is not untypical of some of the cases I have had to confront (professionalism prevents me from giving details of individual cases):

> *[There were]… loud cries and shouting. Her body, which went through a series of elaborate motions, was either in the throes of wild gyrations or catatonically motionless. Her*

legs became entangled, then disentangled, her arms twisted and disjointed, her wrists bent. Some of her fingers were stretched out straight, while others were twisted. The body was either bent in a semi-circle or loose-limbed. Her head at the time was thrown to the right or left or, when thrown back with vehemence, seemed to emerge from a bloated neck. The face alternately mirrored horror, disgust, anger and fury. It was bloated and showed shades of violet in its coloration.

This could all be simulated, of course – but I doubt it.

We can read the following cautionary words of 1583:

Before the priest undertakes an exorcism, he ought diligently to enquire into the life of the possessed, into his condition, reputation, health and other circumstances; and should talk them over with wise, prudent and instructed people, since the too credulous are often deceived and melancholics, lunatics and persons bewitched often declare themselves to be possessed and tormented by the devil; and these people are nevertheless more in need of a doctor than an exorcist.

These wise words are taken from the deliberations of the Synod of Rheims and are as valid now as they were then. Perhaps the only thing we would take issue with is the reference to those 'bewitched', which is to be understood in the context of the age.

THE DIAGNOSTIC EXORCIST

When enquiry has established that indeed there is a sudden and great change in a person, in speech and behaviour, then one must pause for reflection. Ally to this an apparent absence of physical illness and it may be that one has a case of possession. At any rate, these have been my criteria.

People can be obsessed by thoughts of domination by the forces of evil, namely the Devil, which may exhibit itself in a turning away from Christian ceremonies and objects. Though such people feel (literally) that they are demonically possessed, they are really not. In this situation, the exorcist is reminded of the saying, 'Fools rush in ... '. The ever-present danger for clerical exorcists is that, as Portia said, one can 'rush to judgement' – by virtue of the fact that the priest's whole background and moral training predispose him to making moral judgements. It is possible to see sin where none exists. Belief in the existence of malicious spirits is a credo of sacerdotal or priestly education. Because this is so, there are the dangers of a misdiagnosis. Some people are simply mad, and I have come across these cases; they are impervious to a restoration to normality by religious means because they are incapable of comprehension. But these cases are easily diagnosed. They clearly in my judgement needed psychiatric help. Some were obsessed by internal visions of evil spirits. Shakespeare summed it up nicely:

One sees more devils than vast hell can hold,
That is, the madman...

An interesting and valid comment has been made by F. X. Maquart in his article 'Exorcism and Diabolical Manifestation' (*Satan*, ed. Moeller, page 186), where he speaks of inexplicable events that in case of suspected possession 'imply divine intervention'. He says:

> *First we have [events] that nature cannot bring about in any way; second are things that nature could not do in a particular determinate manner (such as giving life to the dead); third, are events which while not above the powers of nature, are produced in non-natural ways [that is, sudden cures].*

It is in the light of these observations that puzzling cases have to be scrutinized.

The analogy between a doctor and an exorcist has often been made, with some validity. There is, however, one difference that must be emphasized. When faced with a difficult case, the doctor can refer the patient to a specialist. This is not an option for the exorcist. He has to adopt a holistic approach, and has to treat all the symptoms (at least initially), not of course to check on the medical opinion, in which he is not qualified anyway, but to ascertain whether all the facts have been covered. F. X. Maquart, *idem*, says:

> *Being habituated to theological reasoning, he [the exorcist priest] will tend to explain the facts by remote, universal, abstract or unobservable causes; his diagnoses will take on a moral complexion…*

Exorcists must always have this thought in the forefront of their minds!

Joseph De Tonquedec, an erudite Jesuit exorcist himself, spoke of unaccountable behaviour in persons who normally were docile and circumspect (Maquart, *idem*, page 193). His experiences were not unlike some of mine. I freely confess I always found this type of behaviour baffling. Here are his own words:

> *I have met with young girls who would spit out the sacred Host after having received It or keep It back in order to profane It in unworthy ways; and people who befouled the crucifix, trod the rosary underfoot…*

This is the reality of true possession. As Maquart (*idem*, page 198) says, 'If the facts already recognized as naturally inexplicable tend to an evil end, the theologian will legitimately conclude to the intervention of the devil.'

Jeanne Fery's Story

One of the most interesting and detailed accounts of a case of demonic possession is given by Pierre Debongnie in *Satan* (ed. Moeller), where he writes of the case of Jeanne Fery in France, 1584. It is well worth reading. Jeanne Fery was one of many well-known cases of the time, where people (usually young women, as Jeanne was) drew attention to themselves as victims of diabolical possession. Her case was apparently particularly interesting as she gained the ministrations of several Roman Catholic clergy. Attempts at exorcism were made, but to no permanent avail (at least initially). In her more lucid moments she wrote an 'autobiography' in which she detailed features of her states of 'possession', but the narrative is confused and contradictory in places, giving rise to suspicions that there was an element of pretence about her 'seizures'. Her exorcists also wrote accounts of her, but they seemed just as confused. Although an ordinary person basically, she clearly had an ambitious streak in her and was something of an exhibitionist.

Extracts from her autobiography are given, and the reports of the exorcists. It is an extraordinary and puzzling story. As the conclusion to the episode points out – what is the truth of the matter? Was it all true or partly so or mere fiction? She was clearly determined to make people believe her and wanted the actual exorcists to write their accounts. There is a large degree of agreement between the two. The main issue, as the conclusion states, is whether her story truly indicates unmistakable diabolic activity. Or on the contrary, was it all a trick, as Debongnie poses, to gain the ear and protection or patronage of high society, embodied in her case by the Archbishop of Cambray, who perhaps unwisely allowed the young woman to take up residence in his house? But that is another matter.

CONVERSATIONS WITH DEMONS

'Conversation' with the demon is believed to be very important. Careful note must be made of it so that analysis, if needed, can be made later. I have remarked earlier on the voice that emanates from the possessed, which is usually quite different from the normal (as one is told), such as a male voice issuing from a female. Many old accounts give quite lengthy and detailed conversation between the exorcist and the demon or between the demon and the possessed – the latter in the style of an interior monologue. This does not appear to happen so much now, perhaps because of the more immediate attention and succour given to victims, which does not allow the Devil to, as it were, gather his thoughts. Cynics, however, might say we are living in less credulous times.

In any event, the exorcist is urged to engage in dialogue with the demon, not the person, even if the conversation turns out to be a trifle one-sided. In theory, the demon should only answer when bidden or when expected, the exorcist trying to speak almost all the time. For example, questions clearly demand an answer. What is your name? How long have you been in possession? Thereafter it should be mostly a series of commands to the demon to obey, to get out and suchlike.

I have questioned possessing evil spirits and been given replies whose authenticity I have *later* disputed. At the time everything has to be taken at face value, without showing any semblance of doubt which would be seized on as weakness by any true self-respecting demon. Tones and timbres of voice can be simulated, even male for female. In the tense and oppressive atmosphere of an exorcism everything is heightened; and it is easy to imagine drastic voice changes even when the change is slight. All 'replies' coming out of the mouth of the patient are abusive, insolent and ambivalent. Sometimes they are almost witty in a malicious way. I have never experienced the small talk which some narratives display.

The above raises the fundamental question: is the personality divided and are there two natures in the one person at the time of possession? There is indeed a lack of communication between the two natures, so from this point of view they are separate. My contention is that at the time the invading spirit is capable of taking over the outward shows of personality but that basically the true nature remains, subservient indeed, but able to assert itself if it is *willing* to be helped by an external religious agency, namely a consecrated and devout priest. Otherwise exorcism could never work. I concur with Oesterreich (*Possession*, page 38) when he writes that 'the only adequate explanation of possession is that postulating a simple alteration in the functions of the ordinary subject'.

Possessed people imbued with the idea that an evil spirit has entered them tend to behave in a way that lives up to this belief. It is in just such a case that conversation of a kind is manifest, sometimes audibly and sometimes between two voices. I have known people seemingly talking to themselves, but on closer analysis there is actually a conversation proceeding between them and the possessor. Is therefore the obsessing personality autonomous, and does it really understand the words of the exorcist? In instances where the possessed rebukes the invading spirit, does the latter understand the rebuke? These are questions to which no blanket answers can be given, for all depends on the circumstances of each individual case, on the data received by the antennae it might be said, of the exorcist at the time.

The difficulty is that oppressed or possessed states tend to become more and more akin to the original nature of the person. It can be a vicious circle; that is why prompt action is needed; indeed, why the exorcist often feels he cannot hang around too long waiting for medical verdicts. But, of course, he has to! I freely admit the power of hetero-suggestion, by which a person may be made to hallucinate; before this occurs, timely intervention by a psychiatrist is desirable. Associated with hallucination is one of the most difficult problems presented in the field of deliverance. This is when an individual is convinced he is motivated by, and under the guidance of, a higher, extraneous supernatural power. One might say he believes himself to be a chosen one.

Finally, I end this section with a cautionary tale to all exorcists, which sticks in my mind, and which would be amusing if it were not so tragic. It concerned one of the clerics involved in the epidemic at Loudun, Father Tranquille, and was recounted by Oesterreich (*Possession*, page 38).

Father Tranquille was a native of Saint Remi in Anjou. He was the most famous preacher of his time. Obedience summoned him to the exorcisms of Loudon. The devils, fearing this enemy, came forth to meet him in order to frighten him if it were possible and caused him to feel on the road such debility in the legs that he stopped and remained where he was.

For four years he was employed as an exorcist, during which time God purified him by tribulation like gold in the furnace. He thought at first that he would expel the demons promptly, trusting in the authority which the Church has received from Our Lord. But having learned his mistake by experience he resolved to have patience and await the will of God. Fearing that his talents were a snare and would be an occasion for pride to him, he desired to abstain from preaching and gave himself entirely to exorcism.

The devils, seeing his humility, were so enraged thereby that they resolved to take up their abode in his body. All hell assembled for this purpose and nevertheless was unable to achieve it, either by obsession or full possession, God having not permitted it. It is true that the demons made sport in his inner and outer senses; they threw him to the ground; cried out and swore by his mouth; they made him put out his tongue, hissing like a serpent; they bound his head about, constricted his heart and made him endure a thousand other ills; but in the midst of all these ills his spirit escaped and was at one with God, and with the help of his companion he always promptly routed the demon who tormented him and who in turn cried out by his mouth: 'Ah, how I suffer!' The other monks and exorcists pitied Father Tranquille in his sufferings but he rejoiced in them marvellously...'

The conclusion is that the devils resolved to bring about his death, which they eventually did by renewing their torments. Father Tranquille died 'in the forty-third year of his age'.

CHAPTER EIGHT

CHANGING ATTITUDES TO THE DEVIL

I n the late eighteenth and early nineteenth centuries, change came much more rapidly than previously, and it was accompanied by increasing secularization, and a lessening of the hold of religion on society. In the void of the more modern psyche Satan began to flourish even more strongly. Medicine and psychiatry made inroads in relieving some disturbed states, but can never truly heal a sick spirit.

Belief in Satan runs parallel to belief in Christ. There cannot be one without the other. Good without bad is meaningless. Indeed, a belief in Satan can be honourable, whereas a belief in Satanism is a perversion and often involves the abuse of children. In every case, these uninvited external forces of evil must always be taken seriously.

Over the centuries, writers – from Dante to C. S. Lewis – were increasingly drawn to the Lucifer legend and the entrancing catch-all character of the Devil. The evolution of the concept of the Devil can be studied through the progression of creative literature; these notable original thinkers and writers were much concerned with the influence of the Church – often critically – and with good and evil. They reflected the past, were part of the present and helped lay the groundwork for the future.

THE DEVIL IN THE PRESENT

Over the last few centuries attitudes to Satan and his followers have changed drastically – but not for everyone! Decline in belief in the Devil and all his works and pomps began with the decline in belief in witches and their maleficia. Increasingly secular attitudes, the growth of materialism, the influence of science, the application of reason, applying rationality to everyday problems and a decline in religious hold over people are some of the reasons for the demotion from high estate of Satan, the Prince of Darkness.

He is, however, far from being a spent force. One who has for so long held so prominent a place in Man's consciousness cannot be easily dismissed. Witnessing the manifest evil exhibited in the world in the twentieth century, one could be forgiven for saying the Devil (and his demons) are still at work, if indeed they are not alive and kicking. No matter how sceptical we are, some would say it would be just as arrogant to deny his present and past existence as it is to categorically deny *without proof* that God does not exist. Shakespeare's adjuration in *Measure for Measure*,

> *Let the devil be sometimes honoured*
> *For his burning throne,*

reminds us that he was once a real and terrifying figure.

The problem is – jumping to the present – that many, if not most, theologians are hesitant to commit themselves to open belief in the Devil. They seem to feel that commitment to a belief in supernatural powers is somehow indicative of an anachronistic attitude which has no place in the modern world. I sometimes feel that they are being economical with the truth, and that deep down they do believe that Satan still stalks the earth. What is major exorcism about otherwise? If they believe in the Bible as Holy Writ, they would have to be selective – which process can be used to justify or deny anything. The Bible has many references to demons, to the Devil and to angels; to ignore all these is to call in question the credibility of all Scripture.

It cannot be denied that there is less instancing today of overt supernatural influence at large in the world than in the Bible, but this fact is not in itself a good enough reason for disbelief, or reluctance to believe, in something that has had immense authority behind it throughout the centuries. I cannot see how one can claim to be a theologian where, on this subject, there is little belief. Reading the Biblical texts makes it apparent that the role of demons (and angels) was to play a major part in the drama of Jesus' life – and, at the same time, to present a real threat to the pursuance of the Christian life. Disparagement of the validity of certain texts in the Bible adduces that these texts are but indications of mythological beliefs around at that time. But this is, I believe, to do the writings of honest men a grave disservice and illustrates again the easy way out: selectivity.

It is sometimes said by theologians that we – that is, they – do not need demons and other spiritual beings, because we understand the role that spirits are intended to play – which is tantamount to saying that since God is the paramount spiritual being, and as it is known what part He intends to play, or has played, on earth, belief in Him is also redundant! Some theologians!

A fitting summing up of the position is given by a proclamation of the Roman Catholic Church which says that:

> *The position of the Catholic Church on Demons is clear and firm... when doubt is thrown these days on the reality of the devil we must... look to the constant and univer-*

sal faith of the Church and to its chief source, the teaching of Christ. It is in the teach-ing of the Gospel and in the heart of the faith as lived that the existence of the world of demons is revealed as a dogma. The contemporary disaffection… is therefore not simply a challenge to a secondary element of Christian thought but a direct denial of the con-stant faith of the church…

Another difficulty is that *ex cathedra* pronouncements of the Roman Catholic Church themselves reveal a wavering in belief in evil spirits, especially in con-nection with possession and exorcism. Older statements (of about the turn of the nineteenth century) still implied an unswerving belief in the reality of demon possession – although counselling caution, of course – while more recent state-ments (of about 1970) put more emphasis on medical interpretation such as psy-chiatry reveals, and rather less on the probability of demonic possession (*The Catholic Encyclopedia*).

It would, however, be idle to deny that belief generally in Satan is undoubt-edly declining. I freely admit that the decline is largely due to the general decline in traditional religious observance. On a more dialectic plane, the idea of a Principle of Evil does not appeal to many for the reason that a Principle that is capable of manipulating – or seeks to manipulate – another's will must itself have a 'will', which as far as we know is possessed only by a person, a human being. This is inherently a difficult concept to justify.

It appears that present-day arrogance would deny the actions, and thereby the testimony, of Jesus Christ, when He seemed from all accounts to be addressing per-sonal beings who, He would have us believe, were demonizing people of His time.

Thus much of the prevailing attitude of moral relativism would, it seems, strive to deny the existence of real evil in the world: a sitting on the fence which proclaims 'I do not know the difference between evil in itself and its manifesta-tions, therefore I refuse to commit myself' – a position which Jesus Himself never adopted. For Christ (and His early followers) the Devil was never a metaphor for evil, as many now claim. To maintain that he is a metaphor is to rob Christianity of any meaningful tradition and definition. And it is to deny one's own claims to be a Christian. Of course, I am talking of people who profess a belief in Christianity, but who are, to say the least, ambivalent in their attitude to the Devil. Non-Christians, or non-believers, must judge by the evidence afforded them in their perception of the world about them.

It must be admitted that in past centuries, illness of mind and body was usu-ally put down to demonic infestation. The advance of science, especially medical science, has in most cases, *not all*, revealed a more mundane cause. Hence, for many people confessing to a belief in demons is thought to be not scientific, and no one wants that!

Another besetting difficulty is that the traditional Biblical Devil is something of a chameleon figure, undergoing drastic change in his progress from the Old to the New Testaments. Accordingly, it is hard to say which Devil we are talking about, any one conception at any one time. In fact, the only thing we are sure about is his historical development. We have to acknowledge that there are many imponderables about the nature of Satan and many questions left unanswered, because they are unable to be answered, at least with any degree of conviction. This leads many people to regard the person of the Devil as a mere figure of speech for a Principle of Evil that causes death and destruction in the world – in which evil is all too clear, too manifest. What made Hitler, Stalin and many other world leaders into the monsters they were? Was it by the direction of a Satanic being within them? Who knows, and who can with authority deny the possibility?

THE IDEA OF A DEVIL

The idea of a Devil is implicit in Christianity. Christianity is the religion instituted by Jesus, about whose existence there is no argument. All He ever did and said testifies to an extraordinary person who appeared to have supernatural powers. The populace of the time, and later the Gospel writers, all acknowledged this power. Whether He was truly the Son of God, a statement which Jesus Himself was never to unambiguously claim, lies in the realm of faith, but there is much evidence to the fact of His divine origin.

Perhaps one of the worse consequences of denying the modern existence of the Devil and his cohorts is the danger it leads us into of thinking of evil as a minor force, a concept that can almost be avoided in conversation or debate. Advocating disembodied evil can result in trivialization, which would be a profound mistake – particularly in our time.

An Extraordinary 'Person'

In speaking to many people of varying educational backgrounds, I have been surprised at how large a proportion believe sincerely in the existence of the Devil, and especially his ability to possess mankind. For as many as disbelieve, there are, it seems, just as many who believe, either as acts of faith or because they have had some experience, often traumatic, which served to convince them. Proofs of the existence of God, according to, say, the Roman Catholic Church, are to such people incontestable and disproofs are flawed. I have to say as an ex-cleric that the proofs for God's existence always seemed to me more convincing and logical than the solipsist arguments (belief that nothing but the self exists) of a contrary nature. There is difficulty in attributing unlimited power to God, His omnipotence, as it is called, because even the Almighty cannot create anything which defies logic; but His power must comprehend evil as well as good, if He made it a hurdle for mortals to surmount and defeat. Evil in the abstract is purely a metaphysical concept; embodied evil is something different altogether. The Devil is the embodiment who creates wickedness in people and destruction in the world.

Goodness itself cannot exist without the exercise of free will (a subject discussed earlier); neither can evil *unless* it is embodied in God with regard to the former, and in the Devil with respect to the latter. Free will allows us to decide between good and evil; between God and the Devil. God made the world; if we accept this, then God created Satan, or allowed him to become Satanic. Allowing connotes a purpose which must be just as valid for humanity today as it was aeons ago. Man has not changed his nature.

In fact, belief or unbelief in such concepts as God and the Devil is an act of faith, one though which from common observance seems to point to an evil entity at large. Allying this to Man's natural proclivity to sinful activity and the fact that many people seem able to rise above this inclination leads us to think there is a corresponding (or compensating) good entity. We do experience good and evil in others as well as in ourselves. The waging of war, preparations for war, the stockpiling of weapons of mass destruction – what impels us to do these things? We know that no one can possibly benefit. What force, then, makes mankind come ever closer to self-destruction? As J. B. Russell so trenchantly puts it (*Mephistopheles*, page 300), 'If Satan does not exist, God must be responsible for evil, at least, natural evil.'

It is common nowadays to say that people who are victimized are 'demonized', which itself suggests at least an echo of the once firm belief in demons. It tends to be used in a derogatory sense, as if entertaining the idea of a Devil encourages a person to regard transgressors as demon inspired. QED: the Devil and his demons do not, or rather should not, exist. The truth is that the use of this term in this sort of context is trivial – unless the person shows the signs of spiritual possession. On the other hand, the common expression may indicate that belief in the Devil and his demons is far from dead!

SATAN IN DECLINE?

Decline of belief in the Devil as a person began, as we have said, as early as the seventeenth century, hastened by the influence of several 'rationalist' thinkers and writers (about whom more anon). The Reformation was not itself responsible for the decline, as most of the influential figures were staunch believers in Satan and all things Satanic. Roman Catholic revivals in the seventeenth and eighteenth centuries failed to redress the balance, as matters had progressed too far and the existence of the Devil remained incredible to many.

Even so, much of Roman Catholic thought remained traditional up to the nineteenth century (and beyond). The pre-eminence of demons in possession and exorcism rites was emphasized in the then current handbook *Rituale Romanum*. Right up to the 1960s the Church defended unabated the reality of Satan's existence. After this time, approximately, the Church has seen a division in its approaches to the concept of Satanism (among other things) and, as in the Protestant Churches, about which we tend to hear so much more, there are two main arms: one espouses the traditional view of the Church throughout the ages; the other advocates a new look at traditional theology, belief and ritual, among which is a debate, rather an uncertainty, about the existence of the Devil and demons. However, the Second Vatican Council (1962–5) made several references to the Devil, contrasting with the Roman Catholic *Encyclopedia*, already mentioned, of 1967, which tended to play down the status of the Devil, regarding him more as a symbolic figure. Scepticism was beginning to show. Selective adductions from the Bible were chosen to bolster that position. Further, it was adduced that belief in the Devil had never been an article of faith; certainly, from the evidence of the deliberations of the Councils of the Church Satan as an entity of moment had not been the focus, except for one or two assemblies.

Naturally, the Devil cannot exist as a person in the accepted sense, and this may be one of the barriers to traditional belief. Certainly, he is not a person as a human being is a person, but the difficulty may therefore lie in the definition or semantics of a word which is open to interpretation. 'Person' can mean several things, but always connoted is the idea of will and intelligence, of which by all accounts the Devil has plenty.

Uninvited Forces of Evil

Modern medicine and psychiatry may indeed explain physical and mental illness more suitably than demonology, but sickness of the spirit they cannot cure. Uninvited external forces of evil may be the answer where the victim is more to be pitied than laughed at, as the saying goes.

As Peter Stanford says in his book *The Devil* (page 229), Christianity, which begat the Devil, has not killed off its creation.

> *He continues to thrive on the margins, in exorcism rituals… in the born-again movement. He retains a place in the popular soul of Christianity, the catch-all character to blame for actions too terrible to ascribe to a loving God and too frightening to put down to dark urges in the human psyche.*

Satan will always be a reality for some people: those who feel, for whatever reason, that they are not truly part of society, and so are looking for some reason why this should be. It is but a short step for many such to believe either that they are 'bedevilled' or that attention to occult forces will help them. This is one reason for belief, but it is not the only one, or even a true one. Satanism and belief in Satan are not necessarily the same thing. Satanism flourishes out of a void in the modern psyche which itself arises from the modern system of values in which God is marginalized. Belief in Satan can be an honourable thing; belief in Satanism is always a perversion.

Satanism by and large still regards its figurehead as a type of monster, giant-sized if possible, with horns and tail, breathing fire and sulphur – all the more to attract, or to terrify, its adherents into submission. Once he was seen as

> *chained to the mouth of hell as a dog to its kennel and yet [he] wields his trident sceptre… a demon more hideous… than pagan art has offered… This image figures the various aspects of infernal sin, by its many faces, having a face on each shoulder and a face at each hip. With long ears like those of a hound, thick short horns of a bull, his legs and arms are covered with scales and seem to issue from the mouths of the faces at his joints. He has a lion's head with tusks and hands like the claws of a bear. His body*

open at the waist reveals a nest of serpents darting forth and hissing. In this monster we find all the elements of a dragon, leviathan, lion, fox, viper, bear, bull, and wild boar. It is a compound of each evil quality in these animals, embodied in a human form. (The Missal of Poitiers, by Didron)

The Devil of today has lost his terrifying aspect, being mostly a disembodied evil spirit. However he is regarded, the Devil is a fascinating figure. If he is dead, for many people he won't lie down. Even in the midst of present-day materialism, he still has an influence over minds that despite their worldly preoccupations cannot forget him – especially when confronted with manifestations of wickedness.

Subjective Devotion

The time was when Man, in order the better to understand his concepts, objectified qualities such as bravery or beauty in effigy, statues and the like. Later ages rejected these practices, trusting more in an intrinsic, inward expression of religious fervour. Individualism became important, subjective devotion, the idea of a personal path to eternal happiness, and, with the advent of the Reformation, a jettisoning of the belief (among its adherents) of the necessity for clerical intervention and papal dictat. On this principle Protestantism was built. For many clergy, truth did not entirely repose in the teachings of the Church, and even the doctrine of papal infallibility was itself fallible. Religious truth lay in what reasonable and devout persons saw with their own eyes; it was an element that could be subjectively appraised and objectively evaluated. It was part of the march forward of religious evolution.

An Objective Measure?

Is there any objective measure of right or wrong? Is there a Principle of Evil? These are some of the fundamental questions that the overthrow of a dominant authority in the sphere of faith and morals threw up. Can they be answered? It may be argued that goodness is manifest only in action – the same with evil. That goodness (or evil) does not exist in principle – only as the deeds of someone. This would if accepted lead us on to belief in God – or Satan. Doubters may claim that the idea 'God' is really at bottom only a guideline, a rule even, for good conduct, and that in the same way, the 'Devil' is just an authority for bad conduct. All is subject to a factual interpretation of the world and its ethereal connotations. This is a dangerous belief. The idea of God is that of final authority, of moral values which *per se* are incapable of mechanical analysis. An immanent God (having only an internal effect) cannot be scrutinized or understood.

Satan is the Antichrist; he is, to quote Carus' words in *The History of the Devil* (pages 472, 488), the representative of rebellion and disorder, but at the same time is 'an indispensable phase in the manifestation of God'. As Carus goes on to say, Satan is part and parcel of the divine dispensation and the Devil is 'the most... faithful helpmate of God'.

OLD ORDERS CHANGING

By the end of the eighteenth century and the beginning of the nineteenth, the hold of religion on the masses, and on the educated, had begun to weaken, so much so that God's influence on everyday matters was no longer accepted uncritically as it had been when the Church of Rome dominated. With it, belief in the power of the Devil also declined. Thinkers of the movement known as the 'Enlightenment' espoused a rational approach to matters of religion and were in the vanguard of the secularization of society, which steadily increased. Much of this attitude was a response to the perceived worldliness of the Church, however. Increasingly, Christianity came to be viewed as largely superstition, whose attribution of hard to understand phenomena to supernatural agency was all but ridiculed. This view was held by the sceptics of the age, the radical thinkers and writers; while on the one hand traditional believing Christians continued to adhere to their age-old beliefs, on the other, liberals partly embraced the old verities and partly accommodated the new.

Where did all this leave belief in the Devil and his demons? The nineteenth century was undoubtedly a time of change, from the French Revolution and its aftermath to the industrialization of populations, particularly in Britain. Making money became the new god for many; perhaps I exaggerate, but new opportunities for the pursuit of wealth tended to displace enthusiasms which until then had often turned on religion. The new urban classes drawn into this struggle dominated by materialism became less receptive to the law of the clergy. Accordingly, views on the Devil became variegated, many either blaming him for unsettling events or, in contradistinction to earlier centuries, absolving him from all blame – because they no longer believed in him. The Bible itself became subject to criticism, or at least critical scrutiny, and some of the major beliefs came to have doubt cast on them. Needless to say, Satan did not come out well from this examination. Demons who possessed might be another matter, though.

Protestant religious thought tended to side with the sceptics in so far as it chose to regard the Devil as a shadowy figure, with little relevance to the modern day and as a Biblical metaphor for evil which then had deep meaning for people of that age (and subsequent centuries). It was otherwise with the Roman Catholic Church. It still clung to traditional thought and belief, defending credence in the personality of the Devil. For the increasingly sceptical masses, those who could read, that is, the long story of the Devil was enshrined not so much in theology as in the literature of that era by writers who became, it seemed, drawn to the Lucifer legend. These writings, which we shall refer to in the last section of this chapter (*see* page 162), reveal the fascination of the Satan story, and as such are valuable to any demonological study.

Satan, however, was not going to curl up and die for anyone. He saw himself in danger of being rationalized out of existence and decided to make a comeback. This rather flippant comment is not meant to disguise the real threat that Satanic activity now poses. It cannot be denied that sects, cults, occult groups of all kinds flourish throughout the world. From a low point, Satan may be regarded as back, even achieving prominence. He wields a fascination as great as at any time in ages past – the only difference being that for most people he is not taken seriously, or as a serious threat capable of interfering in a normal life, whatever that is! One has only to look at the plethora of books and films, to say nothing of features or 'documentaries' available, especially on the small screen, to see what an unending source of interest and entertainment all things devilish are.

THE DEMON OF ABUSE

Satanism which affects no one else apart from the participants is one thing; quite another are Satanic rituals which occasion harm (or death) to others, especially the young. Many of these cults have child abuse as one of their main practices. It is difficult to believe that the perpetrators of this wickedness are not motivated by an evil force: a demon? It seems to me there are three spheres where a demonic spirit is capable of motivating: catastrophic events, often on the world stage, caused by deliberate human agency; the driving mad of a person by possession; and the wilful ritual abuse of children, where proven. This is the Devil at work in the present.

'Accredited' exorcists in the course of their deliverance ministry are called on to deal with extraordinary situations; this goes without saying. Some of these situations are not just extraordinary – they are horrific in their abnormality. Cases of severe disturbance have medical people, social workers, maybe police in attendance, as well as clergy, particularly if the subject has (or had) any religious affiliation with a particular church. I have been called in to suspect cases of severe mental disturbance which might, it was believed, have been due to diabolic influence. Further investigation has revealed that abuse, perhaps ritual, and perhaps Satanic, has been the core problem. All of the victims I have investigated have been female, except for one disturbed young boy who had been born into a family that believed in Satanism. Some experiencing abuse were young; others were older, not at the time experiencing abuse, but, as is so often the case, reliving memories, suddenly surfaced, that they had repressed for years, either consciously or subconsciously. In periods of lucidity they told me stories that were almost unbelievable of sexual abuse, torture, even bestiality. These experiences were indeed enough to drive anyone out of their mind. It made me very sad to think that such evil existed today in what on the surface seemed civilized life. That they were psychologically damaged owing to abuse was not in dispute; was this damage lifelong or could the victims get over it? Could anyone really do anything about 'curing' them? Sometimes I did not feel as though anything permanent could be done to bring them back to 'normality' or to alleviate their suffering for good. Was there a cure? Sometimes I almost despaired.

About half of those whose malady lay in childhood abuse claimed they were possessed by evil spirits. A form of exorcism did offer them some relief, largely I suspect because of the attention given to relieving their obsession (by a priest) and because they felt they were being listened to. True exorcism is efficacious only when an evil spirit is present in the victim; with this category of person it was a repressed memory which could no longer be repressed and which manifested itself in ways suggestive of possession. The awareness of the use of a form of exorcism as a catch-all was personally very strong, especially in relation to these patients. There is a pressing need for the education of clergy in the field of ritual abuse.

Some victims had been so severely traumatized by their early experiences that to all intents and purposes they manifested signs of diabolic infestation. They had developed two personalities: one comparatively normal and lucid; one abnormal and demented. At times, I felt as if I were indeed in the presence of some malicious being, as though deeds of abysmal depravity could induce, 'call up', devils from hell.

One difficulty is focusing the attention on what really matters. Is it ministering to the personal needs of the victim – or trying to discover the truth about the abuse? On reflection, I believed the latter was mainly the remit of social services, counsellors and the like, while the Church should devote its attentions more to the immediate needs of the victim. Of course, neither can really be divorced from the other; it is just a question of prioritizing energies. Dealing with such cases confirmed my belief that there was such a thing as evil within humanity which does not require much to manifest itself – and I am not thinking of the poor tormented victims, but of their torturers.

LITERATURE AND HISTORICAL CONCEPTS OF THE DEVIL

Concepts of the Devil and his demons in a particular epoch are revealed not only in human behaviour and the reaction to them of authority, be it clerical or lay, but just as much in the creative literature of the time which rejected these concepts. Attitudes to the Devil and all things Satanic are revealed clearly in this literature and denote the popular beliefs of the day. The study of writers of importance in this field indicates the fascination of the subject to both literary figures and their readers. One of the interests in looking at this body of imaginative writing is seeing the changing attitudes to and the evolution of Satan and his minions. In some ways, works of fiction, of the imagination, are better indicators of current belief and curiosity in the subject of the diabolic than the treatises, proclamations and bulls emanating from minds that had an axe to grind.

Dante and the *Divine Comedy*

Dante (1265–1321) was the earliest of the great writers who took diabology as a main theme. Dante in his poem *The Divine Comedy* featured the Devil as a force operating in the universe, which encompassed hell and earth. The cosmology of his age has been described in Chapter One; sufficient to say here that his system of belief (like everyone else's) was in the cosmos of Ptolemy; that is to say, that the universe was arranged in concentric circles, with the earth at the centre. In the centre of earth was hell; the very outermost circle contained heaven. The earth was the centre of the universe and everything else went round it. In his system, therefore, Satan was at the hub of the universe, not God. Satan and his followers, who became demons, fell from heaven because of their sinful pride and took up their dwelling in earth's centre. Imprisoned there in ice and cold, the Devil contrasts with the warm love of God. He inhabits the lowest part of hell, reserved for traitors, where he is portrayed as chewing endlessly on other infamous traitors, such as Brutus and Judas. He is a hideous and hateful figure.

Satan played (literally) a major role in many other stage productions throughout the following centuries. The fallen angels supplement the casts, often in the role of named demons. Clearly, many of these plays were written by clerics who wished to keep the fear of the Devil very much in the forefront of the people's minds. In some plays the demons became figures of fun in order to engender light relief before the serious devil or devils reappeared. The demons are often portrayed as asking their leader, variously described as Satan, Lucifer or Beelzebub, about major articles of faith and who exactly is Jesus. Naturally, the answers always discomfort the demons and strengthen the faith of the groundlings. Common themes were of demons frustrated by Christ's power, plotting His downfall and death. They are thwarted in their purpose of trying to carry off Christ's soul and at the Resurrection they are completely routed and confused. God has triumphed yet again.

Rabelais

The next major literary figure to feature the Devil prominently in his writings was the great French writer Rabelais (died 1553), who in *Gargantua and Pantagruel* used his devilish creations to satirize society of his day. His most evil character is the devil-like Panurge, who presages the idea of the Mephistopheles of the later Faust legend, about which there has been a well-nigh continuous outpouring.

Basically the story concerns someone who makes a pact with the Devil in return for worldly power and glory through the agency of Mephistopheles, one of Satan's right-hand men. There is a limit to the reign of self-gratification, however, after which the soul belongs to the Devil. The story is, of course, a cautionary tale about the dangers of worldly allure. It is different, however, in the way it treats the theme, portraying the Devil as somewhat sympathetic to the plight of the victim and almost showing some regret at his own transgression.

Marlowe, Shakespeare and Milton

Christopher Marlowe wrote his great play *Doctor Faustus* around the end of the sixteenth century. In his plot, Mephistopheles is himself more akin to the Christian Devil. Faustus is in many ways the willing agent of his own downfall, led astray by pride and greed. At the expiry of the due time Faustus is dragged screaming by the Devil down to hell.

No account of the literature would be complete without reference to Shakespeare (1564–1616) and his depiction of evil. The Devil and demons do not feature as such in men's affairs, but there are many references throughout his work to spirits. It is clear that belief in evil spirits was very potent in his time.

Many of Shakespeare's plays mention the Devil, or devils, or evil spirits; his ghosts may be thought of as demonic manifestations. It may be that his audiences interpreted the soliloquies in his great tragedies as promptings of the Devil.

The middle to late seventeenth century was a turbulent time for the Church, racked as it had been recently by sceptical figures such as Luther, Calvin and the Reformation – in England spearheaded by Henry VIII and his supporters. Stories about the Black Masses, possession, real or feigned, diabolical rituals, and sexual excess abounded and troubled both Christian Churches.

One who in a sense brought order out of chaotic thinking was John Milton, a Protestant writer. His *Paradise Lost* (1667) showed Satan in a glamorous light, overshadowing his depiction of God. It was not intentional; the intent had been to show the evil of the Devil as very attractive to readers so that they might the better recognize their own tendencies to sin. Milton's portrayal of Lucifer is of a magnificent being, as befits the King of Hell.

Milton traces Lucifer's rebellion and fall from grace. Down in hell Satan joins his host of fallen angels, now demonized. Satan is changed in the course of the poem from a bearer of light into a loathsome creature who dwells in darkness. In this hell, Satan takes council with his demons; ringleaders, such as Belial, Moloch, Mammon and Beelzebub, emerge, counselling various strategies. At last the plan is formulated to get his own back on God by seducing His creation, human beings. Taking the form of a serpent, he successfully tempts Eve into eating of the apple and returns in triumph to his minions in hell. Without a readership (or audience, for poetry in those days was of some moment and would be retold by word of mouth) that was receptive to accounts of the Devil's wiles and would take to heart the morals he was pointing out in his great poem, Milton would not have taken his tremendous theme – for his purpose was as much didactic as it was poetic.

In the next century, the eighteenth, scepticism about the Devil increased and was attacked along with general Christian beliefs. 'Rationalists' such as the philosophers Leibnitz, Schleiermacher and Kant in Germany, Diderot, Voltaire and Rousseau in France, Hume and Locke in Great Britain fuelled this anti-Christian orthodoxy.

Goethe and *Faust*

A rather strange melding of anti-Church and yet traditional views of the 'new' Christianity of the Enlightenment, Wolfgang von Goethe's labyrinthine poem *Faust, A Tragedy*, finished towards the end of his life in about 1830, was enormously influential. His Mephistopheles is not comparable with the traditional Christian Devil. He is too ambiguous a figure, too nebulous to be equated with the Devil we know (or knew). The Faust figure is at first of a diligent man, a scholar who seeks after truth, but in vain: the world will not yield up its secrets to him. Almost in despair he resorts to the spirit world to help him. Mephistopheles appears to him and suggests a pact by which occult powers will be given. Faust gradually comes under the Devil's influence, which causes him to lose interest in abstract reasoning. Instead, sensuality becomes the new obsession. Faust seduces a young woman, Gretchen, who subsequently kills herself. The poem now relates the struggle for Faust's soul: Faust, who has never truly embraced sensuality, wins through at the end. Faust's story is therefore a symbol of a struggling man's battle with evil forces.

LUTHER AND THE DEVIL

The greatest challenge the sixteenth-century Church had to face was that of Martin Luther (1483–1546). The literature of the age mostly reflected the attitude of the Church to religious matters, but apart from some free thinking, it was not seen as a challenge. Luther's was. His writing was not literature as such, but was doctrinal and in opposition to the current beliefs and practices of the Church and its clergy. Luther preached that the Biblical word was sacrosanct and was the literal rule of good conduct. He was a firm believer in the Devil and demons, professing to have seen Satan in person.

He was motivated by a hatred of what he perceived as corrupt and immoral about the Church of his time. Chief among these reprehensible practices, as he saw it, was the sale of 'indulgences' by which remission of sins in the next life could be secured by suitable donations. His was a reforming zeal which led him to write his own ninety-five 'articles of faith' and to pin them prominently on the church door at Wittenberg. The bulk of them were concerned with the sale of indulgences, but most heretical of all was Luther's view that the pope had no authority or right to forgive sins. He became an implacable opponent of papal authority but was not alone in his views. He is rightly regarded as the father of the Reformation.

An erudite man, ordained a priest and subsequently a lecturer in theology at Wittenberg University, Luther was a formidable foe in matters of theology, and rocked the Church to its foundation. One of his lesser transgressions was his attack on the need for celibate clergy. In fact, he later married an ex-nun, thus proving his point! One of his most outrageous beliefs, as far as the Church was concerned, was in the doctrine of predestination and its corollary, the denial of free will. According to this, humanity is always either in God's power or the Devil's; nothing we can do will alter the fact that an omnipotent God has willed everything to happen as He dictates. This claim was of course diametrically opposed to the traditional belief of the Roman Catholic Church. For Luther, the Devil had an important role as the agent by which evil is introduced into the world for God's purposes, so in a way, the Devil does God's work.

Satan was a real, living presence who plagued Luther and tried constantly to divert him from his devotions. The Devil, according to Luther, materialized frequently, often acting like a poltergeist in its manifold distractions. Luther's lead was followed by many, giving pre-eminence to Satan, whose influence was never once belittled. In all of Luther's teaching, the Devil is always regarded as an ever-present threat to Christians. Satan and his demons work through nature.

They exist in water, woods and deserts. They dwell in the air and the clouds and are the cause of bad weather. The Devil causes sickness and depression and can terrify people, awake or sleeping. He is the master of illusion and delusion, leading people astray.

Magic and sorcery were also realities for Luther. They were illustrative of the Devil's power. He believed implicitly in witchcraft, along with everyone else, and felt no compassion for people accused as witches. In these respects he was a child of his time – but there the resemblance ended. In matters of faith and morals Luther was without doubt one of history's most daring thinkers.

CALVIN, AN INFLUENTIAL DISCIPLE

John Calvin (1509–64) was an ardent and influential disciple of Luther, believing in the paramountcy of the Bible as the word of God, and accepting Luther's view of the omnipotence of God, which itself admits, on their view, of disbelief in free will. Like Luther, Calvin believed implicitly in the reality of the Devil and his demons and refused to entertain the idea of demons as being just a figment of the imagination. Satan in Calvin's diabology is not as prominent a figure as in his mentor's, but still loomed large as the doer-of-evil under God's command. He advocated belief in Luther's doctrine of predestination, and denied that anyone had a free and unfettered will to take any (moral) actions. Naturally, the idea that flowed from this was that some people were destined to be saved and that others were destined to be damned. Nothing could be more contrary to the teaching of the Catholic Church.

Largely as a result of the agitations of these men and others of like persuasion, the reform movement came to both Christian Churches, Roman Catholic and Protestant. The two Churches did not react in the same way and there was some deliberately different hardening of attitudes to reform. Throughout all this the Devil lived on in ecclesiastical circles for centuries and his existence was never called into question.

WESLEY AND METHODISM

John Wesley (1703–91) may be regarded as a major figure in the developing Reformation movement, and he is best known as the founder of Methodism. He became a Protestant priest in 1728. He, like Calvin, was inspired by the writing of Luther. Like them, he was very much exercised by the idea of demons and the Devil, which he believed were essential parts of an ordered whole. As fallen angels they were still part of God's empire. They had become evil and as such sought constantly to betray Man in his search for the good. These evil spirits govern the world of sensations under the command of Satan. Like Calvin, Wesley believed in their responsibility for accidents and illness and even in the little things which irritate. He was a firm believer in witchcraft and demon possession. Although the founder of Methodism, he always regarded it as a branch of the true Church, which for him was the Church of England.

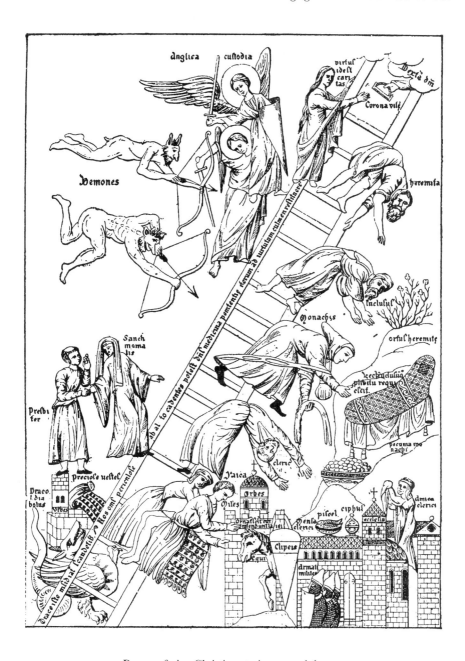

Dangers facing Christians trying to reach heaven

SCEPTICS AND THE DEVIL

With all this debate, and reforming zeal, Roman Catholicism and Protestantism were undergoing quite an unsettling time, which went on for more than a century. Biblical exegesis, or scrutiny, tended to focus on the personality of Jesus, emphasizing that Christ was merely a man of his time with the expected blinkered outlook. This itself threw doubt on the entire validity of the Bible as the inspired word of God. Fuelling the fires of uncertainty and dissent were the views of thinkers mentioned earlier, such as Schleiermacher (died 1834), who was a pastor of the Reformed (German) Church. He devoted much of his energies to proving the non-existence of the Devil and offered practical arguments.

Rousseau (1712–78), baptized a Catholic, was much influenced by Calvinism. His opinion on the nature of evil did not square with that of the Roman Catholic Church, which of course blamed the Devil: Rousseau tended to the view that evil lay within the human heart, or soul, but we can be self-correcting – without the agency of a priest.

By the end of the seventeenth century people were beginning generally to be sceptical about the reality of the Devil's existence. 'Rationalist' sceptics, like Hobbes (1588–1679) and Locke (1632–1704) in England and Descartes (1596–1650) in France, hastened the spread of this attitude, adducing that the existence of spirits could not be proved. Essentially Locke's theory of diabology was that the existence of demons and the Devil could be and should be accepted, but he postulated that they have no influence in nature. Locke stated that Christianity should be rationally scrutinized for anything that is not reasonable – and for him the existence of the Devil was certainly not reasonable.

The three above-named thinkers fundamentally undermined belief in the Devil. Educated people and the uneducated, now being liberated from their rural settings and beginning to settle in the new towns, experienced a lessening of belief in the old dogmas, of which diabology was one.

The great German philosopher Kant (1724–1804) devoted much time and energy to the discussion of evil. His basic thesis was that the only thing that has meaning is something discoverable by the senses. On this view, talk about the Devil (and God) is useless because it is all mere metaphysical speculation. His influential contribution did nothing for belief in the old orthodoxies.

New Values

The all-pervading influence of the Roman Catholic Church continued to abate throughout the eighteenth and nineteenth centuries, as new political and capitalist values began to take shape. The Devil came to be seen in whatever light a particular faction desired: as an enemy if things went wrong; as an ally if things (especially on the world stage) went right – in so far as Satan was to be thanked for the enemy's downfall. A group of writers important in their own right in literature treated the subject of the Devil significantly, and will be discussed in the next chapter (see pages 182 ff). They all contributed towards the scepticism over demonic belief.

A figure of stature in French literature, Baudelaire (1821–67) explored the phenomenon of evil in his work. In acknowledging evil as attractive, he was frequently accused of Satanism and his oftentimes seemingly ambivalent attitude to the Devil and evil made him a target for Christian criticism. But this view is mistaken: Baudelaire essentially took Satan as a symbol of evil in Man.

This fascination with the Devil could not last. By about the middle to end of the nineteenth century, literary interest in the Devil as a major figure in human life and destiny had begun to die out. Religious metaphysics gave way to realism and materialism with the result that belief in a personal devil waned drastically. Before the resurgence of interest in the twentieth century, however, figures important to our theme arose. Among these are the German writers Mann and Nietzsche and the English writers C. S. Lewis and Aldous Huxley. Towering above them in his treatment of evil is the Russian author Dostoevsky, whom we shall leave to a later chapter (*see* page 183).

At this juncture we shall discuss the work of the social and political theorists Marx and Engels, who have had a great influence on late nineteenth-century and early twentieth-century life and conditions.

COMMUNISM AND THE DEVIL

Marx and Engels were atheists, as were other influential thinkers of the age. Outright disbelief in God's existence was a comparatively new attitude that the Churches had now to face. There had been others earlier, such as Shelley, but they were the exception, not the rule. However much leaders of movements, original thinkers and writers had disagreed with the Church in wanting change, they had been fundamentally Christian. Appearing now was a distinctly anti-Christian message, embodied not in literary figures but in the work of people desirous of social change who saw the Churches as an obstacle to their goal.

Marx, Engels and Nietzsche

Karl Marx (1818–83) and Friedrich Engels (1820–95) were the leading lights of this anti-clerical movement. Marxism, which begat Communism, is basically a philosophy of materialism, atheistic in outlook, and dismissive of all belief in the mystic world of religion and the Bible.

Transcendentalism, the concept of God, and spirits, was totally rejected. Marx and Engels argued that humanity was being alienated from material things, possessions and the like, chiefly by the teachings of Christianity, and secondarily by the prevalent values of conditioned society. Capitalism, and the ownership of private property, the accumulation of wealth in the hands of the few, resulting in exploitation, were the chief evils. Only with the advent of true communism will class differences disappear. Along with other Christian beliefs, the notion of the Devil was thrown out. The Roman Catholic Church, though severely battered by these onslaughts, kept determinedly to its belief in the Devil, as did conservative Protestants, though a progressive wing sought to adapt itself to the new ideas.

Nietzsche (1844–1900) developed the theories of Marx and Engels, but without displaying the zeal to reform society. Nietzsche was more a philosopher than the other two, asseverating that the only thing of value is what we directly experience – and this is not much. The ideas of God, spirits, moral standards, are delusions; theology is a non-subject. For Nietzsche, the biggest illusion of all is

Christianity, and one of its worst aspects is that it commands respect from its adherents only out of fear and repression. Although he rejected the idea of the traditional Christian Devil, he still had a role for him as the antithesis of an authoritarian, cold and forbidding God in the sense that he was therefore charitable, indulgent and loving, and more of a friend to man.

Such propositions led into the realm, so far unexplored, of developing sciences such as psychology. Modern movements in psychology tend to play down, if not reject, the idea of religion and its concomitants, preferring to deal with the subconscious or unconscious mind. It follows that concepts such as God and the Devil are regarded as mere mind projection, imaginary atavistic recollections of an age that never was.

THE TWENTIETH CENTURY: C. S. LEWIS

A notable literary figure of comparatively recent times who investigated the subject of good and evil, in particular the Devil, was C. S. Lewis (1898–1963), a convert to Christianity and a subsequent Christian apologist, whose most famous work on our theme was written in the 1940s. Contrasting with the previous two political writers, Lewis is worth mentioning here. He explored in the *Screwtape Letters* and the novel *Perelandra*, in the words of J. B. Russell, 'the struggle between good and evil in the individual soul [which] is the microcosm of the cosmic opposition between God and the Devil, and human sin is part of the great shadow that we call evil' (Russell, *Mephistopheles*, page 274). The main character, Weston, a Faustian figure, in *Perelandra* represents in his wickedness the Devil incarnate, whose power is finally broken, as in the Milton and Dante tradition. The *Screwtape Letters* is a series of letters, as it were, written by a senior demon to a junior, called Wormwood, recommending different strategies for tripping up humans through their foibles and weaknesses. It is apparent from the *Letters* that demons need sustenance, perpetually, for they will not eat the only thing that will satisfy them, the bread of life.

Lewis was concerned with the battle between good and evil, but the individual can make choices. However, because society is materialistic (compare with the text on Marx and Engels above), these value choices are hard to make. In Lewis's view, reality is found in God and the Devil; our material world is a distorting mirror which gives us a misleading picture of the real conflict facing us.

It is clear from a consideration of these writers that sincere belief in, and awe of, the traditional Devil is no longer seen. However, it is equally clear that the concepts of good and evil exercise as strongly as ever the minds of influential writers and thinkers of modern times. If Satan himself as a person is excluded from serious consideration, there is no doubt that Satanism is very much alive.

CHAPTER NINE

THE DEVIL – CRITICS AND SUPPORTERS

S atanists are the ungodly people, often formed into sects, who have been and are the main supporters of the Devil – their 'Prince of Darkness'. Much of the appeal for Satanists must have been that they can do and think as they wish with no restraint of any kind. Their often horrific crimes are reflected in the stories of Gilles de Rais and Aleister Crowley. There are many more, equally matched by the tales of the bewitched and the possessed.

The ground was fertile for Satanism in its many forms to take root. Popes from 1233 issued bulls in attempts to control witchcraft; more such bulls of the late sixteenth and early seventeenth centuries showed increased papal anxiety. The result was a dramatic increase in witch-hunting, with a 'perfect' Satanic twist: it was often the innocent who perished.

Since the Devil seemingly has 'inspired' an immense volume of literature from Mann's *Doktor Faustus* to Dostoevsky's *The Possessed*, as well as much great art and music, should we ask: has this creativity been demonically inspired?

SATANISM

None support the Devil as much as Satanists. The practice of worshipping the Devil (AD) is almost as old as Christianity itself, but in its early days it tended to be a group thing, a cult or sect behaviour. It is still with us today. Throughout the centuries there have been notable tales of people whose crimes were so horrendous that only devotion to Satanism would account for them.

One of the worst was Gilles de Rais (1404–40), a one-time marshal of France, and the richest nobleman in Europe. He also dabbled in magic and alchemy. His constant failure to turn base metals into gold led him to invoke demons, who it seems wanted the killing of children in return. It did not take long for Rais to earn notoriety and to make enemies. When he crossed a member of the clergy, he was arraigned on trumped-up charges of heresy. Rais was an ideal suspect (to find guilty) because he had great wealth and possessions to be confiscated.

He was formally accused of calling up demons and sexual perversions, especially against children. The first charge involved, it was alleged, human sacrifices. These were prefaced by torture, before killing by such means as dismembering and burning. Mutilated bodies were disposed of in ditches and trenches around his many castles. Rais was accused of 'foully committing the sin of sodomy with young boys and in other ways lusted against nature after young girls, spurning the natural way of copulation…'. Parts of bodies he offered to demons as a sign of homage.

Evidence, as was the custom, was obtained by the torture of Rais himself, but especially of some of his attendants. They testified that they had seen their master place his erect penis between the thighs of boys and girls, then on their bellies until 'he emitted his sperm on their stomachs'. Further testimony alleged that Rais killed children while he was abusing them, sitting astride the maltreated bodies and masturbating on them. Afterwards he had their throats cut and decapitated them. Under torture he admitted his greatest pleasure was sitting across the children's stomachs and watching them slowly pass away.

Rais was found guilty on numerous charges and handed over to the lay authorities for punishment. He was strangled (a merciful form of death in those days), and his body tied to the stake. Although it must be said that most of the 'evidence' was obtained by torture, and, as such, it cannot always be given credence, Rais was an evil man and a Satanist who did kill and sacrifice young people. Whether he was guilty of the horrible perversions he was charged with, we will never really know. Rais was a man corrupted by power and vast wealth which he put to evil uses. He almost got away with his crimes and might have done so for ever with his power and influence behind him, had he not made the mistake of thinking he was above the law – laws laid down by the all-powerful Church.

What therefore is Satanism? It can be said to be the worship of Satan by heretical sects, imitating the behaviour of Satan, recognizing his domination of the world. Satan is the 'Prince of this World', as Christ Himself called him, ruling over the world before Jesus came on earth. He is the king of ungodly men as well as king of the fallen angels. Opposed is the Kingdom of God, which Satan's kingdom is pledged to try to destroy. Overt examples of what may be construed as Satanic acts are around us, but the covert promptings of Satan in our hearts are more mysterious – and just as frightening.

There have been, as we have intimated, many sects down the ages which have revered Satan as their king, including believers in dualism, who set up Satan as an equal, albeit evil, to God. From this worship of the Devil grew the belief in witchcraft. Several bulls were issued by popes fulminating against witchcraft; even earlier were proclamations against Satanism. For example, one of the earliest was the bull of Gregory IV, 1233, aimed mainly at activities in Germany, where terrible initiation rites into Satanic sects had come to notice. Three hundred years later the Protestant Reformation was just as obsessed, if not more so, with devilish arts and practices. Witchcraft was regarded as Satanism in practice, manifest in the total dedication of a human body, and soul, to the Devil and his demons. Satanism lives on to this day in various cults and sects; it lives on also in demonic men on the world and national stage.

It appears that 'celebrations' of Black Masses are often the focus of these atheistic groups, which themselves are an excuse for sexual licence. Of recent years there have been accounts of cults devoted to an insane perversion of religion. They have all ended in tragedy for their megalomaniac leaders and their deluded followers. For them Satan remained a person, vivid, embodying evil permissiveness. For many of the rest of us, Satan is a Principle, a personification in the literary figure of speech context; but do we ever really forget that deep down there are those inclinations to perversity, to bad conduct – to put it mildly?

Today, Satanism lies fundamentally in the wilful denial of God's existence and authority; in the claim that Man has autonomy to do and think as he wishes – without restraint. On the one hand there is the abnormal, the profanation, the parody of Christianity, but worse is the belief in modernity, in the reliance on technical skills, on scientific progress, as the answer to all ills: sufficient, without divine guidance. As Jesus Himself said, 'Sufficient unto the day is the evil thereof' (Matthew 6:34). It may be thought that the avowed atheism in much overt writing on the theme and in the failed system of communism indicates a type of Satanism: some do think this. It may be that atheistic writers, particularly novelists, exhibit emotions in their work, of regret for the vacuum in the spirit of man. Maybe.

Corte, a Catholic priest, asks (*Who Is the Devil?*, page 114):

Which way does true realism lie? Is it to be found in watering down... those truths that have reached us by divine revelation... or must it be sought in the faith taught by the Church ever since her foundation?

Corte has no doubt about believing in the second.

Various strands combined – the clerical suspicion of woman as temptress; the outflowing of books and articles on Satanism and witchcraft; the portrayal in art of demonic subjects; the primitive knowledge of medicine; and the delusion of alchemy and related studies – making it no wonder that the ground was laid for sorcerers and Satanists. Men sought remedies for ills: some mysterious cure which might be revealed by the spirit world. The Holy See had become concerned about the growth of Satanism and sought to repress it. Bulls of the late sixteenth and early seventeenth centuries showed papal anxiety about the trend. Magic, sorcery, soothsaying and divination were all condemned and their practitioners denounced as heretics. All these, of course, were believed to be demonstrated only through the agency of the Evil One.

As a consequence, persecution of Satanists (or those thought to be such) was as virulent as witch-hunting. Anti-Satanic measures of whatever kind were, in the Church's eyes, always justified. Even children could be accused, but the death sentence was not passed in the case of pre-pubescents. Sorcery grew by leaps and bounds, especially among the rural uneducated, where it was greatly feared. This evil was always prosecuted with avidity by the Church, as the crime arose out of (perverted) religion.

TRAFFICKING WITH THE DEVIL

In the second half of the seventeenth century some very strange trials of people accused of trafficking with the Devil took place. I give a summary of two which illustrate the credulity of the times. The first one concerns a certain William Drury, tried at Salisbury in England.

Drury's Tale

Drury, an ex-soldier, came to the notice of the law because of antisocial behaviour. He earned a crust from itinerant drumming. Apparently the house of the magistrate before whom Drury had appeared became troubled by strange sights and sounds, but only whenever Drury was in the vicinity. Most of the disturbances consisted of the sounds of beatings on a drum. Drury's drum was destroyed, as he was naturally the prime suspect. However, though the drummings ceased, other unaccountable phenomena took their place as though a poltergeist ran riot: objects of all kinds flew around; lights were seen; drastic changes in temperature were experienced. Blood was found one day, after the discharge of a pistol at a shadow.

Communication with the Devil was established by a system of knocks by means of which the Devil related how he had been set to work by Drury. Ashes on the floor indicated claw-like marks, and the Devil grew bolder, almost manifesting himself on occasions. The drummer was arrested as being responsible by sorcery (Satanism) of causing the disturbances. He was, fortunately for him, sentenced to transportation, but jumped into the sea and swam ashore. He then bought another drum and recklessly went to the magistrate's house and there beat it in bravado. The following day he was again arrested, acquitted of sorcery (belief was clearly dying!), but once again sentenced to transportation as an undesirable. As he did not return this time it is presumed he completed his journey in irons.

Whether Drury was in league with the Devil or whether the disturbances were purely coincidental, we shall never know. The point is that people were being arraigned for Satanism, for being in league with the Devil, with as much conviction as ever – and that they were fitting subjects for severe penalties.

Spatchet Bewitched

The second story concerns one Thomas Spatchet, who came to prominence in 1665. In that year he apparently became quite mad, recognizing no one except a beggar woman, Aubrey Grinset. Naturally, the first thought was that Spatchet had been bewitched, and the handiest suspect was the old beggar woman. She confessed (presumably of her own free will!) to being a witch and to having bewitched to death two persons already. The Devil appeared to her in the form of a handsome man with whom she had 'relations'. Sometimes he manifested as a cat and sucked blood from a secret teat. Driven by the Devil, she had tormented Spatchet by sending an imp to him. On being searched naked, strange scratch marks were found on her body which were interpreted as marks of the Devil.

As Spatchet and the two dead men were regarded as no great loss to society, Grinset was set free. Unfortunately, she did not recover from the Devil's attentions and some two years later, despite being armed with clubs, she was unable to keep Satan off, and died with the skin of her arms scratched or torn off. Spatchet himself made a partial recovery.

All the foregoing could be put down to hysteria and/or imagination except for the fact of the lacerations of Grinset's flesh. Of course, it may all have been an example of self-flagellation; injury inflicted to achieve a sort of status on the part of an otherwise nobody. But if she died as a result of these injuries, what are we to believe? Once again, we shall never know the truth.

FORMS OF SATANISM

Satanism comes in different forms: one group practises cruelty and perversion; another is merely an excuse to be thought different; yet another pretends to a form of Christianity under the guise of religion. Sometimes individuals alone are Satanic. Worship of Satan as a good being is a contradiction; the historical conception of Satan has always been as the embodiment of evil. That is his symbol, his trademark. That is why he was created. Satanism has evolved with the times: through the more or less unified view of the world dominated by one faith; through the advent of materialism and scientific truths, in the eighteenth and nineteenth centuries; through an age in which philosophy and the arts may join with the above to form a new whole. Perhaps; but not just yet. Decline of conventional religious belief has for now made too big a dent in our hearts. We are still seeking answers.

Followers of Satan

Surveys have been taken to try to ascertain the proportions of people involved in Satanism or some kind of occult practice. Results have been illuminating. Adherents came from all groups in society and they were overwhelmingly young; that is to say, under forty years of age. Very few want their real names to be known; perhaps they have something to hide. The Christian Churches certainly think so. The most heinous crime of the Satanists lies in the fact that their philosophy has grown out of the Biblical tradition, which means that they or their forebears originally acknowledged the Christian God. Their Satanism derives from earlier beliefs in Gnostic dualism (see below): the belief that God ruled heaven while Satan was left free to rule the world.

It is an interesting question as to why so many groups have turned to Devil worship down the years. It is something that cannot be answered in a paragraph or two. I have already hinted at some of the reasons in this book. All we can say is that fundamental to all these unconventional sects was dissatisfaction with the status quo, perhaps because results were slow in coming, and the charisma of certain figures who were able to attract followers and who out of pride and misplaced belief in themselves set themselves up as a new and quicker way to salvation. Peripherally, of course, was the licence the new 'rule' gave them to indulge in practices that the traditional Church would have heartily condemned.

The Gnostics, an early heretical sect, basically regarded life on earth as a sojourn in hell and condemned God (Jehovah) as evil for creating Man in the first place. Consequently, Satan was conceived as the adversary of God, and Jesus as the wicked son of a malevolent god. This heresy was carried on later by the Bogomils, who regarded Satan as the Old Testament god of creation. Other heretical groups followed, either eschewing sex or indulging in all kinds of sexual perversion. These deviant sects were ruthlessly persecuted by successive popes and extirpated. The Continent, especially France, was a hotbed of Satanism in the sixteenth and seventeenth centuries. Black magic and Black Masses are perpetuated in the twentieth century. Scientology, founded by Ron Hubbard, is another manifestation of interest in the occult. This fake religion advocates self-improvement in one's physical and mental condition through scientific and psychological means. Another false religion is that of Anton La Vey, leader of the Church of Satan in San Francisco. These churches attract people, often marginalized, who are seeking an easier path to their goals, whatever they may be, in this world, than is offered by conformity to the norms of society or religious belief. Rarely is the goal for a spiritual life aimed at fulfilment in the next. Goals are worldly and material. They are, of course, elusive.

Probably the most notorious figure in the annals of British Satanism is that of Aleister Crowley. He was a truly evil man who dedicated himself to Devil worship with all kinds of concomitant vice. In 1920 Crowley founded the Temple of Black Magic in Sicily, where perverted ceremonies took place, including strange incantations, blasphemy and bestiality. The associated orgies seemed to be a powerful magnet for attracting followers. He produced pornographic books at his own expense. He did not seem to have any difficulty making money; he was a master self-publicist. His was a lifelong devotion to black magic, Satanism in other words. He died in 1947 in penury.

Sometimes places rather than people seem to be a source of Devil worship. Perhaps the most famous place in England where rumours of esoteric activities have been seen is Highgate Cemetery in London. The place had long been in neglect and ravages caused by bombing in the Second World War had made things worse. The cemetery attracted undesirables of all kinds. Strange groups of people congregated there and reports of weird ceremonies were cited. Moreover, vandals broke open coffins and smashed monuments. Soon people began to claim they had seen ghosts. Written accounts stated that the cemetery had become the site of Satanism, black-magic covens and sexual abuse. Investigation did reveal signs of something very strange going on, Black Masses and the like.

Crucifixes and wooden stakes, found in the cemetery, only added to speculation. Most of the initial furore was in the early 1970s, when many people were convinced that Satanism was indeed alive and well in London.

This century has seen the greatest mass killings in history, not all between warring nations. It has also seen the advent of the mass individual killer who murders for fun, or for kicks in modern parlance, often described as a serial killer. Britain and the USA provide many examples. Trying to enter into the minds of such persons, discovering their motive force, is almost impossible, though lawyers and psychiatrists attempt it. The reason may be much simpler, as outlined here (McConnell, *The Possessed*, page 207):

> *No-one asked whether or not the Devil existed, had taken advantage of [the lonely and disadvantaged], possessed and controlled them and then vented their evil on [others].*

Perhaps Anneliese Michel was taken advantage of in this way. She was a young woman in 1976 when she first began to show signs of abnormality. Before this she had always seemed a devout German girl, though somewhat peculiar. She herself was convinced she was possessed by a demon as a result of her sufferings. In fact, she was an epileptic who also suffered from slimming diseases.

However, it was decided to exorcize the girl with all the trappings of medieval ceremony. She was believed to be possessed by six devils. Apparently sex and violence (inducements to, threats of) were characteristic of the exorcisms. Male voices issued from the mouth of the girl, speaking in dialect versions of foreign tongues, and giving vent to the most terrible obscenities.

Nothing, however, did any good and Anneliese's condition worsened, her sexual behaviour becoming more pronounced. She cursed in demonic voices at the sight of sacred objects. As a result of refusing food she became weaker and weaker. After about two and a half months of semi-starvation she died in bed.

The doctor who was called in to issue a death certificate was appalled at what he saw and reported the circumstances to the authorities. The verdict was death by starvation. Neither the exorcists nor the girl's parents had called on a doctor, when it should have been apparent that Anneliese was literally fading away. The court ruled that the parents and the exorcists were guilty of negligence and sentenced them to a short term of imprisonment. All four were convinced that, despite all, they had been dealing with a case of demon possession. How otherwise, they asked, could Anneleise speak in tongues, especially oncs long gone? No one could answer this question.

Satanic Sects

It is probable that instances like this of some practice of accredited Churches going astray with frightful results encourage certain demented people to set themselves up as prophets, as long-awaited messiahs. This, however, in my judgement is one cause; dissatisfaction recently engendered can be 'milked' and turned to the personal advantage of the leader of the movement. Brain-washing is par for the course, by means of which adherents are turned into automatons obeying blindly. The deaths of many followers of David Koresh of the Davidian sect, and of Jim Jones of the People's Temple are illustrations.

Groups tend to fall into two categories: those which deny God; and those which in theory believe in Him. For some followers, Satanism becomes a type of religion; for others their activities seem just an excuse to indulge in profanities. Satanists believe themselves to be in opposition to Christianity and take up an inverse stance, often literally as regards such things as the cross, the Host and other sacred objects. Unfortunately, they tend to be not only anti-religion, but antisocial as well. They cultivate secrecy and misplaced aggression with regard to group activities, but lose no opportunity to steal the limelight where the personal glory of the leader is concerned. Such leaders often claim that it is because we are confronted with so much tragedy and wickedness in the world that it is hard to believe in a merciful God who wills all things. This can only be countered by saying that at bottom evil is man-made, and where it is patently not (as in some disasters of nature), God moves in mysterious ways – the understanding of which is not, as yet, vouchsafed to us.

Along with interest in cults and sects is a revival of interest in witchcraft. This tends not to be the demonic type prevalent for centuries, whereby its practitioners were servants of the Devil. There are many so-called 'white witches' at present who profess to do good, hinting at magical powers. This modern witchcraft is hostile to Christianity, itself claiming a sort of religious aura. Often, however, ancient rites and figures are revived, thus producing a strange amalgam of beliefs. Such people are usually hard put to define what a witch really is or in what the essence or nature of 'modern' witchcraft is – without reference to arcane forces.

Are the leaders of these sects chosen by Satan expressly to lead others astray? It would certainly be a great opportunity to influence hundreds, thousands of souls (used advisedly). Are these leaders already demonized before they begin to make their fantastic claims? Demonization in Biblical times, as we have seen, was overt; one reason given for its prevalence was to show how much the world needed the Messiah's healing hand and the hands of His disciples. In recent centuries, and definitely in modern times, this aspect is not so, with the result that demonization does not need to be overt, so visible, as it once was. This by no means implies that demonization is not as frequent now – only that it is not alluded to in so many words. The word 'demonization' nowadays is mostly used (in general parlance) as a slightly jocular term with a serious connotation: victims or scapegoats, even objects of censure, are said to have been 'demonized' when they have simply been blamed for something.

We may here state that demonization can happen to Christian believers as to non-believers, as much to the devout as to the wicked. History indicates this, though one often finds it adduced that if the faith or spirit is strong enough then the Devil (or his demon) cannot enter. I personally have found many people of a previously well-balanced life whom I believed to be demonized. All the greater is

Satan's triumph if he can, through some little personal weakness, boast of dominating a good person's life! I am not denying that most of the cases I have experience of have some physical or mental sickness at bottom, as I have intimated before. Notice I use the word 'most'. What is similar without doubt to the Biblical act of casting out demons is the immediate aftermath which I have personally witnessed: the sense of relief, of peace, of restoration to normality, and of course the loss of any occult powers the patient may have had.

THE GUARDIAN ANGEL

A concept that I have said little of, if anything at all, is that of the Guardian Angel, a belief, if it may be so called, inculcated into the Roman Catholic child from an early age. The thinking behind this is that as mere mortals, prone to sin, we need constant help. The implication is that the Devil is strong enough and that he or his demons are able to tempt us easily. We may not on our own be strong enough to resist his blandishments. After all, if the evil spirit exists to wreak his wickedness on earth, why not his opponent, created by God to protect us? It may be deduced from this concept that our will is fortified by the imagined presence of an aura of goodness. Perhaps it was by the Guardian Angel's aid or intervention that the mystics achieved spiritual ecstasy.

MYSTICS

We can now consider some of the mystics, scholastics and other groups who played such an important part in the development of the Church and its attitude to demonology.

I have already mentioned some of the scholastics as they were called: Abelard, Anselm, Lombard and Aquinas. They were so called because they looked at Scripture and tradition through the eyes of reason, rather than blind faith. The nature of the Devil came under scrutiny along with other elements, with the result that the Devil as a literary or artistic figure became more prominent, while his role in theology lessened.

These Christian theologians examined the nature of evil, free will, God's position and the existence of evil, *vis-à-vis* the activities of the Devil. They considered the concepts of predestination, and original sin. Redemption and salvation were themes that came into their remit. When and how the devil and his disciples fell; why God created Man – these are great themes. Amid all this, of course, it was taken for granted that the Devil existed – and this belief naturally coloured all their thinking.

Throughout, certain groups were execrated, heretics of course, and non-believers, of whom Jews were foremost. They were 'demonized', to use a familiar term, as representing aberrant, even pagan, beliefs. As demons attack humans in order basically to prevent or at least to hinder God's work, then all non-Christians are in a sense in league with the Devil. The scholastics almost reasoned the Devil out of common man's understanding; perhaps in a way they intellectualized him too much. For most of us, Satan is thought of in more material, corporeal, terms – haunting dreams and darkness.

Mysticism is the doctrine promulgated by scholars that Man may by surrender of the self and spiritual apprehension reach direct communion with God. It also connotes the belief that truth may be apprehended directly by the soul without the intervention of the senses or even of intellect. The doctrine arises from the feeling that there is an ultimate meaning to life, which we are unable to discover by rational means. There is a Supreme Being who can only be known by intuition, and the very highest state of human felicity is known only when an idealized rapturous communion is achieved with God. Mysticism's ecstatic states were only to be attained by contemplation. God is love and the source of all true happiness; the mystics' concept of the cosmos (*see* page 18) was based on the belief that the cosmos is a facet of the ultimate good, God. The implication for the Devil in this belief was that he had no significance in the universe; he is meaningless.

The mystics (or contemplatives) believed they were more vulnerable than most to the attacks of the Devil, by virtue of the fact that Satan loathed above all those people who tried supremely for union with God. They believed they were more susceptible to the wiles of Satan because they were in an intense state of sensitivity (to good). They feared Satan might deceive them into falsely believing they had achieved communion. They felt they were particularly targets for temptation.

Mysticism was at a high point in the fourteenth and fifteenth centuries. The humanists of the late fifteenth and sixteenth centuries felt that the Devil occupied even less of a central place than had the mystics. They jettisoned the belief of earlier times that all seemingly magical events were *de facto* works of the Devil. Humanists offered a more natural view of these things, the occult and the like, and were comparatively modern in outlook (for those times). Pacts with the Devil whereby 'magic' was achieved were in serious doubt. The greatest of the humanists was Erasmus (1466–1536), who believed that the Devil was not an entity, but a metaphor for the propensity of Man for evil. Demons are background figures, real, but of little consequence.

ROMANTICISM IN LITERATURE AND AGNOSTIC WRITERS

The Devil gradually faded in general belief, therefore, except among conservative Christians of both major Churches. A sort of recrudescence of belief in him in the nineteenth century owed much to the fascination the subject of demonology held for writers of the age. This new approach to literature was called romanticism, which emphasized emotional as opposed to rational themes. For the writers of the new movement, exploring the emotions was more important than intellectual insights into character. A romantic idea was that the 'hero' should be depicted as a loner, fighting against a repressive society that was hindering him in his legitimate ambitions. It may be that the romantic admiration for Satan arose because of this concept. Although Satan epitomized the spirit of rebellion that the romantics admired, he was not always an applauded figure, but could be representative of less admirable qualities such as cruelty, indifference, harshness and malice. The romantics' use of the Devil was not ultimately meant as a serious contribution to demonology; as a result their depiction of Satan has not really made a lasting impression on subsequent studies of his nature and being. Nevertheless, the movement's interest in the nature of good and evil did have the effect of bringing to attention the about to be forgotten medieval Devil and led to renewed interest and study of him in the twentieth century.

This in turn gave rise to the gothic novel, so called, which seemed to be emphasizing man's evil that lay just beneath the veneer of civilization. Matthew Lewis's novel *The Monk* (1796) is probably the best-known example of the genre. Other romantic writers of great significance were Byron and Shelley, who reflected atheistic views. In his play, *Cain: A Mystery*, Byron questions the idea of God's omnipotence. Shelley, always a non-believer in dogmatic religion, posed the problem of evil in *On the Devil and Devils* (1821), but shied away from deifying Satan into a hero: Satan was much too vindictive for that. His wife, Mary, wrote the perennially popular *Frankenstein*. Frankenstein's creation was not made a 'devil', as the other characters call him, but learned to be evil from his contact with humans. In art, as in literature, there were few absolutes. Shelley admired Satan's act of rebellion because it represented to him the natural wish of all men to be free.

For the romantics generally, the idea of God had been distorted by conventional Christianity; Jesus had represented true religion, real love and compassion. The God created by the Church was one in whom a conspicuous lack of these qualities was one of the main features. God was not exactly tyrannical, but was at least threatening. Love and freedom were the most important goals, and were attainable by mere mortals, provided they banished the innate evil in their hearts. It is clear that the romantics did experience in their work a feeling of disparity, of dissonance, between the image of God created by traditional Christianity and that of Jesus and His true teaching.

In France the romantic movement was just as strong. The novelist and poet Victor Hugo created a memorable Satan, a sympathetic force, because Hugo could never reconcile the idea of a merciful God with a being who was at the same time a vengeful entity. In his poetic work, Hugo portrayed the Devil as a being who illustrated one of the central romantic tenets: that we do not appreciate the world, our universe, which really is ruled by (God's) love, because we refuse to see that it is our own selfishness and pride that is blinding us.

Other important writers of the period were Gautier, Proudhon and Baudelaire, who all revealed at least an agnostic attitude to the traditional teachings of the Churches. In general, the French writers considered the Devil sceptically, or at least ironically, when they were not employing him as a frightener in their work. In America, the writings of Edgar Allan Poe and Mark Twain indicated the attraction of the Devil as a subject, the former treating him almost flippantly, the latter with his message of pessimism offering a very different perspective. It is clear the Devil has lost none of his malice!

EVIL IN LITERATURE

It cannot be denied that great creativity has been seemingly 'inspired' by the Devil. This is most apparent in the field of literature, where the theme of evil has been deeply and memorably explored in many works.

Thomas Mann

In Germany the most influential writer on our theme was Thomas Mann (1875–1955), whose *Doktor Faustus* (1947) is a secular version of the Faust story. The main character sells his soul to Mephistopheles for twenty-four years of creative musicianship. The Satan depicted by Mann is a veritable protean figure, changing his shape and character to suit the occasion. Adrian, the protagonist, has been very successful in love (or sexual adventure), but eventually his time is up. At the end he is taken away to a mental hospital, there to die, it is presumed.

Mann was brought up a Protestant, but he was never an orthodox believer. He hated Nazism and it was partly as a reaction to this repulsive movement that he began, in 1943, his great work. Reading the novel, one is almost overwhelmed by the images of evil and madness that dominate the book in portrayals of various 'academic' figures. Ironically, the most evil are the professors representative of intellectual dishonesty. One of these professors tries constantly to explain away the problem of evil by sophistry, exhibiting all the time an intellectual deviousness. Mann, it seems, is pointing out that such an obsessive interest in evil is itself a type of concession to evil. These so-called learned men had turned Christianity into a science, not, as it should be, an art of loving.

As in Dostoevsky (*see* below), Adrian has a conversation with the Devil, ostensibly on music and theology, but really on the destiny of Adrian's soul. One character in the book offers the notion that the Devil exists only in Adrian's mind – but we doubt that. The Devil does seem to reflect Mann's view that liberal theologians do not understand religion and that he alone has true comprehension. At Adrian's funeral a shadowy figure is seen – is it the Devil? Mann leaves the question unanswered: demonic power is always focused on man's frailty, this much he acknowledges; whether it is really embodied in Satan or whether it is in our minds, we cannot know with certainty. Towards the end of the book Adrian addresses an assembly come to hear what he has to say:

'*So the Evil One hath strengthened his words in good faith through four-and-twenty years and all is finished up to the last, with murder and lechery have I brought it up to fullness and perhaps through grace good can come of what was created in evil, I know not. Mayhap to God it seemeth I sought the hard and laboured might and main, perhaps it will be to my credit that I applied myself and obstinately finished all – but I cannot say and have not courage to hope for it. My sin is greater than that it can be forgiven me, and I have raised it to its height, for my head speculated that the contrite unbelief in the possibility of grace and pardon might be the most intriguing of all for the Everlasting Goodness, where yet I see that such impudent calculation make compassion impossible. Yet basing upon that I went further in speculation and reckoned that this last depravity must be the uttermost spur for Goodness to display its everlastingness. And so then, that I carried on an atrocious competition with the Goodness above, which were more inexhaustible, it or my speculation – so you see that I am damned, and there is no pity for me that I destroy all and every beforehand by speculation.*

'But since my time is at an end, which aforetime I bought with my soul, I have summoned you to me before my end, courteous and loving bretheren and sisters, to the end that my ghostly departure may not be hidden from you. I beseech you hereupon, you would hold me in kindly remembrance, also others whom perchance to invite I forgot, with friendly commendations to salute and not to misdeem anything done by me. All this bespoke and beknown, will I now take leave to play you a little tune out of the construction which I heard from the lovely instrument of Satan and which in part the knowing children sang to me.'

He stood up, pale as death.

'This man,' in the stillness one heard the voice of Dr Kranich, wheezing yet clearly articulate: 'This man is mad.'

With that he went away.

Leverkuhn… had sat down at the brown square piano and flattened the pages of the score with his right hand. We saw tears run down his cheeks and fall on the keyboard, wetting it, as he attacked the keys in a strong dissonant chord. At the same time he opened his mouth to sing but only a wail which will ring for ever in my ears broke from his lips. He spread out his arms, bending over the instrument and seeming about to embrace it, when suddenly, as though smitten by a blow, he fell sideways from his seat and to the floor. *

Dostoevsky

The greatest literary figure to treat the subject of evil in the modern world was the Russian, Dostoevsky (1821–81). As a young man he was a radical and atheistic. After a somewhat turbulent youth he turned to Christianity, but not enthusiastically, and after a brief period of Roman Catholicism, he found what he was looking for in Russian Orthodoxy. This appeared to offer hope of salvation based on a love and compassion that are obtainable only from a belief in mutual responsibility, a communion of souls that faced squarely humanity's enemies of sin and suffering. To overcome evil, it is necessary first to recognize its existence, and secondly to fight against it with a spirit of love.

Dostoevsky believed that the Devil dwelt in the heart of man, where cruelty and suffering arise and where they are felt. But compassion and love can also arise there so that we are compounded of two sides, good and evil, both striving for mastery. These 'sides' are dominant themes in his writing.

---

* From *Doctor Faustus* by Thomas Mann, trans. H. T. Lowe-Porter. Copyright 1948 by Alfred A. Knopf Inc. Reprinted by permission of the publisher.

Dostoevsky depicts these two sides in the main character of his novel *The Devils* (or *The Possessed*), called Stavrogin. This character leads a life without meaning, cold and dispassionate. His relations with other people are mechanical, without warmth. He seduces a young girl, who later commits suicide, overcome by shame. He himself marries a mental defective as a sort of experiment in the flouting of conventional values. At his confession to a devout priest, Stavrogin admits to seeing and believing in the Devil, who possesses his soul. In the course of the interview Stavrogin confesses to his guilt and seemingly repents. He realizes, however, that his confession has not been made with love (of God, of goodness) and sincerity; he has lived a life of deceit for too long. But he knows that he is doomed, he says so himself, and not long afterwards commits suicide. Like Faust, he had given himself to Satan and could not be redeemed.

The character Kirillov, an engineer, represents the intellectual devil. Here he is in conversation with Stepanovich, an atheist, who is in opposition to society and plans to destroy it, erecting a new one where vice will flourish:

'I am bound to show my unbelief,' said Kirillov, walking about the room. 'I have no higher idea than disbelief in God. I have all history on my side. Man has done nothing to God so as to go on living, and not kill himself; that's the whole of universal history up to now. I am the first one in the whole history of mankind who would not invent God. Let them know it once for all.'

He pointed with feverish enthusiasm to the image of the Saviour, before which a lamp was burning.

'So you still believe in Him, and you've lighted the lamp; to be on the safe side, I suppose?' remarked Stepanovich. 'Do you know to my thinking you believe perhaps more thoroughly than any priest.'

'Believe in whom? In HIM? Listen.' Kirillov stood still, gazing before him with a fixed and ecstatic look. 'Listen to a great idea: there was a day on earth and in the midst of the earth there were three crosses. One on the cross had such faith that he said to another: "Today thou shalt be with me in paradise". The day ended; both died and passed away and found neither paradise nor resurrection. His words did not come true. Listen: that Man was the loftiest of all on earth. He was that which gave meaning to life. The whole planet with everything in it is mere madness without that Man. There has never been any like Him before or since, never, up to a miracle. And if that is so, if the laws of nature did not spare even Him, have not spared their miracle and made even Him live in a lie and die for a lie, then all the planet is a lie and rests on a lie and on mockery. So then the very laws of the planet are a lie and the vaudeville of devils. What is there to live for? Answer if you are a man.'

'That's a different matter. It seems to me you've mixed up two different causes... if the lie were ended and if you realised that all the falsity comes from the belief in that former God?'

'So at last you understand!' said Kirillov rapturously. 'So it can be understood if even a fellow like you understands. Do you understand now that the salvation for all consists in proving this idea to everyone? Who will do it? I!…'

The powerful speech (quoted here from David Magarshack's 1953 translation of *The Devils*, Penguin Books, Harmondsworth) continues on the theme of free will and the nature of (his) godhead. Unable to live with the great mission, Kirillov at the end commits suicide.

In *The Brothers Karamazov*, Dostoevsky bases his novel round the family Karamazov, principally three legitimate sons. An illegitimate son is influenced by the second son, the intellectual Ivan, who argues that because there is no God, there is no Devil either. The brainwashed son, motivated by the theories of Ivan, murders their father, but suspicion falls on the eldest brother.

Ivan has a discussion with the youngest son, Alyosha, about the existence of God. The main plank in his atheistic reasoning is that as individuals can be so cruel, how could God tolerate such cruelty and such individuals? Alyosha cannot reply to Ivan's question: how can God be the architect of a world which exhibits extreme cruelty? Alyosha admits he himself could not be the architect on these conditions. There is only God's love and forgiveness for us. Ivan then tells his brother of an episode where Christ comes to earth a second time, only to be told by a Spanish Grand Inquisitor that He is not wanted; that the Church has authority to deal with anything. The Grand Inquisitor thus becomes a symbol of all that is wrong (in Dostoevsky's eyes) with Christianity and its dogma, and a symbol of humanity which prefers its own prejudices.

Ivan sees the Devil but in different forms. We judge that this Devil is really Ivan himself. Ivan had denied the existence of the Devil, but now he could not. His denial is an attempt to deny demonic elements in himself. The Devil says he is only a figment of Ivan's imagination, but the context tells us that he is in fact real. The discussions between Ivan and Alyosha and between Ivan and the Devil indicate a conflict between belief and unbelief. The author's belief in the Devil and his trust in God shine through the story. Dostoevsky explored the nature of evil more deeply than any fiction writer before or since. The message we come away with from the novels is that evil, great as it is, is not as great as the good created by divine love.

Gogol

Gogol (1809–52) was another great Russian writer fascinated, like Dostoevsky, with the Russian Devil. The central character of *The Government Inspector* is one Hlestakov, who represents the Devil, swaggering and boastful, but in reality he is mediocre and cowardly. His visit to inspect a town dominated by villains throws the town into confusion made worse by Hlestakov's practical jokes. Gogol, however, uses his Inspector to ask the question: who is not at heart such another Hlestakov? Surrounded by the abuses and vices he has himself uncovered, the Inspector seems like a Satan on whom evil spirits dance attendance.

Gogol explores the theme of evil more deeply in *Dead Souls*. The central figure, Tchitchikov, perpetrates a massive swindle by buying a number of serfs who still appear on the registers, but in fact are dead. He pretends to have moved them to another region where they will officially die and then Tchitchikov will receive a large indemnity. The allegory inherent in the book is that just as the Devil makes transactions with God and engages in fighting for souls, in reality he only gets dead, valueless souls.

For Gogol, the Devil resides in our very souls; that is why he is so very dangerous. To show the vices of humanity, it was necessary to oppose them from within. He experienced religious doubt and turmoil all his life. His dream was of a motherland glorying in her form of Christianity, realizing her destiny and achieving an heroic state. It is far from certain that Gogol was successful in his quest, as he abandoned *Dead Souls* before it was finished.

The Devil as 'Inspiration'

The literature involving devil figures throughout the ages is enormous. Above, we have already looked at perhaps the most significant. From them evolved the notion of basing stories round the idea of a pact with the Devil (*see* earlier chapters), which led to the most famous story of all, the Faust legend. At one stage, a humorous view of the Devil was taken. In the twentieth century Satan is often depicted in literature and art as a harmless creature, a portrayal anathema of course to most Christian believers. Ask any exorcist – if they will talk to you! Carus in *The History of the Devil* (page 438) sums up thus: 'Devil stories are myths in which Christian mythology is carried to the extreme'. 'Literal belief' of Christian dogma', he says, 'weaves these pictures…'

The Devil has inspired, if this is the word, much art and much music, especially opera, so that literature has not alone carried the burden. In art, I include sculpture, particularly ecclesiastical, both within and without the walls. Notre Dame Cathedral in Paris is but one, with perhaps the most famous of carved demonic figures. One can believe with the famous French writer Gide that, as he said, no work of art achieves greatness without the collaboration of Satan!

Papini in his book *The Devil* has a very interesting section on books 'inspired by the Devil'. The books considered above may be not so much inspired by the Devil, as by the exploration of diabolic themes by writers who were obsessed by the nature of good and evil. As Holy Scripture was divinely inspired, may it not be, asks Papini, that *human* scripture, some of it, is diabolically inspired? A not totally frivolous question: certain blasphemous works could have been initiated by Satan, so anti-religion are they. Such books are not by any means confined to recent centuries. Materialism and determinism are in fact old themes of books 'devil inspired'. Some names may help to clarify: Machiavelli, Hobbes, Blake, Byron, De Quincy, Poe, Baudelaire, Nietzsche and Kafka.

The question is posed: do these writers recognize the inspiration of Satan behind the writing? Probably not, is the conclusion. But Gide's aphorism, quoted in the preceding paragraph, seems here most apt.

'The collaboration of Satan' appears to indicate that the most interesting works (if not the best!) involve inspiration derived from the Devil – on devilish themes. This, no doubt, is based on the principle that evil is certainly more interesting to read about than good. But rather than just writing about it, some people actively seek the collaboration of Satan. Many spiritualists fall into this category. We shall explore spiritualist phenomena in the next chapter.

CHAPTER TEN

TODAY – STILL A NEED TO BELIEVE

M an needs to believe, and this belief in God is buttressed by a strong faith. Only in this way can men and women repel the evil forces that both surround them and have the capacity to dominate their lives.

These evil forces include the blind alleys of spiritualism, demonization, the occult, clairvoyance and much more. In the case of spiritualism and the supposed communication with the dead, to the Roman Catholic Church this is akin to trafficking with the Devil, and involving oneself in things one ought not to know. Also, these practices, dealt with in depth, can lead to mental unbalance.

As traditional beliefs wavered, the Roman Catholic and the Protestant Churches came to accept a fresh renewal of faith, at the same time recognizing a need to change, as they struggle for relevance in a rapidly changing world.

SPIRITUALISM

The spiritualist movement is a comparatively recent phenomenon whose adherents are increasing as traditional religious belief is decreasing. There is undoubtedly a correlation between growing interest in a spirit world revealed by Man, and declining interest in a spiritual world revealed by God and the Church.

One reason is not hard to find: the greater immediacy offered by a medium. Mediums claim that it is possible to get in touch and converse with loved ones who have passed away. According to practitioners, spirits of the dead want to get in touch with the living, and are seeking sensitive people to do it through. Many are the people who believe that spiritualism is the key to what they most desire: communication with the dead. A comforting belief indeed, but in my opinion always unconvincing.

How a Family Became Spiritualists

The Fox family, in 1848, consisted of the two parents, and two daughters, Margaret and Katie, aged respectively fifteen and twelve, and lived in New York. One early spring, footsteps began to be heard, accompanied by knockings on the walls. The girls, amused by this, began to tap back and in return more mysterious tapping noises were heard in reply. Very soon they had worked out a code: one tap for 'No' and three for 'Yes'. Apparently, they were able to hold conversations by means of this code. Inquiries were then instituted by the parents and it came to light that a pedlar named Rayn had been murdered in the children's room and his body buried in the cellar. It was publicly believed that the spirit of the unfortunate Rayn now haunted the farmhouse and was trying to convey some message. However, no body was found in the cellar. (There is an alternative story which relates that human bones were found.) Unable to stand it any longer, the family moved – but the rappings resumed.

The whole town soon got to know and it was declared that the noises were attempts at communication by spirits of the dead and that the Fox girls had some special facility through which the dead felt able to try to establish contact. The girls became very popular with the local people, who asked them to convey messages to, and receive messages from, their loved ones. The two girls, alive to the possibilities, forthwith held seances and made quite a bit of money. Soon wealthy people from all over America were coming to the sisters.

There was a downside to all this, though; their house was attacked by crowds of people uttering threats against the 'witches' inside. Margaret married, but her marriage was short lived as her husband died not long afterwards. Her husband had been antagonistic to spiritism (or spiritualism) and had repeatedly tried to warn her off it. She did indeed give it up for some ten years, but resumed practice of the art again. From all accounts she began to deteriorate in every way from this moment. Her sister had also married and produced a boy, who suffered neglect by his now alcoholic mother. She died in 1892 an alcoholic and was survived by her sister by only a few months, who also died of chronic alcoholism. The last few weeks of her life were miserable and sordid, when she muttered only profanities.

This is the story of the first spiritualists. Perhaps there is a lesson in there somewhere.

The Medium

It is well known that mediumistic activity is full of fraud, but that equally many gullible people come away with a feeling of satisfaction that they have had visitors from

> *The undiscovered country from whose bourn*
> *No traveller returns…*

This is Shakespeare's belief and that of most people. Roman Catholics condemn spiritualism mainly because in their eyes the practice is trafficking with the Devil and is involvement in things we are not meant to know. Mediums will deny this, alleging that they are only putting people in touch with the harmless, often pathetic, shades of the other world.

The Roman Catholic Church believes that the spirits raised (if they are) are evil intelligences who have never had incarnate bodies. In this sense they are the Devil's emissaries come to snare as many souls as possible. Mediums actively invite these spirits to enter into them (as in cases of possession we have already mentioned), and like them are therefore in great danger. The religion of Jesus Christ loses its meaning. On the other hand, many of the mediums have never been conventional Christians, so spiritism becomes for them a type of religion. Horror stories are legion of the deleterious effect their practices have on them. Maybe this is special pleading by those who have an axe to grind; undoubtedly many mediums are sincere and convinced that what they are doing is both right and helpful.

Mediumship is not far from possession. For the time the seance lasts the medium *is* possessed, if not in the traditional sense of not knowing what one is doing. The danger is that of being so endowed with receptivity to spirit visitation that a state of possession could become permanent. At least, this is a fear of the Roman Catholic Church. Another concern is that dealing in the occult in such depth may lead – and there is some evidence of this – to mental unbalance. Rarely is it claimed that spirit 'response' is by God's agency. For these reasons spiritualism is regarded by the Church as an atheistic pursuit.

I would put it this way. Just as a very small number of 'possessions' are, I believe, genuine cases of demonic infestation, the same proportion of cases of communication with the spirit world could be genuine. If no fraud is detected or suspected, what is the verdict? Does anybody, except the medium, know for sure? Particularly strange are the predictions obtained at seances which come true; how can anyone know the future? Manifestations are susceptible to trickery and one needs to be sceptical. In some cases, however, no inkling of the physical (in life) appearance of the loved one has been given, so a lifelike manifestation is, to say the least, puzzling. It is precisely because there are puzzling cases that the Roman Catholic Church condemns spiritualism. It is regarded as indeed Devil's play. As Summers says in *The History of Witchcraft and Demonology*, 'Modern spiritism is merely witchcraft revived.' This verdict is from a Catholic minister's point of view.

In the early days of spiritualism in Britain the movement experienced attacks from the established Churches and from the law of the land. Despite this, it became established. There have been some notable believers, among them Sir Arthur Conan Doyle in England and Victor Hugo in France. This belief encompasses a conception of the universe in seven planes of existence, the lowest being the physical, and from here the soul can progress to higher planes. Mediums are the movement's embodiment who claim precognition, a type of second sight, and special psychic abilities not given to ordinary people. The ability to 'channel' information about forthcoming events on a world scale is an aspect of mediumistic activity that is of fairly recent origin. Allied to this is the belief that certain places on the planet possess 'energy' where spiritism, especially warnings about the future, is particularly strong. There seems to be a connection between the movement and UFO 'sightings', for example.

An interesting belief is that a good spirit can inhabit a person (a medium) so that the being, called a 'walk-in', can take over the body of someone who has invited possession. The analogy is with the concept of demon possession, but for a different reason. These 'walk-in' phenomena occur when the host has experienced a near-death situation, or has attempted suicide.

Generally speaking, there are two main groups of mediums: those who receive mental impressions and those who act as a means of channelling psychokinetic energy initiated by the dead. The first group interprets messages from the dead for the living. The second group is characterized by bringing about physical manifestations of objects or of persons. A fundamental objection to spiritism is that its practitioners seem to believe that no one ever really dies because they exist in a half world which is neither heaven nor hell.

Most mediums claim to have a guiding spirit through which they work, and in this sense do not communicate directly with the dead. The additional role of the spirit guide is to ensure the welfare of the medium, especially when in a trance where the 'guide' takes over control.

One criticism by lay people is that the belief mediums have of being in contact with those who have 'passed over' is pure fantasy and that their abilities are spurious in so far as they use common principles of behaviour to glean information from their clients – and are therefore duping them. They achieve a false status by their claims. On the other hand, it is acknowledged that we understand only a little of the brain's functions and probably use a lot less than that. On this level, it is possible for people placed in a receptive ambience to intuit feelings, even messages, from others who had been very close to them in life. In such a case it could be claimed that communication is rather between the medium and the client than between the client and a being from beyond.

It has, however, to be admitted that there have been many investigations into mediums and mediumship where allegations of fraud have not been substantiated. 'Proof' of communications from the spirit world is lacking, though some 'evidence' supports the hypothesis. Are there spiritual powers out there that are indeed desirous of communicating? And are they innocuous spirits of the dead? And most important of all, are these spirits speaking by the agency of good or bad demons? Maybe it all comes down to belief – as do so many things in a religion.

Of course, spiritism is expressly forbidden in the Bible; there at least three instances (in Deuteronomy, Isaiah and Leviticus). Jesus Himself spoke about the 'great chasm' fixed between heaven and hell so that no one can cross over it.

A word must be said about extra-sensory perception. It undoubtedly exists, but as an ability peculiar to a medium it is not credible. It may be that such abilities are more highly developed in mediums. This facility, combined with a sophisticated knowledge of human nature, may account for much reliable information given in seances. Much of what is imparted is non-specific, and just like the prophecies of Nostradamus the information is bound to hit the target occasionally. Perhaps the 'hits' are mere coincidence; then again, perhaps they are not.

Appeal of Spiritualism

However, it is not difficult to understand the appeal of spiritualism to people who see in it the answer to communication with the dead that the existing Churches would never countenance. It is an antidote to the functionalism of modern life, whereby Man finds himself devalued. It promises a gateway to the next world, where it is hoped one may find the truth about the meaning of life. Along with the Churches, there is another opponent of spiritualism, some would think a strange bedfellow: scientific thought. Science is opposed to spiritualism because it is basically unprovable.

The Roman Catholic Church, its clergy particularly, condemns spiritualism not because it does not believe in the powers of the spirits demonstrated by the mediums, but because mediums conjure up spirits which are eternal and venerable for our, mere Man's, delectation. They are not puppets to be dangled on a string for our amusement or satisfaction. They are worthy of greater respect. There is of course always the danger of entanglement with Satanic forces. In any case, do the so-called messages really emanate from the particular dead? There is no proof.

Nothing new or significant has ever been revealed from the other world by mediums who insist the messages come via some other entity and not, which is the reality, from their own subconscious. The knowledge they display is derived not from spirits in the other world but from their own power of clairvoyance and intuition. The Roman Catholic Church regards none of the display of mediums as in any way needing the intervention of spirits. No new knowledge has ever been revealed; what has been revealed is something that may be new to the devotee but is not new to some people somewhere.

For us, Roman Catholic clergy, the occult, of which spiritism is the most widely spread, is the equivalent of going down a blind alley. The Church, or Churches, provide the truest guide. Critics of anything to do with a spiritual world will always allege that such belief is fantasy. We have seen it directed at spiritism. But accusations of fantasy have to be proved or the accusers themselves are guilty of the same sin. Belief is one thing; proof is another. Witchcraft is pure fantasy because witches do not and never did exist.

Possession is not fantasy because so many things have happened that cannot be explained in rational terms; exorcism is not fantasy when medical and psychiatric resources cannot help; demons or devils are not fantasy if one accepts the previous clause and if the literal truth of the New Testament is accepted; Principles of Evil are fantastic because they are merely metaphors for something which we do not – and more, cannot – comprehend.

DEMONIZATION – A SCAPEGOAT?

Throughout the ages groups inimical to society or hated by authority have been 'demonized': that is, they are considered to have been driven, motivated, by possessing demons. Such is the case with non-conformist sects through time, and *par excellence* for the so-called witch group. As Cohn points out in his book *Europe's Inner Demons*, much of the demonization of groups is the result of a growing anticlericalism and therefore the Church's need to create a scapegoat for a hostility to Christianity, among which of course the concept of witchcraft was foremost.

In the early days of Christianity, groups also began to form, some with the idea of uniting all followers of Jesus under one banner, as it were. Even in the papacy of Clement, about AD 100, there was concern over the acceptance of leadership of the Church. Writers of the time urged Christians to unite and not to disagree, blaming the Jews for many troubles, who, the writers said, were led into error by 'an evil angel'. Heretical beliefs were being castigated about AD 200 by one of the great early scholars, Irenaeus. Some of these beliefs were questioned in writings that have been discovered in Egypt and Israel since 1945. Some, however, are patently the work of disaffected or even apostaic sects in their claim that, for example, there is no need for 'the Devil' as the God of the Jews is the chief of the fallen angels. These writings have versions, other than the traditional, of the Garden of Eden story, which gave rise to the assertion that ordinary people were being led astray by the rulers; that is, the Church. These heretical views were attacked by Tertullian, among others, as having their inspiration in the Devil. Other discovered writings are at variance on several points with the accepted canon of religious belief as laid down in the Bible.

As Christians we take one person's words as the truth (as 'gospel') and reject another's. Why? Because we are ambivalent in our beliefs, ambiguous as they are. Take the Devil. He is considered by most people as the essence of evil. But, as I have intimated, without him there would be no sin – and correspondingly no demonstrable virtue. It is only because some people are bad that others, by comparison, are good. On this premise, Satan is necessary for Man's struggle to attain everlasting life. Only when Satan incites us to excessive indulgence in sin is his true baseness revealed. Without a fight there is no victory. If the Devil and his demons did not exist, then neither would the saints and angels. If the Devil is supremely powerful in this struggle, then it is futile to blame mankind for anything – a concept completely contrary to the wisdom of the Church. Man has his own nature and because he has free will he must use it to fight back. Satan only profits from our weakness if we are not prepared to fight back. He cannot profit all the time otherwise he would also be omnipotent, and there cannot be two omnipotent beings in the universe. True belief in the existence of the Devil was shown by the saints, those canonized because of their outstanding Christian virtue, and who fought supremely 'the good fight'.

Satan, it is true, influences individual decisions and hopes thereby to influence the many. His power is manifest in the actions and decisions of men which bring disaster to many people. But this is not all. Satan and other evil spirits, according to Christian belief, can and do have power over physical nature: the air, the earth, hell and upper regions (but not heaven). The devils, therefore, are not content with attacking souls; they also attack bodies. Spirits of evil have no absolute powers; those they have are always limited by circumstance. The evil spirit acts by 'using according to his nature things which he is unable to modify – by grouping certain elements, for example, and by arranging the coincidence of apparently fortuitous circumstances' (Joseph de Tonquedec, 'Aspects of Satan's Activity', *Satan*, ed. Moeller, page 49).

CHANGING FACE OF CHRISTIANITY

In the late seventeenth to early nineteenth centuries Christianity became subject to deep scrutiny by some of the greatest minds of the age. Rationality was their watchword.

Justifying Christianity?

Some, such as the learned German philosopher Leibnitz, sought to unite the Christian Churches by justifying Christianity; in his struggle he almost rationalized away its mysteries. For him Christianity was a religious idealism. Other thinkers joined in the line of Leibnitz, also attempting to rationalize, but without any anti-religious bent. In the course of this movement, the role of the Bible as the source of all religious belief tended to be down-played, and ratiocination, a process of reasoning, took its place. Most of these 'reformists', if so we may call them, were Protestant, but there was a sprinkling of Catholics. The Bible came to be looked on as a flimsy document on which to base such a vital thing as a religion.

The Death of God?

Later on in the eighteenth century, another German philosopher, Kant, felt that the reason approach to what is after all a question of faith had gone too far. He tried a counter-argument, but he was swimming against the stream of the 'Age of Reason' and experienced grave difficulty in combating what has very aptly been called the 'secularization of Christianity'. Kant felt that the place of evil, and Man's part in it, had been 'rationalized' too much, so much so that it was in danger of being trivialized. The 'Liquidation of Christianity', to use Lenz-Medoc's phrase, was given impetus by other writers, of whom, as we have seen, Nietzsche was foremost. The phrase 'Death of God' was publicized by Nietzsche in his *Joyful Wisdom* when he writes: 'Where is God? I'll tell you! We have killed him – you and I! We are all his murderers!'

This is an exultation by Nietzsche, a declaration that a transient belief has died out. But it is through the mouth of one of his characters; he himself was apprehensive about a Godless future:

The greatest of recent events – the 'Death of God': in other words the fact that the faith in the Christian God has been stripped of its plausibility – is already beginning to cast its first shadows over Europe.

He felt, however, that maybe a new era would dawn for Man after the death of Christianity.

Revival of Spiritual Life

Instead, a revival of belief happened towards the end of the century. Roman Catholic spiritual life flourished, paralleled by increasing ardour on the part of the Protestant Churches. Rationalism had shot its bolt – to be replaced, at least among the mass of people, by indifference. Confusion reigned among thinkers and people alike. Perhaps we are reminded of that which was promised to the dwellers in the Garden by Satan: 'You will know good and evil…' – and which proved to be a delusion.

Satan himself is above all an agent of delusion who seeks to effect evil. There are two types of evil: the result of natural disasters, illnesses and the like; and that wreaked on fellow humans by the conscious will of an individual. They are not reconcilable. One is superficially fortuitous, the other is deliberate; one is considered simply evil, the other is radical, at the base of character. The latter is irrational to all thinking men; as it is so, is it subject to a controlling force, that is, the Devil? If there is a God who is responsible for the great amount of good in the world, why should there not be a Devil who is responsible for the great amount of evil? We are all too conscious that evil exists; that the world is not morally neutral. Some people are so evil and their actions so destructive that subconsciously we say they are possessed. And perhaps they are. We are chary of stating our suspicions because in this modern age we are frightened of declaring anything categorically, as a fact. Scripture and tradition teach that the Devil exists as the personification of evil. Radical evil cannot be eliminated or even corrected unless and until we recognize Satan for what he is: the adversary of mankind.

This question of evil, as I have said, is *the* important problem. So much so, that evil had to be personified in the form of the Devil, as thousands of paintings, drawings and statues testify. As God was frequently depicted, so it seemed right to depict the Devil. He was a personal enemy, not a principle. God was not objective in this sense; He was too ethereal for that, too representative of a life which was not of earth, worldly. His ministrations had to be interceded by His priests, to be effective; the Devil's attentions were much more immediate and needed no intermediaries. Religious ideas had to take symbolic form and needed parables to communicate them. The notion of God varies according to one's position in the evolution of society: it is different in different epochs; it is different for those who are morally honest and for those who are not.

BELIEF IN GOD

What, we may ask, at this point, is the purpose of a belief in God? It is a question that has been with the human race from time immemorial. It is clearly something that fulfils a need in Man. Without belief, or a system of beliefs, Man feels that much lessened, feels he has little significance against the vast backdrop of eternity or infinity of which somehow he was always conscious. Religion, specifically belief in a god, or gods, has enabled Man throughout the ages to develop his faculties and in so doing to be more than a creature who lives and dies – *finis*! The hope is that this belief will lead to the realization of truth and the mystery that surrounds him.

For the Christian believer there is no doubt about the existence of God; for the non-believer the idea is unscientific – but science cannot reveal or interpret all. However, it may be easier to believe in God than the Devil. A force in opposition to an omnipotent God would have to be a very formidable being indeed – unless he knew he could ally himself to the natural frailties of mankind. Which he can!

In *Mephistopheles* (page 301), Russell writes:

> *In one dimension, the Devil must be seen as an aspect of the cosmos, that God has created and therefore a product of God's will. God could have created a different cosmos, or none at all. But in another dimension, the dimension of space and time in which we all live, the Devil and evil are the antithesis of God, and God wishes us to strive against them with every strength we have.*

Faith, of course, is the buttress; the true Christian should be impervious to the Devil's wiles. But we know he is not, or at least in some cases he is not. Faith alone is not enough; there has to be resolution as well. This in turn comes from conviction – conviction of the truth of the word of God, of the word of Jesus and of His prophets. This conviction imparts meaning to life and gives it a goal. It is often said that belief in the Devil blunts the sense of individual responsibility. I do not believe this. Just because Satan (or his minions) are able to lead us into sin by playing on our weaknesses, this does not mean necessarily that we are forced or tricked into the offence: ultimately it is we who decide on a course of action. Satan exerts a tremendous influence, of course, but this is all it is: an influence, even a subconscious encouragement.

The old cosmology has long since gone and with it the idea of an outer heaven, an inner earth and a central hell; it is presumed the idea of a Devil has gone too, been relegated to the limbo of forgotten theories. Naturally, we understand the concept of the universe better now; we must do with our telescopes and space probes. But because the construct of the universe of medieval man was different, it does not mean that something immanent in nature, changed though it is in description, has vanished with it. A spirit, good or bad, can exist immemorially and permanently, even though Man's conception of its dwelling place changes.

REMY AND WITCHCRAFT PERSECUTIONS

I have alluded to Nicholas Remy, the author of the late sixteenth-century book *Demonolatry* ('Second Book', page 86), which is largely an account of witchcraft persecutions – of which he was an ardent champion. It is interesting to see what he has to say about demon possession in the light of the above paragraphs on spiritualism. This throws light on the beliefs and attitudes of the time, which now seem to us little short of wondrous.

In his 'Second Book', Chapter 1, Remy has a kind of introduction which the chapter proper will elaborate:

> *… it is not in the Demons' power to recall the souls of the dead to their bodies. But since they are the greatest mimickers of the works of God, they often appear to do this when they enter into the bodies of the dead and from within give them motion like that of the living…*

> *History is full of examples of those who have compelled the shades of the departed to return to their bodies and answer in human tongue the questions put to them. When Saul was in doubt… he went to an old woman who was skilled in raising the souls of the dead… and asked her to summon the soul of Samuel from Hell…*

Remy goes on to give several examples of spirit-raising in the next few paragraphs:

> *From time immemorial it has been believed that the souls of the dead can be raised from the tomb and by means of incantations, called back to their bodies. But for my part, I hold that the mortal frame is so dissolved by death that, except by some special favour of Almighty God, it cannot again be knit together… For of a certainty, those apparitions which are raised by incantations cannot be said to exist really in the body, but only in the spirit and in some figure that deceives our sight… Since they are foul and unclean spirits it should not be surprising that they should find their favourite habitation and lodging in stinking corpses. And therefore it is that ghosts, that is, demons, are chiefly to be met with in churchyards and places of execution… it is foolish to believe that souls haunt such places, since there are fixed and constituted places for them to go.*

To all this must be added the fact that Satan is the greatest aper of God's works and it is his chief care to appear to his subjects as nearly as possible God's equal in power and might.

Remy relates examples from history which have a bearing on his theme. He continues:

> *St. Justin Martyr proves the same insane terror against those who profess to be able to raise souls from Hell by their incantations, namely, that they do not see that it is not the shades of the dead but demons they evoke… certain questions are thrown up worthy of consideration as showing the boundless and insatiable ardour of the crafty devil in imitating and copying the functions of humanity…*

He writes next of incubi and succubi, themes which afforded Sinistrari much material in his own book *Demonality*, and makes the following comment expressive of the universal attitude to women at that time:

the rabble of witches is chiefly composed of that sex which, owing to its feebleness of understanding, is least able to resist and withstand the wiles of the Devil.

He next relates a story:

There was... a certain witch [male] who told how he had been led away to such abominable iniquity and by what wiles the Demon had seduced him... 'Being a herdsman I was going my rounds one morning to collect my cattle and one of the girls who used to open the stable doors for them stirred my soul with love more than the rest, so that I began to dream of her more and more both by night and day. At last, while my thoughts were deeply occupied with her as I was alone in the meadows, there appeared one like her hiding behind a bush. I ran up to seize the prize of my desire and embraced her in spite of her struggles and after some repulses she surrendered herself to me on condition that I should acknowledge her as my mistress and regard her as she were God Himself. I agreed to this. I enjoyed her and she at once began to enjoy me to such a degree that I was always unhappily subject to her will.'

ATTITUDE OF THE CHURCHES

Remy's accounts may seem amusing to us now, but much of what he wrote about still has some relevance in modern religious thought. Remy was a Roman Catholic writing in an age dominated by the Roman Catholic Church's way of thinking and behaving. Basically, although there has been an attempt to come to terms with present-day thought, much that the Roman Catholic Church still believes is ancient, laid down centuries ago. Of course, in the light of modern medicine and scientific development things had to change – but not all that fundamentally. The Church of England or Anglican Church, I believe, is more receptive to change, to new ideas, than is the Roman Catholic. The Church of England was born out of a feeling that reform was necessary, so that the movement begun by Luther on the Continent and carried a stage further in the time of Henry VIII in England meant necessarily that the protesting Church – that is, the Protestant Church – had an impetus (to change), while the Roman Catholic Church had not – at least an impetus that was counteracted by the hierarchy of the Church.

To this day the Roman Catholic Church is more bound up with aged tradition than is the Protestant. Take the notion of the Devil. The Anglican Church almost lost faith in an active Satan, sooner and more deeply, than did the Roman Catholic, which has never lost belief in Satan as an entity, even as a personal devil. In fact there has been some resurgence of belief in the Prince of Darkness by both Churches, but especially by the Church of Rome. In effect, the Protestant Church is seen as less dogmatic than it used to be (which was always less than the Roman Catholic) in matters of faith and morals, and to have changed more in this respect than its sister Christian Church. One obvious difference between the two is seen in the edict forbidding marriage for Roman Catholic priests. To sum up, the Church of England is by far less traditional, some would say less hide-bound, than its Roman counterpart. This more liberal attitude does not extend to denying the existence of evil spirits. Possession, for example by a demonic spirit, is not ruled out in a minority of suspect cases.

The Churches: Present Beliefs

Both Churches have experienced a recrudescence of belief in recent times in possession and the efficacy of exorcism. Parallel to the lessening of belief in the Devil was a diminution of trust in genuine cases of possession and thereby the need for exorcism. Under the pressures from the new discoveries in science, medicine and psychiatry and the attacks, real or implied, by political or literary figures, the Churches' traditional beliefs began to waver – but not to crack, especially within the Roman Catholic Church.

Exorcism and the need for it – that is, genuine possession – features strongly in both faiths. More books than ever are being written about these subjects. I feel, however, that it is true to say that the Roman Catholic Church takes the concept of evil spirits having the ability to direct people's lives more seriously, perhaps more traditionally is the better word, than do other Churches. Certainly, to judge by the words of the 1994 *Catechism of the Catholic Church* ('Sacramentals', page 373, quoted by permission of the Vatican) one would think so:

> *When the Church asks publicly and authoritatively in the name of Jesus Christ that a person or object be protected against the power of the Evil One and withdrawn from his domination, it is called exorcism. Jesus performed exorcisms and from him the Church*

A witch divining the future using burning coals and dancing spirits

has received the power and office of exorcizing. In a simple form exorcism is performed at the celebration of Baptism. The solemn exorcism, called 'a major exorcism', can be performed only by a priest and with the permission of the bishop. The priest must proceed with prudence, strictly observing the rules established by the Church. Exorcism is directed at the expulsion of demons or to the liberation from demonic possession through the spiritual authority which Jesus entrusted to his Church. Illness, especially psychological illness, is a very different matter; treating this is the concern of medical science. Therefore, before an exorcism is performed, it is important to ascertain that one is dealing with the presence of the Evil One, and not an illness.

Satan and his demons are clearly still a reality in Roman Catholic ritual.

The Occult

It is also undeniably true that interest in the occult on the part of laity (laity in the sense of being uncommitted to any one particular religion) has grown in recent years. This, as has been said, is partly due to the secularization of society, a society which nonetheless feels the need for some spiritual element in life, maybe to give meaning to life. Occultism is denounced by the Churches as pursuits which may lead to involvement with malevolent spirits and result in psychological problems for the future. It is this very element of devilish agency which is anathema to Christian thought. Many church attenders do not see this, or are not aware of it. Clearly, adherents want to go beyond man's normal intelligence and see visions of the next life.

Accordingly, occult practitioners devote a large amount of their time and effort in attempts to disclose the future. Changes in living conditions and lifestyles, changes in national structures have all played their part in 'the occult explosion' and with it the desire to see what the future may hold. Knowledge of what constitutes matter is a recent development and this has added to people's expectations of experimenting in the occult. In an age which tends to devalue the individual, group activity, such as that encountered in occultism, has an attraction as a means of meeting certain spiritual needs.

In attempting to reassess its attitude to ancient beliefs, the Church (or Churches) have often been guilty of throwing out the baby with the bath water. The Churches know that for many people they do not have the meaning they once had. It is a difficult problem. This struggle for relevance has resulted in some good things, but also in some controversial conclusions: perhaps a surfeit of involvement in social and political matters? In large measure the Churches have only themselves to blame; often they are seen to be not only irrelevant but lacking in moral leadership. Consequently, people turn to something more positive, more immediate: occultism. Ironically, the Churches themselves betray a lack of spirituality. It may be that some of the growth in drug-taking is in essence a seeking after a form of spiritual experience.

'Psychic' powers are assiduously cultivated by occult practitioners – or at least their devotees' belief in them. These powers feature strongly in all forms of divination. The emanation of psychic energy is very demanding on the occultist, we gather, and the reason for the vagueness of the intelligence. One study which claims to divine the future is astrology, a very popular concept. Probability or hindsight interpretation, or difficulty in reading the prognostications aright, probably accounts for most 'accurate' predictions. No one can *know* the future, unless aided by some supernatural intelligence.

Fortune-telling either by palmistry, cards, ouija boards or whatever seems to invite unknown forces to intervene in the lives of people who, if believers, will encounter disturbances. Involvement in occult practices often begins innocently enough, but is the slippery slope to deleterious habits. It has been pointed out that accuracy or 'success' in prediction falls under seven heads: mere chance; conscious fraud; telepathic powers; subconscious implants; external intelligences; departed spirits; evil spirit (Richards, *But Deliver Us from Evil*, page 64).

Of course, a whole raft of phenomena occurs in spiritualist trances: apparitions, hallucinations, levitation and telekinesis (moving an object) which the medium claims are caused not by her (or him) but by the spirits. The strange voice that emanates from the medium when in a trance is not, it appears, recollected afterwards. All this is condemned by the Roman Catholic Church and to a lesser extent by the Church of England.

Even claims of spirit healing are made by some mediums or occultists. Spiritual healing, if it can be demonstrated as genuine and permanent beyond doubt, is something of a puzzle. It is often assumed that this type of healing cannot be found any longer in the traditional Churches, and as a result many have turned to spiritualism. Modern witchcraft and Satanism are offshoots of occultism – especially since the former at least has been legal since 1951. Along with these practices is 'black' magic, the pursuit of selfish aims without necessarily having an anti-Christian bias (Satanism has). Some black-magic purposes are, however, distinctly anti-Christian: the desecration of churches or graves, for instance. Interest in such as the occult and Satanism at least gives incontrovertible evidence of a longing on the part of Man for a search for meaning in life – and death.

One school of belief alleges that occult phenomena – noises, movement, telepathy – are but due to the activity of part of the soul. Humans comprise body and soul, the latter being incomplete without the former. The soul, however, lives on after the body has gone; in a sense, it is the spirit which continues to exist. Death is the severance of body and soul. The soul is immortal, but wants to reunite with its host, the body, at the Resurrection. The life of the disembodied soul is that of a spirit. This conception of 'spirit' is not the same as that in a spiritualist context where it is, it seems, capable of appearing in a semi-corporeal guise. The spirit of the soul we are talking about is entirely incorporeal, not dependent on matter for its being. God is a spirit, as are devils and angels. Spirits need no senses – as man does – to apprehend material or non-material things. Their intelligence, powers of cognition, are much greater than ours. Nevertheless, we are still able to exercise our free will. It is axiomatic that soul spirits are good and that their activity is directed to doing good. In the same way, evil spirits are essentially evil and once having made their choice they are incapable of redemption. In our context of considering occult phenomena, the ability of spirits to move material things is of the greatest importance. This power extends to Man himself, as in possession of the body with concomitant control of his senses.

It is vital to the argument that we understand that disembodied souls can communicate with each other. They can influence each other. They can decide on a course of action – such as in cases of the dead appearing in which the soul takes the form which is most familiar to persons who knew the dead. All phenomena must not be ascribed to the Devil, as is so often the case. It is the lot of fallen Man to be easily influenced by supernatural forces, evil especially, but equally – in theory, at least, considering man's natural concupiscence – by forces for good. Before he fell, Adam possessed preternatural powers which enabled him to apprehend things in a way similar to how the disincarnate soul/spirit does. He, and we, have lost that power now. The soul, however, neither loses nor forgets anything.

Even it cannot see the future. Mediums often act as if they are foretelling the future, but the events foretold are usually vaguely couched or so concerned with tragedy that some of them are bound to happen – or in hindsight are interpreted as correct forecasts. Related to this is telepathy, by which we mean the seeming ability to 'read' another's mind. Mediums have developed the ability to tap into a person's subconscious and speak of events, which to the ordinary person sounds as if the medium is in communication with the dead. In the highly charged atmosphere of a seance it is possible by suggestion to the subconscious mind to make the subject believe almost anything.

Closely associated with this is clairvoyance, which is the disclosure of future events about which no one has any knowledge. (Telepathy is the transmission of thoughts from one person to another.) Clairvoyant powers are generally rejected by the Church, though if they exist, the agent is the spirit of the soul, which is directing its powers to the thoughts of others. There are many other features of spiritualism and occultism, such as are involved in physical manifestations, but these can be interpreted according to the soul/spirit theory advanced. It may indeed be that more secure information is achieved by hypnosis than by the occult! Hypnosis can bring benefits – this is well attested; but it can also bring harm. Some of its less desirable effects are often attributed to a spirit agency of some kind. Obviously not *our* human soul/spirit!

Difficult to categorize are miraculous cures. Many are spurious and some are transitory. Nevertheless, the Roman Catholic Church regards them as essential evidence for canonization. This type of cure, it must be supposed, is due to the agency of good spirits or the spirit of the soul, as I have suggested. Cures effected at seances are founded on the probably subconscious faith of the members. Even so, spiritual powers are invoked. In both categories, these may or may not be miraculous events.

Occultism and the paranormal are usually interpreted as evidence for the supernatural, either diabolic or divine. This is not necessarily true. They do not need to be interpreted in terms of spiritualism either. The phenomena associated with these activities is due to a singular condition which comes about when the spirit of the soul is active.

Interest in the magical and sorcery is of comparatively recent origin in Man's history of evolution. Interest in the occult is more recent still. The thesis seems to be that as Man 'progressed' with Christianity, belief in one remote God became boring and the Devil became more interesting. It has been adduced that this development is only to be expected: Man once knew nature intuitively, as became a favoured creation of God; now he knew nothing. The practice of magic became one aspect; Devil worship another. There were and are a variety of aspects. Sorcery and so-called pacts with the Devil are some. These practices can be seen as an attempt to ape the Creator.

In some ways, occultism is a modern form of dealing in witchcraft. It is, on the surface, less dangerous – or even less arduous – than old-style witchcraft. As belief in Satan has declined drastically in modern times, demystification of his power and influence has replaced old fears of his reality. Satan has, for most people, but not for all, lost his ability to terrify, as we shall see in the next chapter.

CHAPTER ELEVEN

DEMYSTIFYING THE DEVIL

T hat the decline in Christian belief and obedience to its commands in the twentieth century has been to an extent filled by bogus 'religions', such as communism, occultism and many other '-isms', is undoubted. On the part of some people, there is the feeling that humanity is programmed to progress indefinitely, that all is for the best – but we may entertain many grave doubts.

As concern for spiritual matters declines, selfishness, acquisitiveness and megalomania increase. These can be deadly sins. Truth is interpreted according to the fashion of the hour; men of principle find it hard to speak out; all values are relative. The Bible is no longer taken literally, even the reported words of Jesus, even by clergymen. This is the current situation at the end of the twentieth century.

Belief in the Devil has never been an article of faith in the Church(es). It has never been a part of religious dogma. But he has been believed in for two thousand years.

SATAN'S AUTHENTICITY

Prevalent today is the denial of the existence of Satan, and posing of the question – did he ever exist? It is a fashionable thing to ask. But in my experience just as many believe in him. Perhaps it is the result of the many instances of wickedness in the world; perhaps it is the influence of the media, and television and newspapers especially. Many relate personal anecdotes which offer (to them) proof of the Evil One's existence.

It also must be admitted that the Devil's existence often provides a reason for something that is otherwise inexplicable. Denying the Devil is a comforting doctrine: it enables the continual pursuit of criminal ends. It minimizes the great struggle that religion has had to face throughout the ages. It flies in the face of the inspired words of Scripture, an example of which lies in the famous lines of St Paul (Ephesians 6:12), where he says:

It is not against flesh and blood that we enter the lists; we have to do with princedoms and powers, with those who have mastery of the world in these dark days, with malign influences in an order higher than ours.

Nothing could be clearer.

Where he is not denied, he is often perversely lauded. Satanism is an attempt by deluded individuals to copy his rebellion. By denying God, Satan is given a prominence his followers attempt to justify. For the members of Satanic sects and diabolic cults, they have no doubts: Satan is a reality. As for others, as long as people deny God, Satan is content to be denied himself. Of course, many people do not consciously think about their attitude to the Devil (or God for that matter), but their pursuits and way of life tell the story.

Much in society makes little acknowledgement to a religious life; the new gods are technical progress and material gain, dictated by science and technology. Whole systems built on a denial of God exist: communism, for example, and much atheistic literature. Pornography on the Internet, and many magazines, testify to the growing secularization of society. For some, all this is testimony to Satan's existence. One *can* ignore the teachings of Christ on himself and on the Satanic, but it may not be wise.

The Lord's Prayer includes the line 'deliver us from evil' – what is the meaning of this? My interpretation is that we are continually and perpetually assailed by the attacks of the Devil, so much so that we need the constant grace of the Lord to parry them. It follows that Christ wanted us to realize that Satan did exist and always will do. The line also speaks of deliverance, perhaps in connection with possession; in fact, the Anglican Church prefers the word 'deliverance' to the word 'exorcism'. Consequently, the expression 'healing ministry' is likely to be heard more on the lips of Anglican clergy.

HEALING – LAYING ON OF HANDS

Maybe here it is opportune to say something about the 'laying on' of hands in the healing connection. The practice is derived from the New Testament accounts of Jesus' actions in touching physically afflicted people at the time of healing them. 'Faith healing' is well documented and there is little doubt that some people have derived benefit from it. These 'healers' claim that the power to heal comes from their own persons, passes through their hands and so enters the sufferer's body. In some contrast is healing done by clerics, for instance in the bedside ceremonies conducted by hospital chaplains. The Churches discount the psychic or preternatural powers of the healer. Where then does the occasional healing power come from? Some would argue that it is precisely by faith that some are healed; faith in the power of the healer, lay or clerical. The minister would always claim that the healing power is not his, but has been transmitted to him, to pass on to others. Lay healers, if they gave credit to other agencies than themselves, might not allege divine power – or so is the belief of the Roman Catholic Church.

LESS BELIEF IN GENUINE POSSESSION

Growing lack of credence in genuine possession has contributed to the apparent demise of belief in the Devil. Possession is infestation by Satan or his demons. If they are thought not to exist, where does that leave the deliverance ministry? 'Out on a limb' is many people's answer. But we see that people do need, or want, deliverance; the latter is wider than the penumbra or shadows of meaning thrown up by exorcism. Deliverance encompasses the casting out of demons, but also elements of immediate solicitude and aftercare.

I believe that writing off the Devil is vastly premature. As has been seen in the last chapter, the present dabbling in occult practices implies a rejection of the Divine presence, but an increased belief in Satanic influences. There are hundreds of modern accounts of demonic infestation, possession if you will, which when put under the microscope are shown to be susceptible to the interpretations of medical science, particularly regarding states of mental health. But some are not so shown. What *is* possessing them?

THE INFLUENCE OF JUNG AND FREUD

Two great thinkers and writers on the subject who have had immense influence on modes of thought in this area are Jung and Freud. To a large extent they were concerned with the problem of evil in the context of present-day thinking.

Freud

Sigmund Freud (1856–1939) is called the founder of psychoanalysis. He regarded religion as a myth perpetuated by clerics as a control system and as something that could reasonably be explained in these terms. He was, however, fascinated by the Devil and demons and worked on cases of possession in France. As he said, the Devil was nothing other than a personification of 'repressed, unconscious drives'. For Freud, the polymorphous Devil was the cause of many mental illnesses, adducing that possession, for example, was a type of psychological disease (rather than spiritual).

Probably the best-known aspect of Freud's work is that concerned with repressed sexual memories. The Devil became a symbol, in his view, of the abusing father figure, later a hated figure who gave rise to disorders in adulthood. As his thought developed, Freud regarded the Devil as a symbol of the fear of death, but repressed, thus it was so much worse.

Freud was a great enemy of organized religion. In his *Totem and Taboo* (1913) he claimed that religion was neurotic, characterized among other things by the repression of instincts – a behaviour that, as we have seen, he was implacably opposed to. Some of his attacks on religion are based on criteria that are ambivalent – and simply casuistic, intellectually dishonest. Repression *per se* does not always have deleterious effects; in fact, out of it has come much of value in the arts world. In some ways, Freud became obsessed with the Devil as a symbol of hatred on the part of abused children, leading to his central argument that cases of mental disturbance had their origin in childhood abuse.

Jung

The main thesis of C. G. Jung (1875–1961) is that evil can result from the repression of feelings, especially malicious ones, by its creation of a 'negative' force in the personality which can erupt destructively. Keeping quiet about wicked actions is an example.

Jung, like Freud, was a psychologist whose reasoning about evil is of great value. His approach is to delve into the human psyche; here he adduced that the development of the persona led to differentiated aspects of the mind: one tending to good; one tending to bad. Relating this thinking to theology, Jung adduced humanity's conception of God himself, whereby evil represented by the Devil is repressed, while for the moment goodness represented by God prevails. To remove evil the need is for integration, not separation; full understanding of it, so that it is not repressed but suppressed. In this way evil is brought under control. Evil, it is seen, is personified.

Jung, however, disagreed with Freud's virulent anti-clericalism, regarding religious belief as a vital part of the personality. God and the Devil were not for him repressive inventions, but realities. Jung advanced the theory of 'archetypes': unconscious structures familiar to all races which produce similar images.

The Devil, according to Jung (and in distinction to Freud), is not just an entity arising from the repressions of the individual, but is something born out of, or in, the collective consciousness of nations. Jung believed the Church's lack of decisiveness about the problem of evil was just shirking the issue, a non-coming to grips with the real evil in the human personality. Evil is real, just as much as good is real. Evil is necessary for understanding the cosmos – and for trying to understand God. The energy of the Devil is a natural part of the universe, which when repressed (as we have seen earlier) leads on to destructiveness. To Jung, the Devil is a psychological concept, not the metaphysical Christian being. He developed the idea of the 'Shadow', a creature of repression, a force in the unconscious which is impossible to control. The Shadow of a nation, collectively, might reveal itself in mass destruction and be closely allied to absolute evil. An enemy is thereby dehumanized, as Russell puts it (*The Prince of Darkness*), into demons – or subhumans on which we project our Shadow and thus feel justified in destroying them.

Central to Jung's thinking, therefore, were the concepts of suppression and repression; the former is a wholesome process, whereby we thinkingly reject something; the latter is an unwholesome process of unconsciously denying natural feelings which can lead to destructive outbreaks. The Devil for Jung was a much more immediate personality than for Freud, but both regarded possession seriously – as a psychological state. Reality has two aspects: that of God (goodness) and that of the Devil (evil). The latter is a formidable force which, if ignored, will break into destructiveness commensurate with the degree to which he has been repressed by humanity. The converse holds: if he is recognized for what he is, his energies can be tamed towards mankind's greater good. This

Shadow, the more it (or he) is denied the more potentially violent it becomes. We must recognize evil if we are to defeat it.

Jung writes about two types of conscience: the 'positive, right conscience' and the 'negative, false conscience'. The former is, for him, Man's 'daemon, genius, guardian angel'; the latter is 'the Devil, the seducer, the evil spirit'. The voice of conscience can be positive or negative, therefore; either way the demonic is adversarial and will offer challenges. This kind of demonic antagonist seems to be malevolent and dark. Jung uses the symbol of the Shadow to describe these areas of darkness. The demonic is antagonistic satanism which exists to create disruption in the victim. Confronted by a demonic Shadow, we never know whether we can integrate it and thereby make it harmless. We avoid seeing the demonic overtly, claims Ann Ulanov in *Disguises of the Demonic* (Olsen, ed., page 134): 'We either become possessed by it or try to repress it. Either has serious negative implications for us.'

A PERSONAL DEVIL?

'Science nowadays has thrown off the yoke of theology…' This was written more than a hundred years ago by a French doctor. The opinion was premature. It is now acknowledged that science alone cannot explain everything, especially in the domain of the spiritual. For Roman Catholics especially, Satan is indeed a person; he is not a metaphor. At bottom, it has to be admitted that belief in a current Devil is something of an act of faith – a faith, however, which is based upon observance of monstrous evil in individuals and in nations. The puzzle is this: some men and women lead blameless lives, and contribute nothing but good to civilization; others are the complete opposite and are a destructive force to civilization. Why is this? Are some people naturally wicked, even though they have gone through some baptism-like ceremony and even though Christ died for *all* mankind? Or have they been corrupted? And by whom? Philosophers such as Rousseau believed that Man was naturally good; how many have argued that Man is naturally bad? (Original sin is something different altogether.) The possessed person who does not respond to medical science but responds to the ministration of a priest; the disturbed location that seems to lose its menace after an exorcism – what are we to make of these? Perhaps after all it is more than faith that is persuasive.

Atheism, which is arrogance personified, as nothing can be *proved* either way, owes much of its origin to a devotion to modern preoccupations with materialism; by the same coin, the Devil is denied. The spiritual in life is denied by some governments because it diverts attention away from the temporal and transient achievements of a nation's leaders. Much more common is agnosticism, in which a *laissez-faire* attitude predominates in society to the extent that almost anything can happen without raising eyebrows. Even some prominent clerics exhibit agnostic views about some erstwhile article of faith; their beliefs, they know, are regarded as fashionable, and so they court popularity among the 'trendies' – maybe another name for the agnostic arm in the Churches. The ordination of certain groups in society who would never have been considered a few years ago is one sign of this attitude. This position is defended, but it does not have scriptural authority.

It was common decades ago in religious philosophical writing to deplore the 'arms race', the headlong rush to mass extermination of mankind because we had the means. Armageddon was close at hand. Now we tend to speak more of a balance of terror, the likelihood of 'assured mutual destruction' as being the salvation of nations. When we pause to think of this – what a position to be in! Two (if we consider the world as East and West) great evils cancelling out each other! This represents Satan's supreme triumph; we need look no further. The whole world is in thrall to him.

Political and religious conflict have down the ages been the cause of many wars. Political conflict, differing ideologies, territorial expansion as causes we can understand, if not condone; religious conflict often involves differing belief systems, different religions – these too can be understood. What is difficult is dissension between adherents of basically the same religion. The reason for conflict lies in man-made dogmatism, not in the principles or fundamental truths. When Man arrogates to himself the capacity to limn, to embroider, the basic teachings of God and Jesus, is it any wonder that dissidence arises? Many tenets of organized religion are nowhere to be found in the Bible. It is dogma raised to articles of faith that causes conflict. Who or what authorized them in the first place?

Materialism breeds the secular. Preoccupation with acquiring goods fits uneasily with religious concern. For this reason the vow of voluntary poverty is one taken by Roman Catholic priests. The difficulty is that many people look at the cars and big houses of (some of) the clerical hierarchy and begin to wonder. Secularization is the first step on the way to Satanization, among whose distinguishing features is contempt for life – a worldly life which moreover is our only one – so it is alleged. The motive force is materialism, and the sensual; the patron of these is the Devil.

'Modern sophisticated Man gives all the classic signs of not being in control of what he is and does. And if he isn't in control, then who is?' These lines of Kevin Logan (*Satanism and the Occult*, p. 194) sum up the situation nicely. There is undoubtedly much chaos in a world originally created as an earthly paradise. The eternal riddle of the universe is its creation. As well as chaos there is much beauty, but it is of a natural kind: did it all arise accidentally and indeed were the very exact conditions for life on earth purely the result of random forces? The Devil as himself a created creature could not have brought about these conditions. God alone could have done it. If God originally wished to create a perfect world, who, we may ask, would wish to thwart this design?

Free from Further Harm?

The Devil has many objects of his powers. People who have ostensibly been delivered of actual or imagined demonic possession may not be completely free from further harm – either because of regression or because of lack of subsequent support. As we have seen, many people who are thought, either by themselves or by others, to be possessed are in fact victims of childhood trauma, often ritual abuse, or allied traumas. People who offer support to survivors of abuse, usually called carers, find great demands are made on their time, energy and patience. I know; I have been one. Initially, emotional support is paramount; later the reacquisition of social skills on the part of the survivor takes over as a priority. This process cannot be rushed. The patient has been indoctrinated over a long period and is not likely to forget this in a hurry. Most have been brought up to accept Satanism: the belief that the Devil has dominion over the world; that the leaders of the cult or sect are always right; that obedience to Satan is unquestioned and that vows made to him are not to be broken. This is powerful stuff to counteract. Almost illogically, what we cannot do is deny the existence of Satan, the central figure in their life. This would be easier than admitting Satan exists. But we must admit it, because we do believe he exists. This makes the task of committed Christian carers all the more difficult. Combating a mere symbol or metaphor is one thing; combating a reality is another. Thus fear is a powerful emotion on the part of victims: they know that their helpers believe in the demonic and so know that in a sense their (inculcated) beliefs have a basis in reality.

Ideally, there would be a team of counsellors, so all the burden does not fall on one person's shoulders. Naturally this team, or its leader, needs to be assured that the sufferer has broken permanently with the abusing sect or cult. It is more difficult still if the abuse has been within the family, for greater ties then may be involved. One needs to be particularly careful when the victim regresses; that is to say, relives incidents or episodes of abuse. The necessity is to keep the victim in the present, mentally and emotionally. Depression is another commonly experienced syndrome; sometimes the survivor feels suicidal. Then our responsibility as carers becomes very great indeed. The whole process boils down to love and compassion for the victim: the substitution of divine care for demonic abuse.

PRESENT POSITION OF THE CATHOLIC CHURCH

This next section is derived mainly from the *Catechism of the Catholic Church* (1994), which 'is a statement of the Church's faith and of Catholic doctrine, attested to or illumined by Sacred Scripture, the Apostolic Tradition and the Church's Magisterium' (the college of Cardinals, Bishops and so on, which interprets the word of God).

I have had a few harsh words to say about dogma, but this does not mean to say that all dogmatic statements in religions are to be censured. I therefore propose to begin with this subject as being in many ways the most important subject in Roman Catholic belief.

First, it must be emphasized that nothing is promulgated by the Church without undergoing thorough examination. Regarding dogmas, the Catechism (88) states that:

The Church's Magisterium exercises the authority it holds from Christ… when it defines dogmas, that is, when it proposes truths contained in divine Revelation… in a form obliging the Christian people to an irrevocable adherence of faith.

The section goes on to elaborate:

There is an organic connection between our spiritual life and the dogmas. Dogmas are lights along the path of faith; they illuminate it and make it secure. Conversely, if our life is upright, our intellect and heart will be open to welcome the light shed by the dogmas of faith.

Divine Revelation means the Word of the Holy Scriptures. The Church states (Catechism, 29) that God inspired the human authors of the sacred books. To compose them:

God chose certain men who all the while he employed them in this task made full use of their own facilities and powers so that although he acted in them and by them it was as true authors that they consigned to writing whatever he wanted written and no more.

It is interesting to note that in the Catechism there is no mention in the index of demons – you have to look up 'Angels'. Neither are there entries for possession or for deliverance. Sorcery gets a one-word mention, but there is no entry for witchcraft. The only mention of demons is in the above-quoted paragraph on exorcism and in the section dealing with the fall of the angels – surprisingly little considering the tremendous influence demons have had on Roman Catholicism for centuries. Now the emphasis is on good spirits, namely the angels. It is instructive to see what the present-day Church has to say on angels, however, in default of any substantial reference to demons. Clearly, the Church views demons as having relevance now mainly in relation to states of possession.

The Fourth Lateran Council (1215) (so called because it was held in the church of St John Lateran in Rome) affirmed that God at the beginning of time created the spiritual (angels) and the corporeal (humans). The existence of the angels is 'a truth of faith'. As spiritual creatures angels (like devils) have intelligence and will and are immortal creatures. Throughout history, angels have announced the divine plan for salvation, protecting and facilitating. The whole life of the Church, states the Catechism, benefits from the mysterious and powerful help of angels. The idea of the Guardian Angel is expressed.

In view of earlier comments I have made about body, soul, spirit, it is apposite to quote from the section 'The Profession of Christian Faith' (Catechism, 317):

Sometimes the soul is distinguished from the spirit. St Paul for instance prays that God may sanctify his people wholly with 'spirit and soul and body'… The Church teaches that this distinction does not introduce a duality into the soul. 'Spirit' signifies that from creation man is ordered to a supernatural end and that his soul can gratuitously be raised beyond all it deserves to communion with God.

The problem of where evil comes from is next discussed. Even, we are told, St Augustine had no answer. A telling passage (Catechism, 385) attempts to explain its existence:

Only in the knowledge of God's plan for man can we grasp that sin is an abuse of the freedom that God gives to created persons so that they are capable of loving him and loving one another.

It is in the following section on the fall of the angels and Original Sin that most mention is made of the Devil and demons. The being who seduced the first humans was a fallen angel called 'Satan or the Devil'. The Lateran Council of 1215 summed up the position, which has remained unaltered to this day: 'The Devil and the other demons were indeed created naturally good by God, but they became evil by their own doing.' The tempter is the Devil, who 'has sinned from the beginning; he is a liar and father of lies' (1 John 3:8). The Catechism (395) quotes John again: 'The reason the Son of God appeared was to destroy the works of the Devil.' A significant passage follows:

Although Satan may act in the world out of hatred for God and his kingdom in Christ Jesus and although his action may cause grave injuries – of a spiritual nature and, indirectly, even of a physical nature –… the action is permitted by divine providence… It is a great mystery that providence should permit diabolical activity…

One significance is the reference to physical injury, which may refer to injury caused to the victim in states of possession – as well as general injury which could be occasioned by misadventure as a result of being misled by the evil spirit.

Reading further, it is clear that modern Roman Catholic theology is not very different from that of centuries ago. A possible retort is: Why should it be? The Magisterium by no means discounts the story of Adam and Eve as mankind's first parents. As it says, 'The Church, interpreting the symbolism of Biblical language in an authentic way, in the light of the New Testament and Tradition, teaches that our first parents, Adam and Eve…' Man was 'tempted and seduced' by the Devil in his desire to be like God. All men are implicated in Adam's sin. The text (Catechism, 403) continues: 'The Church has always taught that the overwhelming misery which oppresses men… cannot be understood apart from [its] connection with Adam's sin…' By our first parents' sin 'the devil has acquired a certain dominance over man…'; Man was not prevented from sinning because, as St Leo the Great, pope 440–61, said, 'Christ's inexpressible grace gave us blessings better than those the demon's envy had taken away.'

Adam's sin had left mankind perpetually damaged. Henceforth, all would be tainted by original sin. As a consequence, the Devil now had the power of death.

A profound statement (Catechism, 407) testifies to the fact that ignorance of Man's 'wounded nature', now inclined to evil, 'gives rise to serious errors in the areas of education, politics, social action and morals'. More attention to this pronouncement (Catechism, 2116) by leaders of society and nations would, I am sure, pay dividends:

> *Man, enticed by the Evil One, abused his freedom... he still desires the good... but he is now inclined to evil and subject to error.*

The occult (and divination), subjects which we have already discussed, are 'to be rejected'. The future can only be revealed to God's prophets or to other saints. Consulting horoscopes, astrology *et al.*, recourse to mediums and so on 'all conceal a desire for power over time, history and... other human beings, as well as a wish to conciliate hidden powers'. The Church could hardly be more censorious. All practices of magic or sorcery (still used!) (Catechism 2117),

> *by which one attempts to tame occult powers so as to place them at one's service and have a supernatural power over others... are gravely contrary to the virtue of religion... even more to be condemned when accompanied by the intention of harming someone or when they have recourse to the intervention of demons.*

Obviously, the Church of Rome has not lost any of its belief in demonic powers; it just talks about them less. 'Spiritism often implies divination or magical practices; the Church warns the faithful against it.'

When we discussed witchcraft the aspect of sacrilege and blasphemy often occurred. The Catechism (2120) has something of importance to say on these subjects. Sacrilege in the eyes of the Roman Church 'consists in profaning or treating unworthily the sacraments... as well as persons, things or places consecrated to God'. Blasphemy, which we have seen is typical of states of possession, 'consists in uttering against God... words of hatred, reproach, or defiance, in speaking ill of God... in misusing God's name... the prohibition of blasphemy extends to language against Christ's Church, the saints and sacred things'.

I spoke earlier of Revelation, that last book of the New Testament. In it John, the prophet, writing about AD 100, gave us his vision of the future. He did not use the word 'Antichrist', but gave many intimations of its impending presence. It was John, who called himself 'the Elder', the author of the Second Letter, whose theme was a warning against welcoming itinerant teachers of false doctrines, who used the word. He said in verse 7:

> *For many deceivers have gone out into the world, men who will not acknowledge the coming of Jesus Christ in the flesh; such a one is the deceiver and the Antichrist.*

The authors of the Catechism too speak of Christ's second coming, after the Church has passed through a final trial. There will be a religious deception

offering men an apparent solution to their problems at the price of apostasy from the
truth. The supreme religious deception is that of the Antichrist, a pseudo-messianism by
which man glorifies himself in place of God…

The words of Pope Pius XI (died 1939), who was over forty years of age at
the turn of the twentieth century, are particularly apt as the second millennium
approaches with all its projected pomp and ceremony, glorifying man's worldly
achievements. He said then, as the twentieth century dawned:

The Antichrist's deception already begins to take shape in the world every time… a mes-
sianic hope [is claimed]… The Church has rejected even modified forms of this falsifi-
cation of the kingdom to come under the name of milleniarism, especially… the
political form of a secular messianism.

NEW DEMONS

For many people there are new demons to be faced. They are not the spiritual
beings of old but are on the contrary very tangible. For Christians these new
demons are the modern pursuit of material possessions, power, wealth, scientific
advance, sexual pleasure, selfish goals; for others these new demons are the new
gods which they assiduously cultivate.

The relative morality which characterizes so much of modern ecclesiastical-
ism seems to smack too much of sitting on the fence when people want decisiveness, and authoritative statements from Church leaders about issues of the
moment. These issues should mainly have to do with such as faith and morals,
though it is right to speak out on social matters on the appropriate occasion. I am
not so sure speaking out on political matters is a good thing. It leaves the Church
which does this open to the charge of bias, of meddling in things which do not
concern it, and, above all, the charge of getting involved as mere tokenism, an
indication to the masses that the Church is relevant. This tends to show the contrary: religion cannot stand on its own two feet as a guiding belief system, but
needs secular props to bolster it up. Perhaps more talk of the Devil and demons
is needed: old *and* new.

We are living in a time of rapid change – nothing new in that statement –
and indeed religion is having a hard time of it to keep up. But it is my contention
that religion *is* keeping up. This may not always be manifest in church attendance, but it is in people's hearts and minds, where it matters. Many things have
weakened traditional belief. Some have been mentioned: among these urbanization, going back a century or two, was a principal one; the age-old bond with
nature was broken and the new urban dweller looked at his new god, the factory
or the mill, rather than at the land or sky created by the Lord. It was the beginning of materialism. The nature of people's work was different also: it was
mechanical and aimed at a specific end – mainly, making money for the owner.
It no longer involved any sort of commune with nature; it was barren and often
soul-destroying. Thus work is more and more being seen as a small contribution

to a nation-wide or world-wide business, which reduces the individual significance of Man still further. No longer was he able to see his life, his religion and
beliefs against a backdrop of eternity, reflected in the stars and the apparently
limitless fields. It was, and is becoming more, a technical work experience, dominated by technological progress. Comparatively few people now relate to what is
natural in their everyday life; most of what they do relate to is mechanistic and
artificial.

When people's lives were largely rural and their occupations mainly agricul-
tural (only some two or three centuries ago), and their horizons literally bounded
by woods, hills and streams, it was natural for uneducated men and women to
see, or imagine they saw, strange shapes in the dark shadows. After all, the teaching of the Churches was that evil spirits could be anywhere and what the Church
said went. All natural features had their devils: dryads, spirits of trees;
hamadryads, spirits that lived and died with the trees they inhabited; and ner-
eids, spirits of rivers and streams – there are many more. The people's folklore
was dominated by evil, mostly in the shape of demons. When the Industrial
Revolution came, they were unable to see these spirits and so credence faded too.

Money of course had always been important to the peasant – and to the
villein before him. Many of the poorest had been paid, partly at least, in kind,
gifts of produce or carcasses of meat, from the feudal lord, later lord of the
manor. Now for many that had all gone and the new labourer had, by the sweat
of his brow, to earn money to live.

This was by no means the only or major change in lifestyle for the masses (as
they had now become). Accompanying this change was an altered outlook on
life, morality and all things societal. In largely rural communities, family life and
close bonds dominated; in the new urban society this was no longer so – or not to
the same extent. Opportunities increased for relaxing a moral code of behaviour
that by and large had ruled for centuries. To an extent, expediency replaced personal honesty as allegiance began increasingly to be seen as something owed not
so much to God as to mammon, in the shape of the State. Ally this with the
increasing perception that economic power often meant political power and
indeed the secularization of religion had begun. It had a long way to go to reach
the present. Belief in demons round every corner and in the trees had gone, but
they existed still in people's minds – and still do now, as the following news item
from a couple of years ago reveals.

Sandie – A Victim

When fourteen-year-old Sandie was found stabbed to death, it was at first
thought to be the work of a maniac. There was no obvious motive, such as sexual assault, and the body was fully clothed. Sandie had multiple stab wounds to
the upper body and genital area and had been found at a local beauty spot.
Inquiries revealed no evidence of enemies who would want to kill such a young
girl. Her distraught parents could shed no light on motives. The police interviewed the dead girl's friends and acquaintances, among whom was a somewhat

strange twelve-year-old girl known as Liz. Further inquiry revealed that Liz had grown up in a family disposed to occult practices, though not devoted to any cult or sect, as far as could be ascertained. Liz's companions had always regarded her as something of a loner and were a bit wary of her.

In the course of visiting Liz's home, the police found a diary. It had been kept by Liz. It was as good as a confession, and, confronted by it, she admitted killing her friend. In it she wrote of dreams in which demons had appeared urging her on to evil ways. Apparently she chose Sandie as her victim because of the instigation of the demons and because of the fact that she was jealous of Sandie's popularity and good looks. She had, she said, seen the Devil in her mirror, who had told her to kill Sandie. Liz, the twelve-year-old, seemed to believe this was a good enough reason for committing murder and for her not to be found guilty. She clearly believed in the Devil and his power. She was sent for life to a secure hospital for the mentally unbalanced. Satan had claimed another victim (names have been changed.)

Whether Liz had really dreamed about demons or had really seen the Devil in her mirror we shall never know. Most people will regard it as a fantasy, one however with tragic consequences. But for others a doubt remains: they would claim that this is how the Devil works now. Christianity had clearly lost its meaning for Liz – and presumably for her parents as well. Perhaps it was all a myth and the only reality was Satan. Why, might we ask, does it seem as if religious, Christian belief has declined, while belief in the demonic and diabolic has re-emerged reinvigorated? Partly it has to do with the debunking of history, of tradition, of old beliefs, of ancient authorities, where these are seen as restrictions on personal freedoms which now are all in all. Satan has always represented liberty and licence and progress – of a kind.

PROGRESS?

Progress, for some, is the antithesis of oldy-worldly obscurantism of the kind propagated by the Church down the years. For some it is a seductive argument. This is the real myth. Progress cannot be areligious because it is precisely in the light of spiritual vision that advancement is made. Devotion to making 'progress' may make people on the surface less religious; the question to be asked is what is progress? Is it the ability to kill more people, create more destruction, prolong life and make monstrous clones? Is progress only to be measured in physical things? History teaches that it is the intangible which counts in the long run. There is directed and misdirected progress. One is permanent and of value; the other is transitory, and leads down a blind alley. The need now is to discern between the two.

A modern parallel to this progress in society's increasing deprivation of clerical character is the growth of mindless violence, resulting in injury or death to innocent people. Not institutionalized violence such as that perpetrated by some dictators, but individual, personal attacks. Many of these criminals claim to hearing demonic voices telling them to kill and hope thereby to escape their just deserts. The Devil is the favourite scapegoat and he is obviously as keenly believed in as ever – at least by people who have something to hide – but sometimes the scapegoat is God!

Most people have heard about the English 'Yorkshire Ripper', as he was dubbed. He claimed that God had instructed him to rid the streets of prostitutes, as a result of which he killed thirteen women, not all prostitutes, however. He was trying to claim he was on a divine mission by stating that he had been receiving instructions from God all his adult life. Of course, Sutcliffe, as he was called, was hoping to convince the jury that he was schizophrenic, as he knew that demonic possession could not be pleaded in law: one is either mad or suffering from diminished responsibility.

Sutcliffe was found guilty and was eventually transferred to Broadmoor. The interesting point about all this is that he reportedly underwent several exorcisms while in prison. It was clearly believed that a man so evil must have been possessed by the Devil. Blaming God had not worked. Roman Catholic priests had believed that the 'voices', if they existed at all, must have been demonic. It is not on record whether or not Sutcliffe is a changed man.

The important point is that demonic 'voices' (in Sutcliffe's case, divine voices) were alleged, and that exorcism was resorted to – a mere couple of decades ago. There have been even more recent examples. Sutcliffe, a lapsed Catholic, had lost faith in the Church, but had placed it in God or Satan, we'll never know which. He clearly preferred a person to an institution. Many people do now, but without resorting to Sutcliffe's horrendous crimes. For some, faith in a cult figure is all-important (Stalin, Hitler, Mao, Saddam, for example). But they are not necessarily all bad figures, it must be said; it just seems as though they are because the bad figures are more newsworthy.

Leaders of political parties can be charismatic to some. Politicized devotees of such people can have their own belief system which may take the place of religious belief. Adherents often feel the need for a sort of religious belief which for them is met by politics. The trouble is that there are political parties which can and do differ in outlook and aims. In these circumstances, religion can be seen as a guarantor of order, of established morality – a way of behaving which offers truth and permanence.

We could do with what is on offer in the above sentence! Despite our 'progress' we are conscious of difficult problems and grave issues in the world: pollution, population, energy supplies and national militancy. Bad news seems to bombard us every hour from all parts of the world; we have hardly time to digest it before there is something new. In a sense, we are too preoccupied with the present. An antidote would be no bad thing: re-creating the religious and the sacred. As Ellul says in his book *The New Demons* (page 205), 'man is recapturing an ancient experience. He is in gear once again with a known movement [religion]'.

There is, as I have mentioned, a danger in intellectualizing religion to the extent that it becomes a movement almost chameleon-like in its nature, so that it is interpreted as fashion and the hour dictate. The modern verdict would be that

Christianity is going through a fundamental process of change from which it may emerge better – or worse. I certainly do not believe the latter, and I am not sure I believe the first! To return to our initial theme, secularization there certainly is, but it is more to do with objects and spurious beliefs than true religion. Science and rationality may be around us, but they are not necessarily enemies to religion; only if we want them to be are they so. Christianity cannot afford to allow gaps to appear and to be filled by the other 'religions' of materialism, technology and politics. It must show itself ready to fight. In-fighting between Christian religions is totally non-productive – so is navel-gazing, whereby churchmen are fixated on nit-picking, lacking in confidence, too self-critical. Religion has just as much a claim to importance in life as science, history, politics *et al*. It is no use being apologetic. The new gods are only idols, after all.

CHAPTER TWELVE

THE WILES
OF SATAN
VERSUS THE BIBLE

As always, the Devil still attacks in ways too numerous to recount. He knows our weaknesses; he may be the tempter from outside, or he may seek to activate our natural predilection to evil. We can become stronger by being able to understand the Devil, so we know the scope of the evil we are facing, and by recognizing the immense power of the angels for effecting good in affecting our lives.

Control over the power of demons – indeed, trying to understand their nature – has exercised the greatest minds mankind has ever known. There are several approaches to demonology, and to those beings that seem to insist on being centre stage for most of the time.

Looking at excepts from the the Bible, the Catechism and literature gives us the widest possible view of demonology, from the horrific to the humorous, and of the healing power of Christian belief. Jesus believed implicitly in the power of demon possession in this never-ending battle with the Evil One, a battle in which the sorcerer and the exorcist are placed at either extreme.

UNDERSTANDING THE DEVIL

The first thing to say is that it is impossible to understand the Devil – to be able to do so would necessitate a knowledge of the very essence of good and evil, eternity and infinity, permanence and transience – which no human possesses or ever has possessed. The belief that anyone can be 'saved', even the worst sinner, is a fundamental Christian concept. Do we draw the line at Satan, however?

It has been argued that the Devil himself can be saved – if he wants to be (Papini, *The Devil*). Following Origen and St Jerome, Papini bases his argument on the fact that the Redemption was for everyone and for all things. Orthodox theologians take the position that when the apostate angels rebelled they did so as supremely intelligent beings whose actions cannot be recalled (as we have stated earlier). But this may not be sound, says Papini. At the end of time, when the Day of Judgement dawns, all (evil) will have to disappear including hell and its inmates, of which of course one is Satan. It is a nice point – and interesting. It raises the question of the permanence of evil and its nature – and why it exists at all. Often evil-doers appear to prosper in this world, and perhaps they do on a material plane. According to God, according to religious doctrine, this is not what counts. We remember the words of Jesus about the rich man and the eye of the needle. Naturally we are talking about a very long time scale – at least we believe we are!

One of the problems is that as humans we are unable to understand the meaning of eternity – and infinity. Our intellects are not up to it. God always existed (incomprehensible also), and heaven, we suppose, but hell certainly did not; it came into being as a result of the angels' fall. Therefore it is finite: it had a beginning and it follows that it will have an end. Also, it may be argued that as God is all-merciful, He could, faced with repentance, grant forgiveness, even to a deadly enemy. This view, I hasten to add, is not accepted by the Roman Catholic Church – at the moment, but thinking may change. An associated difficulty is that concerned with the punishment of sinners: is it really eternal for those who die in a state of sin? There appears to be a lack of fit somewhere. I am not urging the point of view which says Satan can be saved; I simply record it.

Satan, like his followers, is a fallen angel; that is to say, he is pure spirit, ageless and perennially vigorous. He cannot feel injury and pain as we can; the only way we can hurt him is emotional – by rejecting him. His only dependency is on God as his Creator. Just as we cannot hope to understand the meaning of God, we cannot hope to understand Satan – though this has not stopped us trying for the last thousand years. Satan is a formidable enemy, as becomes the foremost Seraph. We deny him because we do not understand him.

Equally we could say that Satan, or Lucifer as he then was, did not understand, with all his intellect, the nature of God. How could he hope to be equal? My contention is that he didn't: he wanted to share power, albeit as second in command. When he sinned, he sinned from pride, as theology has always stated. An irrevocable choice it was, unless we agree with Papini above. His real pain then was loss: loss of the ineffable love of God; and his damnation was a figurative hell – or real one, depending on the theology chosen. With him went his deceived followers, now literally demonized, into hell's community. There untruth reigns supreme. And therein lies the difficulty for mankind: nothing can be believed that has its origin in evil – evil that in multifarious ways has misled Man for centuries.

Possibly there is more evidence for believing in the malignancy of demons in the world of Man than there is for the Devil. Certainly, if Scripture is taken as the foundation of belief then the activity of demons is well documented – look at the many cases adduced of possession and exorcism. We have already discussed this topic adequately, I trust. The present Roman Catholic position is a compromise; it is sceptical, but allows for the possibility of genuine demon possession. Reaction on the part of a sufferer to what he believes is sacred, but is not truly so, only weakens belief in the demonic; unfortunately this happens. I believe I am right in stating that the Protestant Churches do not have as much faith in the reality of demon possession. On the other hand, if human survival could be proved (by spiritualism for example), this would be an excellent argument for the existence of spirits, probably not good ones – which act as the 'control' for the medium.

It is, however, clear from pronouncements of Pope John Paul II that for him – and, it follows, for all Roman Catholics – Satan exists. Satan is a 'dark power of evil' and is the enemy of Man. The reality of demon attacks has for centuries been well attested. Dismissal of evidence of such entities is often blind prejudice or, worse, arrogance. There is just as much testimony for the reality of angelic beings. Disbelief without proof or evidence, in the face of testimony from holy witnesses, is in reality a sign of an unmanageable fear – that the phenomena might indeed be true.

MORE ON DEMONIC POWER

The power of demons has been a changing subject over the centuries. Have they real power? Is it independent? Is it controlled by Satan or by God, or both? Can Man make use of them – by calling them up? By making pacts? Are they merely agents? Of God? Of the Devil? Such questions have exercised the greatest minds, Christian and other, since Biblical times. The answers, if there are any, vary according to the theological perspective taken up. Maybe the answer to all the questions is yes; maybe it is no. The power of the sorcerer and that of the exorcist, apart from their utilization for very different ends, are poles apart, if only in their source. It is the issue of control over demons which dominates all thinking in this sphere.

The point of view has been expressed that demonology is capable of four approaches (Ferguson, *Demonology of the Early Christian World*): (1) Demons never existed. (2) Demons have always existed and still do. (3) Demons did exist in the early days, but do not now. (4) Demons still exist, but with limited powers. All viewpoints can be argued. Two and four are not mutually exclusive, but one and three are. The view of the Roman Catholic Church now would be consonant with the second approach, leavened somewhat by approach number four, adducing that at a very special time in Christianity, namely the time of Christ's ministry, demon activity, possession and subsequent exorcism had to be demonstrated; now there is not so urgent a need for this demonstration, though it is still allowed to occur at certain times and in certain circumstances, if only to testify to the existence and power of God. The overcoming of demons is a sign of the defeat of Satan.

Demons started out life in pre-Christian times as animals or had a very close association with them. Later they took distorted or half-animal, half-human form, especially in the Christian era. With regard to Satan, as we have seen, very few references to his majesty are to be found in the Old Testament. He grows in stature as in malignancy in the New. He gains physical attributes. He is by no means just a personification of the evil tendency in man. One of the main impulses for the belief in, and creation of, Satan arises from the theological position, current today, that God as the origin of all things could not be considered responsible for all the wickedness in the world; there had, as we have intimated, to be a scapegoat (somewhat frivolous, I own) – better, to be a cause in its own right: the Devil.

It must be admitted there is some ambivalence in the attitude of today's Church towards Jesus as exorcist expelling demons. A certain temporizing is apparent. Not all individual members of the practising Church today agree, however. The divine power by which Jesus exorcized, once accepted without question, is often attributed to His charismatic, overpowering personality on disordered minds. It is by the power of faith that the miracles of healing at a distance were effected – or so it is said. Many questions remain – unsolved, and probably unsolvable, if divine power is denied.

Belief in demons always had a very close association with sorcery, magic and all sorts of divination, hence it was only to be expected that the Church(es) did not, and still do not, approve of them. What powers these early magicians had, it was believed, derived from Satan (whom Jesus, it is clear, firmly believed in as being head of the kingdom of evil). In the same way, the adoration of idols, 'graven images', apart from being forbidden by the first commandment, is regarded as a gravely sinful act precisely because it is regarded as the worship of demons.

The Devil attacks mankind in many ways, always through his weaknesses. These are manifold, though in the Church's eyes the flesh is particularly vulnerable to attack. The flesh is viewed as the root of evil desires which may lead to sin. Consequently, the teaching has always been that sexual activity outside of marriage is forbidden. As a result, the question is frequently put: why is the Church so much against sex? As it is an organization that regards celibacy as one of its major virtues (at least for its pastors), this attitude is not surprising. The commentary on the sixth commandment in the Catechism (1352) makes this very clear:

> *sexual pleasure [should not be] sought outside of the sexual relationship which is demanded by the moral order and in which the total meaning of mutual self-giving and human procreation in the context of true love is achieved.*

THE WILES OF SATAN

Whether the Devil leads us astray acting as an outside tempter or whether it is our natural predilection to sin as an internal urge, we do not know for sure. The truth, as always, lies somewhere in the middle. Possessed persons, for example, in the eyes of the Church are of two kinds: those who are invaded and those who invite in the demon. Genuine possession is believed in by both major Christian Churches. There is naturally a contrary point of view. It is well expressed by Langton in *Essentials of Demonology* (page 155):

the main factors accounting for demon possession in the Gospels are: pathological conditions of body and mind, such as hysteria and epilepsy; a strong popular belief in the power of demons to take possession; subconscious activity of the mind; the existence of psychic states which can assume the appearance of individuality; together with some measure of hallucination and autosuggestion.

– but is it the whole truth?

It is often forgotten how much good powers feature in the Gospels. These are, of course, the angels. God created them first, but because bad news is always more readable, the Devil and his demons have taken centre stage down the centuries. There are many references to the important presence or intervention of the angels, but not as many as to demons, it must be admitted. The function of angels in the divine plan is firmly supported by the Church just as much as demons as part of the diabolic plan.

'Demythologizing' is an 'in' word at the moment. As applied to Scriptures it can mean disbelief in such as angels and demons, the Devil and related activities and utterances. It is pertinently asked: where is the line drawn? If one thing is doubted there is the danger that the whole edifice of revealed truth will come crashing down. This putative situation is patently absurd. The Bible represents wisdom and truth accumulated over centuries and written by inspired men of

Behemoth, the biblical demon of animal strength

God. Times do change and with them modes of expression. Much of the Bible is allegorical and metaphorical. That is why we do not *need* to take all it says literally. We can if we want to. If we do not want so to do, the essential message remains; only, some things we can understand – some we cannot.

BEELZEBUB, THE BIBLE AND HEALING

On this question of belief (in the Bible), literal truth cannot be proved or disproved. Much may be allegorical or metaphorical. None of it, I am certain, is (or was) calculated to deceive. It is confusing and mystifying to pick and choose what we find convenient to accept or not accept. Most people, however, now do this very thing. The Pharisees of Jesus' time chose to believe in only what they already knew and found acceptable. Casting out demons through divine agency was a concept they could not accept, for it went against received knowledge as they understood it. Their minds were closed to the truth.

From Matthew 12:22–4:

> *Then a blind and dumb demoniac was brought to him, and he healed him, so that he spoke and saw. All the people were amazed and said, 'Can this be the Son of David?' But when the Pharisees heard it they said, 'It is only by Beelzebub, the prince of demons, that this Man casts out demons.'*

The name Beelzebub was obviously a common name for the Devil in Jesus' time. The Pharisees were an ultra-orthodox sect of Jews who tended to keep themselves aloof from the 'ordinary' Jew; they had a reputation for hypocrisy, however, and clearly saw Jesus as a threat to the status quo.

Matthew continues the Bible narrative (Matthew 22: 25–8):

> *Knowing their thoughts, Jesus said to them, 'Every kingdom divided against itself is laid waste and no city or house divided against itself will stand; and if Satan casts out Satan he is divided against himself; how then will his kingdom stand? And if I cast out demons by Beelzebub, by whom do your sons cast them out?... But if it is by the Spirit of God that I cast out demons, then the kingdom of God has come upon you.'*

No one reading this passage can be in any doubt that Jesus believed implicitly in demon possession. He insinuated rather than stated outright that His power came from God – notice the small but significant word 'if'. The interpretation of this passage, though, is that Jesus was making acknowledgement to his Father, from whom He derived His powers. This episode is retold in Mark (it may be that Matthew retold it following Mark, since Bible scholars believe that Mark's was the first Gospel) (Mark 3:20–3):

> *Then he went home and the crowd came together again so that they could not even eat. When his family heard of this they went out to seize him, for people were saying, 'He is beside himself'. And the scribes [probably Pharisees] who came down from Jerusalem said, 'He is possessed by Beelzebub, and by the prince of demons he casts out demons.'*

Mark's narrative continues in the same way as Matthew's, regarding Jesus' reply.

Luke in essence repeats the accounts of Mark and Matthew. but adds the significant passage about seven demons returning to the victim. The pericope (extract) given is that following Christ's statement that the kingdom of God has come upon them (if they believe in his divinely inspired power) (Luke 11:24–6). Jesus continues:

> When the unclean spirit has gone out of a man that spirit passes through waterless places seeking rest; and finding none he says, 'I will return to my house.' When he [the demon] returns he finds it swept and put in order. Then he brings seven other spirits more evil than himself, and they dwell there, and the last state of that man becomes worse than the first.

Jesus is emphasizing here the absolute necessity for something to replace the evil that has left a void; that something has to be love and faith – the succour of religion. In modern exorcism it is also the need for aftercare, as we have said.

The next passage is quite extraordinary, for it shows the ability of Jesus to heal at a distance – an occurrence which has no parallel in the present day. We have alluded to it earlier in connection with faith healing. Even so, it is not apparent how the mother's faith in Jesus could have worked a cure on her daughter, who lay at home some distance away. Indeed, He was no ordinary exorcist (at that time it seems there were many itinerant exorcists); His powers were too great for that alone. Jesus was able by the powers of concentration, divinely inspired, to heal when the sufferer was not actually present – an ability not attested to anyone else in the Bible. Mark writes (Mark 7:24–30):

> From there Jesus arose and went to the region of Tyre and Sidon… he entered a house… a woman whose little daughter was possessed by an unclean spirit came and fell down at his feet… and begged him to cast the demon out of her daughter. 'Let the children first be fed… it is not right to take the children's bread and throw it to the dogs.'
>
> 'Yes, Lord,' she answered, 'yet even the dogs under the table eat the children's crumbs.'
>
> 'For this saying,' he replied, 'you may go your way; the demon has left your daughter.' The woman went home and found the child lying in bed, and the demon gone.

One of the most famous passages in the New Testament follows. It indicates Jesus' belief in the origin of the Devil, the temptation in the Garden of Eden, and the deceit of the Devil which brought about Man's sinful nature. Jesus is speaking to a crowd of Jews, mainly Pharisees (John 8:42–5):

> If God were your Father, you would love me, for I came forth from God; I came not of my own accord, but he sent me. Why do you not understand what I say? It is because you cannot bear to hear my word. You are of your father, the devil, and your will is to do your father's desires. He was a murderer from the beginning and has nothing to do with

the truth, because there is no truth in him. When he lies he speaks according to his own nature for he is a liar and the father of lies. But because I tell you the truth, you do not believe me.

Peter, 'an apostle of Jesus Christ', wrote (so we believe) his first Letter from Rome to the Christians of the then Asia Minor (modern Turkey) when they were experiencing persecution for their faith (Peter 5:8–9):

Be sober, be watchful. Your adversary the devil prowls around like a roaring lion seeking someone to devour. Resist him, firm in your faith…

Reminiscent of the quotation above from the Gospel of St John is this extract from the first of St John's Letters to the Christians in Asia Minor (John 3:4–8). He says:

Everyone who commits sin is guilty of lawlessness… He who commits sin is of the devil, for the devil has sinned from the beginning… no-one born of God commits sin; by this it may be seen who are the children of God and who are the children of the devil.

The last Book of the New Testament, Revelation, makes several references to Satan or the Devil. This Book was reportedly written by a prophet named John (not the apostle John, therefore) about AD 100 and speaks of a brave new Christian world. He is addressing his words to the churches in Asia Minor (John 2:9–10):

I know your tribulation and your poverty… and the slander of those who say they are Jews and are not, but are a synagogue of Satan. Behold the devil is about to throw some of you into prison that you may be tested…

Belief in Satan or the Devil as a formidable adversary was clearly fixed in the minds of early AD prophets.

THE ROMAN CATHOLIC CATECHISM

From the words of Scripture as illustrative of our theme we may turn again to the modern Catechism of the Roman Catholic Church whose pronouncements have the blessing (no pun!) of Pope John Paul II, in order to examine the current dogma. Our theme is, of course, demons and demonology (including to an extent the angels as in a sense forebears of demons). In the Catechism Pericope 328 is quite explicit: 'The existence of the spiritual, non-corporeal beings that Sacred Scripture calls "angels" is a truth of faith.'

In the sections 'Fall of the Angels' and 'Original Sin', especially paragraphs 391 to 398, the Church's unmistakable belief in the historic truth of angels and demons is patent:

Scripture and the Church's Tradition see in this being [a seductive voice, opposed to God] a fallen angel called 'Satan' or the 'devil'... the devil and other demons were indeed created naturally good by God, but they became evil by their own doing.

We may have heard this before, but it is so important a declaration that it is worthy of repetition.

Paragraph 392 continues:

Scripture speaks of a sin of these fallen angels... The tempter's words [to Adam and Eve]: "You will be like Gods". The devil has sinned from the beginning; he is a liar...

Paragraph 394:

The reason the Son of God appeared was to destroy the works of the devil. In its consequences the gravest of these works was the mendacious seduction that led Man to disobey God.

The essence of paragraph 395 has been given earlier when we first considered the Catechism; concerning the power of Satan – that it is not infinite.

Paragraph 397:

Man tempted by the devil let his trust in his Creator die in his heart and, abusing his freedom, disobeyed God's command.

Paragraph 398:

In that sin Man preferred himself to God and by that very act scorned him... Seduced by the devil he wanted to be like God, but without God, before God and not in accordance with God.

We may read this in conjunction with the pronouncement of the Ecumenical Council in 1965, which stated that 'Although set by God in a state of rectitude, Man enticed by the Evil One abused his freedom at the very start of history.'

In the section 'The Profession of the Christian Faith', Jesus' temptation in the desert is mentioned in terms that leave no doubt about Catholic attitudes to the reality of Satan. Satan is a living tempter; whether he appeared in an adapted shape we are not told. Jesus' defeat of Satan in the desert presages the latter's defeat in the Redemption. Paragraph 538 says this:

The Gospels speak of a time of solitude for Jesus in the desert immediately after his baptism by John. Angels minister to Him... Satan tempts Him three times... Jesus rebuffs these attacks... and the devil leaves him until an opportune time.

Paragraph 539:

Jesus is the devil's conqueror... His victory over the tempter in the desert anticipates the victory at the Passion, the supreme act of obedience of his filial love for the Father.

Paragraph 540:

Jesus' temptation reveals the way in which the Son of God is Messiah, contrary to the way Satan proposes to him and the way men wish to attribute to him.

MACHINATIONS OF THE DEVIL

It might be instructive (and interesting) at this juncture to look at what the machinations of the Devil meant for ordinary people of the sixteenth century in Britain. The credulity displayed in the following is almost beyond belief. It concerns the indictment on various charges of two 'witches', Jenny Pearce and Elizabeth Gordon. The main charge was naturally that of bewitchment. It transpired in evidence that the two women, who lived together, agreed to give their souls to the Devil in return for malevolent powers. That night they each received three 'familiars' and at the same time the Devil appeared in the form of a tall black man, telling them that the imps (familiars) he had given them had the power to kill man or beast provided the imps were allowed to suck the women's flesh every night. Before he went, the Devil had intercourse with them, but as usual he was unpleasantly cold and rough. The imps soon got to work and caused the deaths of several neighbours and their animals. The women, of course, confessed under torture, but in court denied their confessions. However, they were found guilty. As usual with these cases, the charges were naturally fabricated out of malice or out of cupidity if the accused persons were worth anything. The two women, living together, had acquired a reputation for immorality. Apparently they said that the Devil had appeared several times to them and gave them new imps which sucked a teat or piece of red flesh in their privy parts (so the evidence relates). This was found by women who examined them. They had, it seemed, killed some thirty people, men, women and children. Stories were told of their power of being able to make people dance naked in public and to make women's dresses fly above their heads. They boasted, so it is said, that their master, the Devil, would not allow them to be executed. In this they were disappointed as they were hanged as witches, cursing and raving.

It is horrifying that juries up and down the land found such stories believable and were prepared to sentence people to death on this kind of evidence (especially when they knew that torture had been employed to get confessions).

ALLUSIONS TO THE DEVIL IN LITERATURE

The Devil, demons and fiends have always been mentioned in literature particularly when writers wished to heighten dramatic effect. The instances are innumerable in poetry, drama and fiction. Invoking Satan, authors knew they were sure of a response – generally alarm and fear, if the context was serious; amusement if not. The great number of instances where the Devil or his cohorts are mentioned is significant in that it indicates throughout the centuries a belief (sometimes residual) in: (a) the awesomeness of the Being and the terrors that his demons could bring; and (b) the fact that almost all readers would be believers in the Dark Prince and that therefore they would be all the more impressed by the author's credentials, as it were.

Let us look at some of these instances, among the most notable and memorable quotations in English literature. We may begin with William Blake's comment (about 1800) on Milton's *Paradise Lost*, where we saw a brilliant depiction of Satan. He wrote:

> *The reason Milton wrote in fetters when he wrote of Angels and God, and at liberty when of Devils and Hell, is because he was a true poet, and of the Devil's party without knowing it.*

This comment goes a long way towards explaining Milton's greatness in his epic poem, it may be thought!

I am sure Papini would agree with the Elizabethan writer Thomas Lodge's well-known line: 'Devils are not so black as they are painted.' Shakespeare, of course, has many references to devils in his plays. He could take it for granted that the people believed implicitly in the Devil and demons so he was indeed dramatically increasing tension. Here are some of them (*Troilus and Cressida*; *Henry V*):

> *Sometimes we are devils to ourselves*
> *When we will tempt the frailty of our powers*
> *Presuming on their changeful potency.*

> *Give them great meals of beef and iron and steel; they will eat like wolves and fight like devils.*

Frequently in literature (and in common parlance) the references to devils or demons relate to superhuman abilities: 'work like demons'; 'like things possessed'; 'diabolic insult' and so on.

There is the famous passage from *A Midsummer Night's Dream*:

> *The lunatic, the lover and the poet*
> *Are of imagination all compact;*
> *One sees more devils than vast hell can hold,*
> *That is, the madman…*

In *Henry V* there is the deathbed scene of Falstaff:

> *Boy: 'Yes, that a' did; and said they were devils incarnate.*

Hostess: A' never could abide carnation…

Boy: A' said once, the devil would have him about women.

Othello, finding his wife Desdemona dead, said:

'This look of thine will hurl my soul from heaven
And fiends will snatch at it…
Whip me, ye devils,… '

Kipling, writing about 1910, speaks of Tomlinson, who yammered:

'Let me in…
I borrowed my neighbour's wife to sin the deadly sin';
The Devil he grinned behind the bars, and banked the fires high;
'Did ye read of that sin in a book?'
And Tomlinson said 'Ay'

Poor Tomlinson was doomed to the fires of hell for his sin of the flesh.

Browning (1812–90) adduces the devils in a serious connotation in his poem 'The Lost Leader':

One more devils' triumph and sorrow for angels,
One wrong more to man, one more insult to God!'

Isaac Watts, writing about 1720, sums up then current belief in his serious poem 'Heaven and Hell':

There is a dreadful Hell
And everlasting pains;
There sinners must with devils dwell
In darkness, fire and chains.

Robert Burns, not known for his piety, alludes to the Devil generally amusingly in his poems (see 'Tam O'Shanter') as in this one called 'Address to the Devil':

O thou! whatever title suits thee
Auld Hornie, Satan, Nick or Clootie.

Burns was writing (about 1790) not only from the perspective of an agnostic (to say the least), but at a time when general belief in the terror of Satan was in decline.

Blake, writing at about the same time, shows a similar attitude to Satan in his

'Gates of Paradise', a religious poem typical of his later period:

> *Truly, my Satan, thou art but a dunce,*
> *And dost not know the garment from the man…*
> *Though thou art worshipped by the names divine*
> *Of Jesus and Jehovah, thou art still*
> *The Son of Morn in weary Night's decline…*

Blake, after his little humorous excursion, refers in the last two lines to Satan as a 'Fallen Angel', still retaining some original majesty and power.

The word fiend is always used as a synonym for evil – namely the Devil, and in the plural for demons. The fiend as tempter is well expressed in Shakespeare's *Merchant of Venice*, where Launcelot speaks:

> … *'my conscience says, "Launcelot budge not." "Budge," says the fiend. "Budge not," says my conscience. "Conscience," say I, "you cannot counsel well; fiend, say I, you counsel well".*

The foul fiend is encountered several times in *King Lear*. Here is one instance:

> *Keep thy foot out of brothels, thy hand out of pockets, thy pen from lenders' books, and defy the devil.*

Perhaps one of the most famous instances occurs in *Macbeth*, where, after hearing the prophecies of the witches, Macbeth, showing distrust, speaks of the 'juggling fiends' that mislead us in a 'double sense'.

John Bunyan (1628–88), the Quaker author of *Pilgrim's Progress*, presented the difficulties facing a seeker after salvation. Christian encountered the Devil in many guises. One such was Apollyon, who 'straddled over the whole breadth of the way': 'A foul fiend coming over the field to meet him' [Christian].

'The Ancient Mariner', by Coleridge, writing in the early nineteenth century (though about events presumed to have happened centuries before), tells of a mariner who brings down misfortune on his own head. He cannot escape even when he leaves the ship: he is doomed to be

> *Like one that on a lonesome road*
> *Doth walk in fear and dread*
> *And having once turned round walks on*
> *And turns no more his head*
> *Because he knows, a frightful fiend*
> *Doth close behind him tread.*

George Meredith (died 1909) has some beautiful rhyming lines in his poem 'Lucifer in Starlight', reminiscent of Milton's blank verse *Paradise Lost*. The most famous passage speaks of Satan (or Lucifer):

> *On a starred night Prince Lucifer uprose.*
> *Tired of his dark dominion swung the fiend…*
> *He reached a middle height, and at the stars,*
> *Which are the brain of heaven, he looked, and sank.*
> *Around the ancient track marched, rank on rank,*
> *The army of unalterable law.*

It seems fitting to end this section with a quotation from John Milton's greatest poem. His is an inimitable description of Satan:

> *High on a throne of royal state which far*
> *Outshone the wealth of Ormus and of Ind,*
> *Or where the gorgeous East with richest hand*
> *Showers on her kings barbaric pearl and gold,*
> *Satan exalted sat…*

After his Fall, Satan's shape:

> *… black it stood as night*
> *Fierce as ten furies, terrible as hell,*
> *And shook a dreadful dart; what seemed his head*
> *The likeness of a kingly crown had on.*

Finally:

> *So eagerly the fiend*
> *O'er bog or steep through strait, rough, dense or rare,*
> *With head, hands, wings, or feet pursues his way*
> *And swims or sinks or wades or creeps or flies.*

THE REALITY OF DEMONS

Demonology is not some arcane study, like astrology, or some outmoded science like alchemy. Demonology is the study of phenomena which have puzzled the world since its inception. Its fascination lies in the fact that no one can with authority claim demons do not, or never did, exist; and on the other hand, no one can incontrovertibly claim that they do, always did, exist. There is evidence to support the view that evil spirits exist today. Conversely, some people would explain away the Biblical instances of demon possession in terms of modern medical science. On one side of the 'argument' are atheists, agnostics, sceptics, scientists who have no religious belief; and on the other, traditional Christians who believe everything if it is in Scripture. Notice I said 'traditional', because there are committed Christians who are to say the least hesitant in declaring for

The Wiles of Satan versus the Bible ≈ 233

the Devil and his demons. We cannot just write off the word of pious men who were in ecclesiastical eyes divinely inspired; just as we cannot believe everything that is allegorical and patently metaphorical. Christ taught largely by means of parables, which by their very nature are not to be taken at face value. Ultimately, we are faced with choice and belief, which itself is dictated by faith. Science and the reasoned approach cannot explain matters spiritual, of faith. It can explain demonstrable fact – but our study has not been about tangible facts. Non-belief in the materialization of the Devil is something else. This non-belief in no way affects belief in the powers of evil spirits which can exist in spirit form.

I would like to quote some words of St Thomas Aquinas as a conclusion. The following was written in the second half of the thirteenth century and forms a part of his monumental study of God and man's relation to His purposes. It is from *Summa Theologiae* (page 158), one of the greatest books ever written in any language. The subject is devils:

> *To tempt means properly to test or try out and the immediate goal of testing is knowledge... The devil tests in order to harm people and throw them into sin: indeed this sort of tempting is regarded as his special job and when anyone does it he or she is regarded as an agent of the devil. The world and the flesh are sometimes called instruments of temptation because how a person reacts to desires of the flesh and worldly possessions shows what kind of person he is and therefore the devil employs them in his temptations... the devil has caused all our sins because by instigating Adam's sin he made the whole human race prone to wickedness... however the devil does not cause every sin because some are committed from free choice and weakness of the body: the devil has not instigated them. Even without the devil, we would have the urge for food and sex... which can cause disorders unless they are controlled by reason. Whether we keep such desires in order is a matter of free will. There is no need to blame everything on the temptations of the devil.*

We end with the inspirational words contained in the Letter of James (3:13–17), written in about AD 45, over a thousand years before St Thomas Aquinas addressed the scattered Christian communities:

> *Who is wise and understanding among you? By his good life let him show his works in the meekness of wisdom. But if you have bitter jealousy and selfish ambition in your hearts, do not boast and be false to the truth. This wisdom is not such as comes down from above, but is earthly, unspiritual, devilish. For where jealousy and selfish ambition exist, there will be disorder and every vile practice. But the wisdom from above is first pure, then peaceable, gentle, open to reason, full of mercy and good fruits, without uncertainty or insincerity.*

APPENDIX 1

EXORCIZING THE POSSESSED

(Source: the *Rituale Romanum*, Roman Ritual (1619), of Pope Paul V [1605–21], reproduced by permission of the Vatican.)

The priest robed in surplice and violet stole one end of which is placed round the neck of the possessed person, bound if he is violent, sprinkles those present with holy water. Then the service begins.

1. The Litany
2. Psalm 54 (Save me O God…)
3. Adjuration imploring God's grace for the proposed exorcism and a caution to the demon to speak his name, and hour of departing
4. The Gospel (John, Mark, Luke)
5. Preparatory Prayer
   Then the priest protecting himself and the possessed by the sign of the cross, placing part of his stole round the neck and placing his right hand on the head of the possessed resolutely shall say:
6. First Exorcism
   I exorcize thee most vile spirit… in the name of Jesus Christ to get out and flee from this creature of God. He Himself commands thee… Hear therefore and fear, Satan, enemy of the faith, foe to the human race… Why dost thou stand and resist when thou knowest that Christ the Lord will destroy thy strength?
      Making signs of the cross on the forehead of the possessed, the priest says: Depart therefore in the name of the Father, Son and Holy Ghost…
7. Prayer for success, making the sign of the cross over the demoniac
8. Second Exorcism
   I adjure thee, thou old serpent, by the judge of the quick and the dead…that thou depart quickly from this servant of God whom the Almighty hath made in His image. Yield therefore; yield not to me but to the minister of Christ… let the image of God be terrible to thee…
   For it is God who commands thee
   The majesty of Christ commands thee
   The sacred cross commands thee…
   Go out therefore thou transgressor… O most dire one, give place; give place to Christ… who hath cast thee into outer darkness…
   But why truculent one dost thou withstand? Thou art accused by Almighty God… by the human race… Therefore I adjure thee, most wicked dragon, to depart from this man [sign of the cross]…
   Tremble and flee at the invocation of the name of the Lord…

The word made flesh commands thee. Jesus of Nazareth commands thee...

Therefore, adjured now in His name, depart from this man whom He hath created... The more slowly thou go out, the more the punishment against thee increases.

9. Prayer

10. Third and final exorcism

I adjure thee most vile spirit... in the name of Jesus Christ... that thou stop assaulting him whom He hath formed from the dust of the earth... Therefore yield to God... who condemned thee in Judas Iscariot the traitor. For thee and thy angels is prepared the unquenchable fire... because thou art the chief of accursed murde... Go out thou scoundrel, go out with all thy deceits... Give honour to God... give place to the Lord Jesus Christ... Give place to the Holy Ghost...

Now therefore depart, thou seducer... Be humbled and prostrate. For behold the Lord approaches quickly and His fire will glow before Him... He expels thee... to whose power all things are subject...

He excludes thee, He who hast prepared for thee and thy angels everlasting hell...

Final prayers, including canticles, creed, and various psalms.

(The complete version is to be found in Summers' *The History of Witchcraft*, in the chapter 'Diabolic Possession'.)

There is a shorter form of exorcism, authorized by Pope Leo XIII (1878–1903), found in later editions of the *Ritual*:

After the customary invocation, In the name... the rite begins with a prayer to St Michael; the solemn adjuration of some length follows with versicles (short verse recited by the minister and the congregation alternately) and responses; a second prayer is next recited; and the whole concludes by three aspirations from the Litany: 'From the deceits and crafts of the Devil. O Lord, deliver us. That it may please thee to rule thy church so it shall always serve Thee in lasting peace and true liberty; we beseech Thee, hear us.' The place is then to be sprinkled with holy water.

Other short forms of exorcism (for use in the Anglican Church) are authorized by the *York Report* [Archbishop of York's Study Group, 1974, The Christian Ministry of Healing and Deliverance]. These consist of only some three or four sentences (apart from prayers).

John Richards in *Exorcism, Deliverance and Healing* gives some guidelines for Anglican exorcizors. He divides the rite up into three sections:

1. Preparation;
2. Deliverance;
3. Conclusion.

1. When all are assembled the minister may begin: In the name...
   One or more may be read of the following: Psalm 54; parts of the Gospels.
   The minister may then say: Let us confess our sins to Almighty God.
   [Prayer follows, in which all assembled may join in]
   The people assembled may then say a short prayer.
   The minister may then conduct an act of recollection.

2. The minister and assistants shall stand round the sufferer while the minister intones: In the name of Jesus of Nazareth, I bind you evil spirit and command you to leave this person.
   Repeat the exorcism as necessary.
   The sufferer should now make a confession of his sins.
   And the minister should call upon God to grant forgiveness.
   The minister should now encourage the sufferer to make an act of renunciation and of faith.
   The minister and one of the assistants shall then lay their hands on the head and shoulders of the person, saying: Christ be with you.

3. The service may conclude with the Lord's Prayer, an act of recollection, and the blessing.
   The person should be prepared by his priest for Baptism and/or Anointing and/or Holy Communion at the earliest suitable time.

In the case of the exorcism of a place the above is still done but the rooms or places are sprinkled with holy water, and a prayer or appeal is made along the lines: Visit we beseech you, O Lord, this place and drive far from it all the snares of the enemy...

APPENDIX 2

RITE OF THE ORDINATION OF EXORCISTS

(In the Catholic Church an exorcist is ordained for the work by a bishop)
(Source: the Roman Ritual, which lays down the procedure.)

Before the ceremony can begin a Catholic Missal and/or a Book of Exorcisms or a Pontifical (book of rites performed by a bishop) must be available. Subsequent to ordination by the bishop, priests can be 'initiated'. The bishop dons his mitre and takes his seat at the Epistle side of the altar (the right-facing side) and the Missal is brought to him. He reads the Gradual (a song or psalm coming between the Epistle and the Gospel) or the Alleluia. The Gradual is sung by the choir. When finished, the bishop takes off his mitre and reads the third Lection (a portion of Scripture). Two chaplains assist. The Archdeacon summons the ordinands (those about to be ordained into the exorcism ritual), who hold lighted tapers in their hands and kneel before the bishop, who addresses them as follows. 'Dearest children who are about to be ordained to the office of Exorcists, ye must duly know what ye are about to undertake. For an Exorcist must cast out devils... Ye receive also the power... and the words of Exorcism by which unclean spirits are driven out from the bodies of those who are possessed. Be careful therefore... that ye banish all uncleanness and evil from your own bodies... truly will ye rightly control those devils who attack others... may the Lord vouchsafe to grant ye this...'

The bishop then hands to each a Missal or Pontifical, saying 'Receive this... and have power to place thy hands upon energumens' (people possessed by a spirit). All kneel, and the bishop, wearing again his mitre, stands and prays. 'Dearest brethren, let us humbly pray the Almighty that He may bless his servants to the office of Exorcists that they may have the power to command spirits... through His only begotten Son Jesus Christ...' Then he removes his mitre, turns to the altar, saying, 'Let us pray', while the new exorcists kneel and a prayer is said over them. 'Eternal God, vouchsafe to bless these thy servants to the office of Exorcists, that by the imposition of our hands and the words of our mouth they may have power and authority to govern and restrain all unclean spirits...'

Then they return to their places.

Thus the Exorcist is ordained to cast out demons and given dominion over evil spirits. It is a very solemn ceremony and clearly the Order is taken very seriously. The office is one of the minor orders into which a priest is initiated but in practice exorcisms now tend to be performed by senior clerics. However, all priests may in theory be called upon to exorcize, especially parish priests, but they must carefully abide by the rules of the Roman Ritual. The Roman Catholic Church is very thorough in its rules for exorcism and does everything in its power to avoid mistakes.

We have already mentioned some of the qualities that the exorcist must possess: he himself must be mature and prudent; he must be capable of scrupulous preparation; he must be learned and cautious; faithful to the divine will; wise in judgement and selection of witnesses; not credulous; painstaking; fervent and authoritative; assured; confident in desired outcomes; conscious he is using the words of Scripture; attentive at all times to a productive line of questioning of the demon; careful over the use of sacred objects; prepared to repeat the exorcism if need be.

APPENDIX 3

GUIDELINES FOR MINISTERS IN THE FIELD OF EXORCISM

(Source: Michael Perry's *Deliverance*. In this book the author refers to people, lay or clerical, who may be called on to investigate a case as 'Counsellors', a less emotive word. He gives comprehensive guidelines, as he calls them. They are worth mentioning here.)

1. Treat every approach made to you seriously and listen attentively.
2. Pray inwardly for the person concerned.
3. Keep calm.
4. Investigate the background of all concerned.
5. Make notes of the case.
6. Call in professional help if it seems warranted.
7. Make the client feel welcome.
8. Ensure renunciation by the client of any occult involvement.
9. Use the means: prayer, laying-on of hands, anointing – after an initial diagnosis.
10. Bring in a Christian group, especially if it is felt that demonic activity is involved.
11. Be attentive to the need for aftercare.

Longer-term aims should involve counsellors in:

1. Obtaining some training;
2. Making use of the resources of the diocesan adviser or group;
3. Encouraging the spiritual Christian life in the client (Perry's word);
4. Using the prayers of the Christian community;
5. Preaching the gospel of the caring, Christian life;
6. Recharging spiritual batteries by retreats, personal prayer and so on;
7. Training themselves in Christian tradition and thought.

Perry also lists dangers, such as:

1. Concentration on self and residual doubt;
2. Being in awe of the Powers of Darkness;
3. Psychic attacks (from Satanic groups, say);
4. Difficulty in keeping a balance between the rational and the intuitive;
5. Over-reliance on the efficacy of objects;
6. Finding demons because we are looking for them;

7. Danger of physical assault (by the possessed);
8. Danger of sexual blackmail (in visiting homes);
9. Danger of 'bringing work home';
10. Misrepresentation by the media;
11. Rushing into a situation and not allowing adequate time;
12. Not keeping careful notes.

The latter should include, apart from name, address, age, marital status, of course, such data as children, how many and so on; description of house; employment, education, religious affiliation; the problem itself; friends and the not so friendly; health, physical and mental; previous involvement in the occult if any; what action it is intended to take; and any advisers mooted.

APPENDIX 4

PREPARATION OF SUBSTANCES USED IN EXORCISM RITES
(Source: Roman Catholic Ritual Handbooks.)

Exorcism of the salt
I exorcise you, creature of salt, by the living God, so that you may be fit for the healing of mind and body of all who use you. Wherever you are sprinkled may all evil and wicked thoughts depart, all works and deceits of the evil one be driven away, and all unclean spirits be cast out by Him who is ready to judge the living and the dead.

Exorcism of the water
I exorcise you, creature of water, in the name of God the Father Almighty, in the name of Jesus Christ His Son our Lord and in the power of the Holy Spirit, that you be fit to put to flight all the power of Satan and to root out and expel Satan himself and his fallen angels; through the power of the same Lord Jesus Christ who shall come to judge the living and the dead.

Blessing of the salt
Almighty and Eternal God, graciously bless and make holy this creature of salt. May it give health of body and mind to them that use it. Let all touched or sprinkled with it be protected against all that is sinful and against all attacks of spiritual wickedness. Through Jesus Christ Your Son, our Lord.

Blessing of the water

Almighty God, Father Eternal, hear our Prayers and Bless and make Holy this creature of water, that it may serve You for the casting out of devils and in the driving away of sickness of mind and body.

Grant that whatever is sprinkled with this water may be cleansed from all that is foul or harmful. Let no sickness abide there, and cause all the power of the unseen enemy with his cunning and deceits to go away.

Through this water dispel all that is contrary to the health and peace of Your people, so that, protected by the invocation of Your Holy Name, they may be secure against every adversary; through Jesus Christ Your Son our Lord.

Making Holy Water

Salt, in quantity enough to cover a two-pence piece [a level teaspoon or four pinches], is placed on a piece of paper. Water, in suitable quantity, in a bowl or jug, stands beside the salt. The salt is exorcised and blessed first and then the water. After this they are mixed by pouring the salt into the water and the Last Prayer is said. It is well, when a house or place is being dealt with, to carry out this blessing in the presence of those concerned so that they come to understand that Holy Water is not 'Christian Magic' but the symbol of the Prayers that are offered to God as it is blessed.

As the officiant pours the salt into the water he says:

May this mixing of salt and water be done in the Name of the Father and of the Son and of the Holy Spirit.

After the mixing he says:

Almighty Father, look with mercy on this creature of salt and water and of Your loving kindness sanctify it. Wherever it shall be sprinkled with the invocation of Your Holy Name may the attacks of evil spirits be repelled and the fear of evil be kept far away. May the presence of the Holy Spirit be given to all who seek Your mercy; through Jesus Christ Your Son our Lord, who lives and reigns with you and the same Holy Spirit, ever one God, world without end.

APPENDIX 5

WITCH INTERROGATION

(Usual pattern)… and penalties (about 1500 *floreat*)

The preliminary question was commonly the following:

Do you believe in witchcraft?

This was a trick question. As it was a grave heresy in the eyes of the Church to deny the existence of witchcraft, the accused could not answer in the negative without risking death. If the answer was in the affirmative, the accused was already part way to being 'proved' guilty and was therefore in a position to answer the questions to follow. Answers had to be given; failure to reply was seen as an admission of guilt.

How long have you been a witch?
Why did you become a witch?
How did you become a witch and what happened on that occasion?
Who is the one you chose to be your incubus and what was his name?
What was the name of your master among the evil demons?
What was the oath you were forced to render him?
How did you make this oath and what were its conditions?
What finger were you forced to raise?
Where did you consummate your union with your incubus?
What demons and what other humans participated at the sabbat?
What food did you eat there?
How was the sabbat banquet arranged?
Were you seated at the banquet?
What music was played there and what dances did you dance?
What did your incubus give you for your intercourse?
What devil's mark did your incubus make on your body?
What injury have you done to such and such a person and how did you do it?
Why did you inflict this injury?
How can you relieve this injury?
What herbs or what other methods can you use to cure these injuries?
Who are the children on whom you have cast a spell?
Why have you done it?
What animals have you bewitched to sickness or death and why did you commit such acts?
Who are your accomplices in evil?
Why does the devil give you blows in the night?
What is the ointment with which you rub your broomstick made of?
How are you able to fly through the air?

What magic words do you utter then?
What tempests have you raised and who helped you to produce them?
What plagues of vermin and caterpillars have you created?
What do you make these pernicious creatures out of and how do you do it?
Has the devil assigned a limit to the duration of your evil-doing?

Penalties for witchcraft
Those who practise invocations of evil spirits:
For:
any purpose – death

Those who practise witchcrafts and sorceries:
For:
divination of treasure trove;
recovery of lost or stolen property;
murder;
bodily injury;
intent to cause the two above and destruction of goods;
destruction of goods and livestock;
unlawful love;
destruction of cross;
theft of corpses.

All these were punishable by death and the confiscation of property.

APPENDIX 6

INITIATING A PROCESS

(Source: Heinrich Kramer and James Sprenger, *Malleus Maleficarum*, 1486, trans. Montague Summers.)

The first question then is what is the suitable method of instituting a process on behalf of the faith against witches. In answer to this it must be said that there are three methods allowed by Canon Law. The first is when someone accuses a person before a judge of the crime of heresy or of protecting heretics, offering to prove it and to submit himself to the penalty of talion (retalion) if he fails to prove it. The second method is when someone denounces a person but does not offer to prove it and is not willing to embroil himself in the matter, but says he lays information out of zeal for the faith or because of a sentence of excommunication inflicted by the Ordinary [Bishop]; or because of the temporal punishment exacted by the secular judge upon those who fail to lay information.

The third method involves an inquisition, that is, when there is no accuser or informer, but a general report that there are witches in some town or place; and then the judge must proceed, not at the instance of any party, but simply by virtue of his office.

Here it is to be noted that a judge should not readily admit the first method of procedure. For one thing it is not actuated by motives of faith nor is it very applicable to the case of witches, since they commit their deeds in secret. Then again, it is full of danger to the accuser, because of the penalty of talion which he will incur if he fails to prove his case. Then again it is very litigious.

Let the process begin with a general citation affixed to the walls of the parish church or town hall.

(Here the lengthy citation is given whose purport is to encourage people to come forward and testify to the existence of witchcraft in their midst. About half way comes the following.)

By the authority which we exercise in this district, and in virtue of holy obedience and under pain of excommunication, we direct, command, require and admonish that within the space of twelve days... the first four of which shall stand for the first warning, the second for the second and the third for the third warning; and we give this treble canonical warning that they should reveal it unto us if anyone know, see, or have heard that any person is reported to be a heretic or a witch or if anyone is suspected especially of such practices as cause injury to men, cattle, or the fruits of the earth, to the loss of the State.

(The citation is finished, more rules are stated and then the 'process' itself can begin in this manner:)

In the year of Our Lord... on the... day of the... month, in the presence of me the Notary and of the witnesses subscribed, N [name] of the town of... in the diocese of... as above, appeared in person at... before the honourable judge and offered him a schedule to the following effect.

He appeared and laid information to the judge that N of the town or parish of... in the diocese of... had said and asserted that he knew how to perform or had actually done certain injuries to the deponent or to other persons.

After this he shall immediately make the deponent take the oath in the usual manner either on the Bible or on the Cross in witness of the damnation of his soul and body that he will speak the truth in his depositions. When the oath has been sworn he shall question him as to how he knows his depositions are true and whether he saw or heard that to which he swears. And if he says that he has seen anything, as, for example, that the accused was present at such a time of tempest, or that he had touched an animal, or had entered a stable, the judge shall ask when he saw him and where, and how often and in what manner and who were present... and the Notary shall set down a record of them after the aforesaid denunciation. Finally he shall be enjoined by virtue of his oath to keep secret whatever he has said there, or whatever the judge has said to him.

The third method of beginning a process is the commonest and most usual one, because it is secret and no accuser or informer has to appear. But when there is a general report of witchcraft in some town or parish, because of this report the judge may proceed without a general citation or admonition as above, since the noise of that report comes often to his ears; and then again he can begin a process in the presence of the persons, as we have said before.

[Note: 'talion' means retaliation (law of).]

APPENDIX 7

(Source: Johann Weyer, *De Praestigiis Daemonum* (Witches and Devils in the Renaissance), 1583, trans. John Shea.)

Book one: the Devil, his origins, aims and powers
A few statements of the Fathers concerning the Devil's machinations... also why God has established the demons as adversaries of men

> *So that the aims of the demons may become more widely recognised, I have decided to include a few statements of the Fathers which are relevant to this problem. St Clement teaches that unclean spirits love to cling to the bodies of men so that they may fulfil their own desires. Directing the soul towards things they themselves desire, they compel obedience to their own lustful desires, until men are made entirely into vessels of demons.*

Book two: Magicians of ill repute
Uneducated physicians attribute their own ignorance to witchcraft

> *I do not deny that the refuge of some incompetent [doctors] when they do not know the nature of an illness, is to assert at once it is a case of witchcraft. Thus they cunningly cover up their own ignorance... and often the afflictions degenerated into a degree of malignancy because of the ignorance of those men... By referring to evil doing or witchcraft as a pretext, they try to divert malicious accusations, or legal actions, when they are really the evil doers.*

Book three: Lamiae [female serpent demons]

The demi-gods were born like other mortals and no-one is born or conceived without intercourse and the seed of the male and female

A possible reason for the name 'Demi-gods' is that they were procreated from the seed of the gods above; men imagine them born from the union of gods or demons with human beings and therefore to have an in-between nature, neither gods nor men. Not only among Christians but among pagans, some divinities are terrestrial, some celestial, some in the middle.

So, neither a human being nor an animal can be born except from the sexual congress of male and female. To believe otherwise would contradict not only the revealed truth and religion, but also the nature of the universe. Sexual difference, and coition have no other purpose except that all living creatures who are mortal, might be preserved by successive generations.

Book four: Testicles cannot be removed by a charm but the devil can induce sexual impotence

As to the fact that some men are thought to be bound by enchantment and made impotent, as though they had been emasculated, this can result naturally when the sexual organs are impaired. This flaw should not always be ascribed to enchantment nor should an innocent person be put under suspicion. However, I certainly admit that the genitals can be made unsuitable for intercourse by a demon, but I deny this can be done by the ill will of a vile old woman, although she herself, persuaded by a demon, may believe it. The demon is also responsible for the fact that a man may be allowed to have intercourse on many occasions with one special woman and his organs are left free to function, while with another woman he is inhibited and his sexual organs are impeded. The demon needs nobody's help in this activity.

Book five: Treatment of persons possessed

Demonic healings are counterfeit but they are sometimes allowed by God... because of the credulity of foolish people

It is clear that the demon sometimes confers a healing that is counterfeit. The spirit who works among the children of unbelief freely ceases from the torture which he himself has caused and thus ensnares the gullible minds of men... His chief aim is that those whom he has deceived should judge him worthy of divine honour. We believe that God often allows certain things because of men's stubborn unbelief...

Book six: The punishment of witches

A description of the confessions made by three poor women who were burned to death for their belief in witchcraft

To clarify a matter that is obscure in itself and wrapped in darkness, I have chosen to give the confessions of poor women who were imprisoned and put to death by burning a few years ago.

One woman confessed she had deserted the Lord and joined herself to the Devil... and that her demon lover was named Bernard. She said that she once gave an apple to a married woman thus causing her to have six miscarriages. She also confessed she had used maleficium to kill a man's daughter; that she had injured the wife of another man, all by means of maleficia, so that the injured woman is now confined to bed. Because of this confession, the magistrate sentenced the accused to be burned – a warranted solution – if it had been truly demonstrated that she had indeed perpetrated those crimes!

Book six: The punishment of witches

Examples of poor innocent women punished because they were suspected of maleficium

Add to the above the case of the official who had as many of these poor deluded women as possible arrested and punished on the information of a soothsayer. This soothsayer promised the official privately that he would give information against one more woman who was guilty of maleficium. The official readily agreed, but the informer accused the official's wife, saying that he would give proof. He appointed a time at which her husband might see for himself that she was present at the assembly and dances of other witches. The official agreed, and invited some friends to dine at the same table with himself and his wife at an appointed time, not disclosing why he was having the meeting. Then at the time appointed by the soothsayer, he rose and bade his guests to remain with his wife and not move from their places. Then he was taken by the soothsayer to a spot chosen by the latter where he thought he could see assembled witches and dancers, and his own wife among the assembly pursuing the same delights as the others. Returning home at once, he found his friends and wife sitting happily where he had left them. When he asked whether his wife had left, he was assured she had not moved. At this the official revealed the whole affair, and repented too late of the punishment he had in the past inflicted on innocent women. Instead he condemned the accusing soothsayer to death.

BIBLIOGRAPHY

Note: An asterisk in the following list indicates that I am indebted to the publisher and/or author concerned for permission to quote from the work in question.

Alexander, Marc, *The Devil Hunter*, Sphere, London, 1978.*

Alexander, W. Menzies, *Demonic Possession in the New Testament*, Ward & Downey, Edinburgh, 1902.

Allen, Thomas, *Possessed*, Doubleday, London, 1993.

Andriano, Joseph, *Our Ladies of Darkness*, State Universities Press, Penn., 1993.

Aquinas, Thomas, *see* McDermott, T.

Ashley, Leonard, *The Complete Book of Devils and Demons*, Barricade Press, N.Y., 1996.

Ashton, John, *The Devil in Britain and America*, Constable, London, 1896.

Baker, Roger, *Binding the Devil*, Arrow, London, 1975.*

Basham, Donald, *Can a Christian Have a Demon?* Hodder & Stoughton, London, 1979.

Beard, John, *Autobiography of Satan*, Williams & Norgate, London, 1872.

Beloff, John, *The Relentless Question*, Jefferson, London, 1990.

Bernheimer, Richard, *Wild Men of the Middle Ages*, Harvard University Press, Cambridge, Mass., 1952.

Beyersdorf, Eunice, and Brady, J. D., *A Manual of Exorcism* (translation from the Spanish original of 1720), Hispanic Society of America Press, N.Y., 1977.

Bible in English, The, 1589. Miles Coverdale, London. (Known as the Great Bible.)

Binsfeld, Peter (Binsfeldius, Petrus), *Tracat von Bekantnuss der Zauberer und Hexen: Ob und Wie Viel Denselben Zu Glauben*, H. Bock, Trier, 1590.

——, *Tracatus de Confessionibus Maleficarum et Sagarum Recognitus and Auctus*, H. Bock, Trier, 1591.

Boyd, Andrew, *Blasphemous Rumours*, Fount, London, 1991.

Brady, J. D., *A Manual of Exorcism for RC Priests* (translation from the Spanish), Hispanic Society of America, N.Y.,1975.

Carus, Paul, *The History of the Devil*, Bell Publishing, N.Y., 1960.*

Cawthorne, Nigel, *Satanic Murder*, True Crime Publishing, London, 1995.

Cervantes, Fernando, *The Devil in the New World*, Harrap, Edinburgh, 1994.

Charles, R. H., *English Bible Apocrypha and Pseudepigrapha*, Vols 1 and 2, Oxford University Press, Oxford, 1913.

Cohn, Norman, *Europe's Inner Demons*, Chatto & Windus, London, 1975.

Conway, Mercure, *Demonology and Devil-Lore*, Vols 1 and 2, Chatto & Windus, London, 1879.

Core, Dianne, *Chasing Satan*, Gunther Books, London, 1991.

Cornwell, John, *Powers of Darkness: Powers of Light*, London, Viking, 1991.*

Corte, Nicholas, *Who Is the Devil?*, Burns Oates, N.Y., 1958.*

Coulange, Louis, *The Life of the Devil*, Alfred Knopf, Edinburgh, 1929.

Cristiani, Luigi, *Satan and the Modern World*, Barrie & Rockcliff, London, 1961.

Dames, Helen, *Psychic Phenomena*, Arthur Stockwell, London, 1930.

De-la-Noy, Michael, *The Church of England*, Simon & Schuster, London, 1993.

Del Rio, *Disquisitionum Magicorum*, Vols 1 to 3, Lovanii, Cologne, 1589/60.

De Plancy, Collin, *Dictionnaire Infernal*, Fogola Press, Turin, 1976.

Dickason, Fred, *Demon Possession and the Christian*, Crossway, Eastbourne, 1987.*

Eitrem, Samson, *Some Notes on the Demonology of the New Testament*, Universitets-
    forlaget, Oslo, 1966.

Ellul, Jacques, *The New Demons*, Mowbray, London, 1975.*

Ewen, L'Estrange, *Witchcraft and Demonianism*, Muller, London, 1970.

Ferguson, Everett, *Demonology of the Early Christian World*, Edwin Mellen, N.Y.,
    1980.*

Fishwick, Marshall, *Brief History of the Devil*, Harper, N.Y., 1962.

—— *Faust Revisited*, Harper, N.Y., 1963.*

Forsythe, Neil, *The Old Enemy*, Princeton University Press, Princeton, N. J., 1987.

Fox, Rory, 'Can there be a reason for belief in Angels and Demons?', *Downside
    Review*, Autumn, 1997.

Gauld, Alan, *Mediumship and Survival*, Heinemann, London, 1972.

Goodman, Felicitas, *How About Demons*, Indiana University Press, Ind., 1988.

Graf, Arturo, *A Story of the Devil*, Macmillan, London, 1969.*

Greenfield, Richard, *Traditions of Belief in Late Byzantine Demonology*, Adolf M.
    Hakkert, Amsterdam, 1988.

Guazzo, Francesco, *Compendium Maleficarum*, 1626, second edition, *see* Summers, M.

Hall, Fred, *Pedigree of the Devil*, Trubner, London, 1896.

Harpur, Patrick, *Daimonic Reality*, Viking, London, 1994.

Heron, Benedick, *I Saw Satan Fall*, New Life Publishing, Luton, 1997.

Holizer, Hans, *Encyclopedia of Witchcraft and Its Present Day Counterparts*, Octopus,
    London, 1994.

Howell-Everson, Douglas, *Handbook for Christian Exorcists*, Christian Exorcism
    Group, London, 1982.*

James I, *Demonologie*, Edinburgh University Press, Edinburgh, 1966 edition.

Kane, Richard, *Didactic Demons in Modern Fiction*, Associate Universities Presses,
    N.Y., 1988.

King, Francis, *Witchcraft and Demonology*, Hamlyn, London, 1991.

Kramer, Heinrich, and Sprenger, James, *Malleus Maleficarum*, 1486 (translation
    M. Summers), Dover Publications, N.Y., 1971 edition.

Langton, Edward, *The Supernatural*, Ryder, London, 1934.

—— *Essentials of Demonology*, Epworth, London, 1949.*

—— *Satan*, Skeffington, London, 1945.

Leahy, Fred, *Satan Cast Out*, Truth Trust Press, Edinburgh, 1990.*

Leek, Sylvia, *Driving Out the Devils*, W. H. Allen, London, 1976.*

Levack, Brian, *Possession and Exorcism*, Vol. 9, Garland Press, N.Y., 1987.

—— *Witchcraft and Demonology in Art and Literature*, Vol. 12, Garland, N.Y., 1982.*

—— *Studies in Witchcraft, Magic, Religion*, Garland, N.Y., 1992.

—— *Witchcraft in the Ancient World*, Garland, N.Y., 1992.

Logan, Kevin, *Satanism and the Occult*, Kingsway, Eastbourne, 1994.*

Lowe-Thompson, *The History of the Devil*, Kegan Paul, London, 1929.*

Lurker, Manfred, *History of Gods and Goddesses*, Routledge, London, 1987.

McConnell, Brian, *The Possessed*, Headline, London, 1995.

McDermott, Timothy, *Aquinas: Summa Theologiae*, Eyre & Spottiswoode, London, 1989.*

McGrath, Alister, *Renewal of Anglicism*, SPCK, London, 1993.

MacLachlan, Lewis, *Memorable Providences*, A. James, Evesham, 1967.

—— *Miracles of Healing*, A. James, Evesham, 1968.

Maple, Eric, *Domain of Devils*, Robert Hale, London, 1966.

Maquart, F. X., 'Exorcism and Diabolical Manifestation', in *Satan*, ed. Charles Moeller (q.v.)

Mode, Heinz, *Fabulous Beasts and Demons*, Phaidon, London, 1975.

Moeller, Charles (ed.), *Satan*, Sheed & Ward, London, 1951.*

Newton, Michael, *Raising Hell*, Warner, London, 1994.

Newton, Toyne, *The Demon Connection*, Badgers Press, Worthing, 1993.

Oesterreich, Traugott K., *Possession*, Trench & Traubner, N.Y., 1966.

Olsen, Alan (ed.), *Disguises of the Demonic*, Association Press, N.Y., 1975.*

Omand, Donald, *Experiences of a Present Day Exorcist*, Kimber, London, 1970.

Oplinger, Jon, *Politics of Demonology*, Associated University Presses, London, 1990.

Oppenheimer, Janet, *The Other World*, Cambridge University Press, Cambridge, 1985.

Origen, *Contra Celsum* (translated and with an introduction and notes by Henry Chadwick), Cambridge University Press, Cambridge, 1980.

Owen, Alex, *The Darkened Room*, Virago, London, 1989.

Pace, E. A., Walsh, James J., Guilday, Peter, Wynne, John J. and Blanche, Kelly (eds), *The Catholic Encyclopedia*, Gilmary Society, N.Y., 1936.

Pagels, Elaine, *Origin of Satan*, Allen Lane (Penguin), London, 1995.

Papini, Giovanni, *The Devil*, Eyre & Spottiswoode, London, 1955.

Parker, John, *At the Heart of Darkness*, Sidgwick & Jackson, London, 1993.

Perry, Michael, *Deliverance*, SPCK, London, 1987.*

Petitpierre, Robert, *Exorcism*, SPCK, London, 1972.*

Pithoys, Claude, *Exposure of Superstition*, Martinies, The Hague, 1972.

Remy, Nicholas, *Demonolatry*, 1595 (translation E. A. Ashwin), Rodber, London, 1930 edition.*

Reville, Albert, *History of the Devil*, Williams & Norgate, London, 1871.

Rhodes, Henry T. F., *The Satanic Mass*, Ridert & Co., London, 1954.

Richards, John, *But Deliver Us from Evil*, Darton & Longman, London, 1974.*

—— *Exorcism, Deliverance and Healing*, Grove Books, Bramcote, 1976.

Robbins, Rossell Hope, *Encyclopedia of Witchcraft and Demonology*, Hamlyn, London, 1984.*

Russell, Jeffrey Burton, *The Devil: Perception of Evil*, Cornell University Press, N.Y., 1977.
—— *Lucifer: The Devil in the Middle Ages*, Cornell University Press, N.Y., 1984.*
—— *Mephistopheles*, Cornell University Press, N.Y., 1986.*
—— *The Prince of Darkness, Radical Evil and the Power of God*, Cornell University Press, N.Y., 1988.*
Sargant, William, *Man, Myth, Magic*, Heinemann, London, 1971.
—— *The Mind Possessed*, Heinemann, London, 1973.*
Scott, Reginald, *Discoverie of Witchcraft*, 1584; Treatum Orbis Terrarum, Amsterdam, and Da Capo Press, N.Y., 1971.
Scott, Sir Walter, *Letters on Demonology and Witchcraft*, Routledge, London, 1830.
Sinason, Valerie, *Treating Survivors of Satanic Abuse*, Routledge, London, 1994.
Singer, Kurt, *They are Possessed*, W. H. Allen, London, 1976.
Sinistrari, Ludovico, *Demonality* (translation M. Summers), Constable, London, 1989 edition.
Spufford, Francis, *Chatto Book of Devils*, Chatto & Windus, London, 1992.
Stanford, Peter, *The Devil*, Heinemann, London, 1996.*
Storm, Rachel, *Exorcists*, HarperCollins, London, 1993.
Summers, Montague, *The History of Witchcraft and Demonology*, Routledge & Kegan Paul, London, 1969.*
Tertullian (Quintus Septimius Florens Tertullianus), *Prescription* (translation Stanley C. Greenslade), SPCK, London, 1956.
Tonquedes, Joseph de, 'Aspects of Satan's Activity', in *Satan*, ed. Charles Moeller (q.v.).
Tote, Tim, *Children for the Devil*, Robert Hale, London, 1970.
Twelftree, Graham, *Jesus the Exorcist*, J. C. Mohr, Tübingen, 1933.*
Underwood, Peter, *Dictionary of the Supernatural*, Harrap, Edinburgh, 1978.
—— *Exorcism!*, Robert Hale, London, 1990.*
Vatican, *Rituale Romanum* (translation Father P. Weller), 1950.*
Vatican, *Catechism of the Catholic Church*, Geoffrey Chapman, London, 1994.*
Walker, Daniel, *The Ancient Theology*, Duckworth, London, 1972.
Wall, Charles, *Devils*, Methuen, London, 1904.
Wheatley, Denis, *The Devil and All His Works*, Hutchinson, London, 1971.
Weyer (or Wier), Johann, *De Praestigiis Daemonum*, 1563 (translation John Shea), Binghamton, N.Y., 1991.
Wiesinger, Alois, *Occult Phenomena*, Burns Oates, London, 1957.
Wilson, Colin, *After Life*, Harrap, London, 1985.
York Report, Study Group on the Christian Ministry of Healing, Church of England, 1974.

The above are books I have found most useful – and accessible. There are of course many more on the subject. For older, classical works see the extensive bibliography in M. Summers, *The History of Witchcraft and Demonology* (listed above), such as editions of Guazzo, Del Rio, Binsfeld and other demonologists of earlier centuries.

The list given in Summers of books on spiritism is well worth reading, remembering that the first edition of the book was in 1926.

A very full bibliography of scholarly references is to be found in J. D. Russell's books, listed above.

Translations from the original Latin 1909 edition of salient parts of the *Rituale Romanum* are given in several of the books mentioned in this list.

General Reference

Here are some useful general reference books.

Brown, Raymond; Fitzmyer, Joseph; and Murphy, Roland, *New Jerome Biblical Commentary*, Geoffrey Chapman, London, 1991.

Reader's Digest, *Encyclopedia of World History*, Reader's Digest Association, London, 1996.

Reader's Digest, *Bible*, London, 1990.

And, finally, Miles Coverdale's *The Great Bible*, London, 1539.

INDEX

Page numbers in *italic* refer
to the illustrations.

A

Abelard, Peter 179
Abraham 12–13
Adam and Eve 15, 16,
    19–20, 24, 29, 56, 60, 75,
    76, 93, 212
agnosticism 208
Ahriman 19, 31, 43
Ahura Mazda *see* Mazda
Albertus Magnus 57
Alexander, W. M. 114–15
angels 8, 15, 219–20; cre-
    ation 20–1, *223*; fall of
    19, 226–7; good angels
    21; Guardian Angel 179,
    211; hierarchies 18;
    Roman Catholic
    Church's present position
    211
animals: demons appearing
    as 46, 101–2, 104; witch-
    es' familiars 88–90, *89,*
    228
animism 44
Anselm, St 60, 179
Anthony, St 59, 100
Antichrist 159, 213–14
Apocrypha 16, 19–20,
    26–7
Apostolic Fathers 17, 55–7,
    61
Aquinas, St Thomas 8, 10,
    24, 40, 53, 58, 59, 80, 85,
    179, 233
art 186
Asmodeus 12, 38, 79, 140
Assyrians 43
Astaroth 38
astrology 201, 213
atheism 208
Augustine (of Hippo), St 8,
    20, 25, 40, 53, 56–7, 80,
    212

B

Babylonians 43
Balberith 38
Barnabas 55
Baudelaire, Charles 168,
    181, 186
Beelzebub 12, 21, 38, 104,
    163, 164, 224
Behemoth 21, *223*
Belial 21, 164
Belias 38
Belphegor *39*
Benedict XIV, Pope, 133
Bible 154; Christ's power
    over Satan 22–3; demons
    in 34–7, 48, 51–2; exege-
    sis 166–7; miracles 32–3;
    references to possession
    30, 34–7, 48, 99–103; ref-
    erences to witchcraft
    79–80; Satan in 10,
    11–13, 16, 22–3, 27–8
black magic 201
Black Masses 92, 164, 173,
    176
Blake, William 186, 229,
    230–1
blasphemy 213
Bogomils 20, 60, 176
Borley Rectory 128
The Brothers Karamazov
    (Dostoevsky) 185
Browning, Robert 230
Bunyan, John 231
Burns, Robert 230
Byron, Lord 181, 186

C

Cain: A Mystery (Byron) 181
Calvin, John 72, 164, 166
Carnivean 38
Carreau 38
*Catechism of the Catholic
    Church* 210–14, 226–8
Cathars 60
Catholic Church *see* Roman

Catholic Church
child abuse, Satanic rituals
    161, 210
Christianity: decline of
    belief in God 160; Devil
    in 11–12, 15–33, 53–62;
    early Church 16, 53–62;
    Incarnation 65–6, 115;
    Rationalism 194–5; 'secu-
    larization' 194–5, 218
Church of England 106,
    111, 124–5, 129, 132,
    166, 198–9, 201, 205
Church of Satan 176
clairvoyance 116, 202
Clement, Pope 55, 193
Coleridge, Samuel Taylor
    231
Communism 169
cosmology 17–18, *17,*
    162–3, 196
Creation 20–1
Crowley, Aleister 171, 176
cults 60, 63, 160, 173, 210
cures, miraculous 202

D

Dante 153, 162–3, 170
Davidian sect 178
De Quincey, Thomas 186
Dead Sea Scrolls 26–7
Dead Souls (Gogol) 186
deliverance 122–5, 205,
    206; *see also* exorcism
demonization 117–19,
    178–9, 193–4
Demonolatry (Remy) 71,
    196–8
demons 34–52; appearance
    30, 45–6, 56–7; in the
    Bible 34–7, 48, 51–2;
    classification 40–2, 46;
    conversations with 150–2;
    and the early Church
    44–7; hierarchies 38–9;
    manifestation 42–4;

names 43, 46, 143; night-mares 47–8; power 34–7, 221–2; reality of 232–3; representation of 37–9; Roman Catholic Church's present position 211; summoning 94–5; *see also* Devil; exorcism; possession

Descartes, René 72, 168

Desert Fathers 39, 66

Devil (Satan) 9–10, *36;* ancient origins 11–33; appearance 16–17, 21, 23, 29–30, 140, 158–9; belief in 156–8; changing attitudes to 153–70; in Christianity 11–12, 15–33, 53–62; Communism rejects 169; definitions 12; denial of existence of 204–5; in literature 162–5, 168–9, 170, 171, 180–7, 228–32; in Luther's teaching 165–6; in modern world 50; in New Testament 10, 11–13, 16, 22–3, 27–8; in Rationalist philosophy 168; selling one's soul to 112–13; tempts Jesus 18–19, 22–3, 227–8; trafficking trials 174–5; understanding 219–21; wiles of 222–4; and witchcraft 78, 81, 87, 88; worship of 63–5, 71, 171–4, 175–9; *see also* demons; possession

The Devils (Dostoevsky) 184–5

Devil's Mark 87–8, 98

Diderot, Denis 164

divination *199,* 200–1

The Divine Comedy (Dante) 162–3

Doctor Faustus (Marlowe) 163

Doktor Faustus (Mann) 182–3

Dostoevsky, Fyodor 169, 171, 183–5

Doyle, Sir Arthur Conan 190

Drury 174

dualism, Gnostic 175, 176

E

Engels, Friedrich 169

Enlightenment 106, 160

Enoch, Book of 19, 62

epilepsy 106–7, 111

Erasmus 180

Eve *see* Adam and Eve

evil: Day of Judgement 220; demons 49–50; denial of 155; Jung and 207–8; in literature 182–7; nature of 76–7; Principle of Evil 155, 156, 159; types of 195; understanding 25–7

exorcism 72, 120–34, 135–52, *144;* case histories 105, 107–8, 118, 128–9; conversations with demons 150–2; and deliverance 106, 122–5; *The Exorcist* 126, 141; failures 135–6, 142; God's permission for possession 125–6; guidelines for ministers 238–9; inexplicable cases 137–8; Jesus as an exorcist 35–7, 51–2, 99, 100–3, 120, 130, 136–7, 222, 224–5; of places 123, 128, 131, 137, 138, 144–5; preparation for 136–7; rite of the ordination of exorcists 236–7; rituals 120–2, 124–5, 130, 131–3, 142–3, 147, 234–6, 239–40; Roman Catholic Church and 106, 121–2, 124, 125, 199–200; Solemn Exorcism 121, 135, 137, 142–3, 147, 200; 'Yorkshire Ripper' 217; *see also* possession

extra-sensory perception 191–2

F

False Memory Syndrome 138–9

familiars 88–90, *89,* 228

fasting 136, 137

Faust 112, 163, 164–5, 182, 186

Faust (Goethe) 164–5

Fery, Jeanne 149–50

fortune-telling 201, 202

Fox family 189

Frankenstein (Mary Shelley) 181

free will 56, 57, 58, 60–1, 145, 156–7, 179, 193, 201

French Revolution 160

Freud, Sigmund 206, 207

G

Gargantua and Pantagruel (Rabelais) 163

Gautier, Théophile 181

ghosts 131, 137, 145

giants 19, 41, 64–5

Gide, André 186

Gnosticism 32, 175, 176

God: belief in 195–6; cosmology 18; decline of belief in 160; Gnostic dualism 175, 176; mysticism 180; permission for possession 125–6; proofs of existence 156; Romantic view of 181; 'secularization of Christianity' 194–5

Goethe, Johann Wolfgang von 164–5

Gogol, Nikolai 185–6

Gordon, Elizabeth 228

Gospels 13, 18–19, 27–8, 61, 99, 100, 101, 115, 223, 224–5

The Government Inspector (Gogol) 185

graven images 64, 222

Greece 14–15, 23, 44, 64

Gregory I, Pope 59

Gregory IV, Pope 172

Gressil 38

Grinset, Aubrey 174–5

Guardian Angel 179, 211

Guazzo, Francesco 40, 87, 92, 112

H

Hades 15
healing 201, 205, 225
Hebrews 13–14, 16, 49,
  125–6; *see also* Jews
Hell 18, 23, 220
heretics 20, 53, 60, 62, 70,
  74–5, 82, 85, 176, 193
hermits 37–8, 59
Highgate Cemetery,
  London 176–7
Hitler, Adolf 156, 217
Hobbes, Thomas 72, 168,
  186
Holy Spirit 126, 128, 131
Hubbard, L. Ron 176
Hugo, Victor 181, 190
humanism 180
Hume, David 164
Hussein, Saddam 217
Huxley, Aldous 169
hypnosis 202
hysteria 104, 107, 112, 116,
  140

I

Ignatius of Antioch 55, 61
Incarnation 65–6, 115
incubi 30, 38, 40–2, 47, 76,
  91, 197
indulgences 165
Innocent III, Pope 84
Innocent VIII, Pope 67, 83
Inquisition 53, 74–5, 81–6,
  96–8
Invart 38
Irenaeus, St 55, 61, 193

J

Jacob 79
James, St 233
Jeanne des Anges, Sister
  114
Jehovah 49
Jerome, St 56, 219
Jesus Christ 12; divinity 20;
  as an exorcist 35–7, 51–2,
  99, 100–3, 120, 130,
  136–7, 222, 224–5; healing 225; Holy Eucharist
  73; Incarnation 65–6,
  115; Lord's Prayer 205;

on original sin 225–6;
  parables 27–8, 51, 233;
  Resurrection 28, 29,
  62–3, 163, 201, 213–14;
  struggle with the Devil
  18–19, 22–3, 227–8
Jews 12–13, 18, 23, 24, 31,
  43, 61, 179; *see also*
  Hebrews
John, St 32, 61, 226
John of the Cross, St 72
John Damascene 59
John the Divine, St 35,
  53–4, 100, 213, 226
John Paul II, Pope 221, 226
Jones, Jim 178
Jubilees, Book of 19
Judaism 24; *see also* Jews
Judgement Day 28, 54–5,
  62–3, 101, 220
Jung, C. G. 206, 207–8
Justin Martyr, St 55, 61, 197

K

Kafka, Franz 186
Kant, Immanuel 164, 168,
  194
Kipling, Rudyard 230
Koresh, David 178
Kramer, Heinrich 67, 83,
  95, 134, 242

L

La Vey, Anton 176
Last Judgement 28, 54–5,
  62–3, 101, 220
Lateran Council, Fourth
  (1215) 211, 212
'laying on' of hands 143,
  147, 205
Leibnitz, Gottfried Wilhelm
  164, 194
Leo I, St, The Great, Pope
  212
Leo XIII, Pope 235
Leviathan 21, 38
Lewis, C. S. 153, 169, 170
Lewis, Matthew 181
Lilith 13, 15, 21, 45, 76
literature: Devil in 162–5,
  168–9, 170, 171, 180–7,
  228–32; Romanticism

  180–1
Locke, John 72, 164, 168
Lodge, Thomas 229
Lombard, Peter 57, 60, 179
Loudun 104, 109, 114, 140,
  151–2
Lucifer 12, 15, 18, 21, 24,
  163, 164; *see also* Devil
Lucius III, Pope 82, 84
Luke, St 61, 225
Luther, Martin 62, 63,
  71–2, 164, 165–6, 198

M

Machiavelli, Niccolò 186
magic 82, 94–5, 213
maleficia 94–6
Malleus Maleficarum 67, 83,
  90, 95, 134, 242
Mammon 164
Mann, Thomas 169, 171,
  182–3
Mao Tse-tung 217
Mark, St 33, 61, 224–5
Marlowe, Christopher 163
Marx, Karl 169
Marxism 169
materialism 169, 170, 209,
  214–15, 218
Matthew, St 61, 136, 224–5
Mazda 43
mediums 188–92, 201, 202,
  221
mental illness 126–8,
  145–6, 148, 158, 206
Mephistopheles 25, 112,
  163, 164–5, 182
Meredith, George 231–2
Mesopotamia 13
Methodism 166
Michel, Anneliese 177
Milton, John 164, 170, 229,
  231, 232
Moloch 164
The Monk (Matthew Lewis)
  181
Moses 13
murder 177, 215–16, 217
mysticism 60, 179–80

N

New Testament *see* Bible

Nicholas V, Pope 82
Nietzsche, Friedrich
  Wilhelm 169–70, 186,
  194–5
nightmares 47–8
Notre Dame, Paris 186

O

occultism 200–3, 213
Oeillet 38
Old Testament *see* Bible
Olivier 38
Omand, Rev. Donald 128–9
On the Devil and Devils
  (Shelley) 181
ordination of exorcists
  236–7
Origen 56, 61, 62, 219
original sin 16, 60, 65, 208,
  212–13, 225–6

P

paganism 92, 94
Palestine 13–14
Pan 14–15
Paradise Lost (Milton) 164,
  229, 231, 232
Paul, St 10, 27, 61, 73, 75,
  79, 204–5
Paul V, Pope, 133
Pearce, Jenny 228
People's Temple 178
Perelandra (C. S. Lewis) 170
Peter, St 226
Petitpierre, Dom Robert
  130–1
Pharisees 224, 225
Pius XI, Pope 214
Pius XXII, Pope 82
places, exorcism 123, 128,
  131, 137, 138, 144–5
Plato, 15
Poe, Edgar Allan 181, 186
Poirier, Hélène 108
political parties 217
poltergeists 38, 131, 137,
  138, 145, 146, 174
Polycarp 55, 61
possession 72, 99–119; in
  the Bible 30, 34–7, 48,
  99–103; conscious and
  unconscious possession

109–10; conversations
  with demons 150–2; as a
  coping mechanism
  145–6; decline of belief
  in 206; exorcism 105–6,
  107, 120–34; God's per-
  mission for 125–6; mass
  hysteria 104; in modern
  times 111–12; proving
  demonization 117–19;
  Roman Catholic Church
  and 199–200; seances
  190; selling the soul
  112–13; signs of 113–17,
  141, 147–8; 'voluntary'
  and 'involuntary' possession 105
priests 44–5, 71
progress 216–18
Protestantism 63, 72, 73,
  82, 159, 160, 198
Proudhon, Pierre Joseph
  181
psychoanalysis 206
psychology 170

R

Rabelais, François 163
Rais, Gilles de 171–2
Rationalists 164, 168,
  194–5
Redemption 28, 29,
  219–20, 227
Reformation 70, 72, 82,
  157, 159, 164, 165, 173,
  198
Remy, Nicholas 71, 95, 134,
  196–8
Renaissance 30, 82
Resurrection 28, 29, 62–3,
  163, 201, 213–14
Revelation, Book of 34–5,
  53–4, 100, 213, 226
Rituale Romanum 121, 122,
  132, 133, 157, 234–7
rituals: exorcism 120–2,
  124–5, 130, 131–3,
  142–3, 147, 234–6,
  239–40; Satanic 161
Roman Catholic Church:
  belief in the Devil 32,
  157–8; Catechism

210–14, 226–8; on
  demons 154–5, 221;
  exorcism 106, 120, 121,
  124, 125, 132, 133, 143,
  199–200; Inquisition
  81–87; opposition to spiritualism 190, 192, 201;
  present position 210–14;
  resistance to change 198;
  and sexuality 222
Romans 55, 61, 64
Romanticism 73, 180–1
Rosier 38
Rousseau, Jean-Jacques
  164, 168, 208

S

sabbats 71, *84*, 85, 88,
  90–2, *91*
sacrifices 64
sacrilege 213
Salem 104
Samuel 79
Sandie 215–16
Satan *see* Devil
Satanism 171–4; forms of
  175–9; rituals 161; sects
  and cults 205; trials for
  trafficking with the Devil
  174–5
scepticism 71–4
schizophrenia 110, 112, 140
Schleiermacher, Friedrich
  Ernst Daniel 164, 168
scholasticism 59, 179–80
science 196, 208, 218, 233
Scientology 176
Screwtape Letters (C. S. Lewis)
  170
seances 190, 201, 202
Second Coming 28, 29,
  62–3, 163, 201, 213–14
sects 60, 63, 73–4, 160, 173,
  176, 177–8, 210
selling the soul 112–13
Septuagint 12
seven deadly sins 38
sexuality: incubi and succubi 40–2, 76, *91*; and possession 104–5, 107, 110,
  146; Roman Catholic
  Church and 222; and

witchcraft 87–8, 90, 91,
  91
Shakespeare, William 88,
  148, 154, 163–4, 189,
  229–30, 231
she-devils 21
Shelley, Mary 181
Shelley, Percy Bysshe 169,
  181
Sinistrari, Father 40, 41–2,
  197
Sonneillon 38
sorcery 42–3, 70–1, 81, 82,
  213; *see also* witchcraft
soul 44, 47, 112–13, 180,
  201–2
Spatchet, Thomas 174–5
spirits 201–2
spiritual healing 201, 205
spiritualism 188–92, 197,
  213, 221
Sprenger, James 67, 83, 95,
  134, 242
Stalin, Joseph 156, 217
succubi 30, 38, 40–2, 47,
  91, 197
suggestibility, possession
  115–16
Surin 109–10, 114
Sutcliffe, Peter 217

T

Talmud 13
Taylor, Michael 128
telepathy 201, 202

Teresa, Doña 109
Teresa of Avila, St 72
Tertullian 55–6, 61, 62, 193
Torah 13
torture, witches 83–4, 96–8,
  99
Tranquille, Father 151–2
Trent, Council of 73
Twain, Mark 181

U

urbanization 214–15
Uz, Anna Maria 117–18

V

vampires 47
Vatican Council, Second
  (1962–65) 157
Verrier 38
Verrine 38
violence 216–17
voices, possession 141–2,
  147, 150–1, 177, 217
Voltaire 164

W

warfare 209
Watts, Isaac 230
Wesley, John 166
Weyer, Johann 67, 95, 106,
  133–4, 244–6
witchcraft *76*, 78–98,
  133–4; belief in 78–80;
  'confessions' 84, 85–7;
  Devil's Mark 87–8, 98;

divination *199;* familiars
  88–90, *89,* 228;
  Inquisition 81–6; interrogation of witches
  241–4; maleficia 94–6;
  pact with Devil 78, 81,
  87, 88; penalties 242;
  persecution 67–70, 86,
  87–8, 93, 98, 228; and
  possession 106; punish-
  ment 245–6; revival of
  interest in 178; sabbats
  71, *84,* 85, 88, 90–2, *91;*
  torture practices 83–4,
  96–8, *99;* Trial by
  Ordeal 92–4; trials in
  Britain 88; 'white witches' 8, 95, 178
women: Adam and Eve 15,
  16, 19–20, 24, 29, 56, 60,
  75, 76, 93, 212; attitudes
  to 75–6, 197–8; exorcism
  146; incubi and succubi
  40–2; Lilith 13, 15, 21,
  45, 76; persecution of
  witches 67–70, 86, 87–8,
  93, 98; possession 103–5

Y

York Report 124–5, 235
'Yorkshire Ripper' 217

Z

zombies 46
Zoroastrianism 43